Understanding
FEDERICO GARCÍA LORCA

Understanding Modern European and Latin American Literature

JAMES HARDIN, *Series Editor*

UNDERSTANDING

FEDERICO
GARCÍA LORCA

CANDELAS NEWTON

UNIVERSITY OF SOUTH CAROLINA PRESS

Published in Columbia, South Carolina, by the
University of South Carolina Press

Manufactured in the United States of America

Library of Congress Cataloging-in-Publication Data

Newton, Candelas.
   Understanding Federico García Lorca / by Candelas Newton.
      p. cm.—(Understanding modern European and Latin American
   literature)
      Includes bibliographical references and index.
      Contents: Introduction: Lorca, his country and times—The major
   poetry—The major plays—Lesser-known poetry—Lesser-known
   plays—Prose works, visual arts, and music—Conclusion.
    ISBN 1-57003-020-0
    1. García Lorca, Federico, 1898–1936—Criticism and interpretation.
   I. Title. II. Series.
   PQ6613.A763Z7775 1995
   868'.6209–dc20   94-18708

for my brother Roberto,
in loving memory (1955–1992)

CONTENTS

EDITOR'S PREFACE

*U*nderstanding *Modern European and Latin American Litera-ture* has been planned as a series of guides for undergraduate and graduate students and nonacademic readers. Like the volumes in its companion series *Understanding Contemporary American Literature,* these books provide introductions to the lives and writings of prominent modern authors and explicates their most important works.

Modern literature makes special demands, and this is particularly true of foreign literature, in which the reader must contend not only with unfamiliar, often arcane artistic conventions and philosophical concepts, but also with the handicap of reading the literature in translation. It is a truism that the nuances of one language can be rendered in another only imperfectly (and this problem is especially acute in fiction), but the fact that the works of European and Latin American writers are situated in a historical and cultural setting quite different from our own can be as great a hindrance to the understanding of these works as the linguistic barrier. For this reason the UMELL series emphasizes the sociological and historical background of the writers treated. The peculiar philosophical and cultural traditions of a given culture may be particularly important for an understanding of certain authors, and these are taken up in the introductory chapter and also in the discussion of those works to which this information is relevant. Beyond this, the books treat the specifically literary aspects of the author under discussion and attempt to explain the complexities of contemporary literature lucidly. The books are conceived as introductions to the authors covered, not as comprehensive analyses. They do not provide detailed summaries of plot because they are meant to be used in conjunction with the books they treat, not as a substitute for study of the original works. The purpose of the books is to provide information and judicious literary assessment of the major works in the most compact, readable form. It is our hope that the UMELL series will help increase knowledge and understanding of European and Latin American cultures and will serve to make the literature of those cultures more accessible.

J. H.

PREFACE

This study will attempt to elucidate each individual work and its links with other works within the Lorcan oeuvre, paying special attention to poetic images, since they constitute the author's unique language and point to the major concerns in his writings. One of those concerns is the question of writing itself as a complex semiotic system. An understanding of Lorca's art has to take into account the author's own exploration of the nature of writing, of his experience of what it entails to articulate a world of meaning through words. This book will thus draw on Lorca's own critical statements about his work; it will also highlight those moments when the artist points to his art as a created work. Finally, Lorca's vision of poetic language also implies his vision of the reality beyond the artistic creation. Therefore, this book will explore the evolution of Lorca's aesthetics as it illuminates the distance between creation and representation, between the work of art and the world.

Chapters 1 and 2 deal with the most renowned works in the Lorcan canon, the poetry collections *Poem of the Deep Song, The Gypsy Ballads,* and *Poet in New York,* and the dramatic trilogy *Blood Wedding, Yerma,* and *The House of Bernarda Alba.* The two-volume bilingual edition, *The Poetical Works of Federico García Lorca,* ed. Christopher Maurer, trans. Greg Simon and Steven F. White and Francisco Aragón et al. (New York: Farrar, Straus & Giroux, 1988, 1991), and *Three Tragedies: Blood Wedding, Yerma, Bernarda Alba,* trans. James Graham-Luján and Richard L. O'Connell (New York: New Directions, 1955), provide the basic texts for the commentary in these two chapters. Chapters 3 and 4 deal with poetical and dramatic works in the Lorcan corpus that have received less critical attention, but which attest to the breadth and variety of the author's production. Due to the number of works under consideration in these chapters, the analyses are necessarily more succinct than in the first two. While English translations are available for most of these works, this study takes into consideration the difficulty of Lorca's imagery as expressed in his native language. The approach thus used pays close attention to the text while also providing background information that contributes to the elucidation of each of the works. For the poetry collections a detailed textual analysis is offered of one or more representative poems.

Chapter 5 addresses a variety of artistic areas in Lorca's production: music, plastic arts, cinema, and prose. Christopher Maurer's translation of Mario Hernández's book, *Line of Light and Shadow: The Drawings of Federico García Lorca* (Durham and London: Duke UP, 1991) provides a backdrop for the discussion of Lorca's drawings. Besides Lawrence H. Klibbe's translation of Lorca's first book of prose, *Impressions and Landscapes* (Lanham, New York, London: UP of America, 1987) the basic text for Lorca's lectures, speeches, and interviews is *Deep Song and Other Prose,* ed. and trans. Christopher Maurer (New York: New Directions, 1980). The basic text for Lorca's correspondence is *Selected Letters,* ed. and trans. David Gershator (New York: New Directions, 1983). The heterogenous nature of the works considered in chapter 5 is counterbalanced by an attempt to delineate the development of Lorca's aesthetic theories through an analysis, in chronological order, of his lectures.

ACKNOWLEDGMENTS

I wish to thank Christopher Maurer, Vanderbilt University, for his useful commentaries to an early draft of this manuscript. My gratitude goes also to my friend and colleague Kathleen McNerney, at West Virginia University, for her editorial suggestions. Andrew A. Anderson at the University of Michigan, Ann Arbor, greatly improved chapter 4 with his insight, for which I am grateful. My appreciation goes also to Juan Loveluck, at the University of South Carolina, for first bringing the series Understanding Modern European and Latin American Literature to my attention. I am further indebted to Cecelia J. Cavanaugh, at Chesnut Hill College, Robert N. Shorter, at Wake Forest University, and Justus Harris for their reading of sections of this book and to Michael Rahman, friend and computer wizard, for facilitating the computerization of this project while patiently enlightening my technical ignorance. Last but not least, I am indebted to my daughter Isabel Gala, whose insightful commentaries kept me in touch with the student-reader audience.

CHRONOLOGY

1898   Born in Fuente Vaqueros, near Granada, 5 June.

1907   Family moves to Asquerosa (today, Valderrubio), a village in Vega de Zujaira.

1909   Family moves to Granada. Attends the Sacred Heart of Jesus School and the Granada Institute. Studies piano with Antonio Segura Mesa.

1914   Enrolls in the College of Liberal Arts and Law School at the University of Granada.

1916-17   Takes study trips with his "Theory of Literature and the Arts" class under Professor Martín Domínguez Berrueta; meets Antonio Machado in Baeza and Miguel de Unamuno in Salamanca.

1918   *Impressions and Landscapes* published.

1919   Moves to Residence of Students in Madrid; meets future film director Luis Buñuel. Begins friendship with musicianManuel de Falla.

1920   *The Butterfly's Evil Spell* staged 22 March in Madrid.

1921   *Book of Poems* published.

1921-23   Works on *Suites,* not published until 1983.

1922   Delivers lecture "Deep Song: Primitive Andalusian Song" 19 February as part of the Deep Song Festival. (In the period 1930–33 this lecture will be repeated in Cuba, various cities in Spain, and Buenos Aires). Finishes first draft of *The Billy-Club Puppets: Tragicomedy of Don Cristóbal and Miss Rosita.*

1923   Presents a children's festival at his house, to commemorate the Epiphany, in collaboration with Manuel de Falla. Completes law degree from the University of Granada. Meets painter Salvador Dalí. Begins work on *Mariana Pineda,* produced in 1927.

1925   Spends Easter in Cadaqués, at the home of Salvador Dalí. Writes a series of prose dialogues influenced by Dalí and surrealism.

1926   *Ode to Salvador Dalí* published. Delivers lectures "The Poetic Image of Don Luis de Góngora" and "A Paradise Closed to Many, Gardens Open to Few. A Gongorist Poet of the Seventeenth Century."

1927   *Songs* published in May. Includes poems written during the period 1921–26. Travels to Barcelona in June for the production of *Mariana*

Pineda. In October this play is produced in Madrid. Exhibits twenty-four drawings at the Josep Dalmau Gallery in Barcelona, 25 June–2 July. *St. Lucy and St. Lazarus* published in December. Travels to Seville with other poets to commemorate the tercentenary of Don Luis de Góngora's death. Works on avant-garde review *gallo* during this and the following year.

1928   *The Gypsy Ballads,* written during the period 1921–27, published. *Solitude* and parts 1 and 2 of *Ode to the Most Holy Sacrament of the Altar* published. *Buster Keaton's Outing* and *The Maiden, the Sailor and the Student* published in May; *Suicide in Alexandria* and *Submerged Swimmer* published in September. Delivers lectures "Imagination, Inspiration, Evasion" and "Thoughts on Modern Painting" in Granada and "On Lullabies" at the Residence of Students in Madrid.

1929   Travels to New York in June. *Beheading the Innocents* published. Writes film script *Trip to the Moon* (published in 1980). Works on plays *Once Five Years Pass* and *The Public,* and writes poems that will comprise *Poet in New York,* published in 1940.

1930   Arrives in Havana in March; publishes *Beheading the Baptist*; lectures and writes most of the play *The Public.* Returns to Spain in June. *The Shoemaker's Prodigious Wife* is staged in December in Madrid. Dictator Primo de Rivera resigns early in the year.

1931   *Poem of the Deep Song* published. Begins to work with university theater group La Barraca. *Once Five Years Pass* finished in August.

1931-34 Works on *The Diván at Tamarit,* published in 1940.

1932   Lectures throughout Spain from March to May. *Blood Wedding* finished.

1933   *Blood Wedding* opens in March in Madrid and *The Love of Don Perlimplín and Belisa in the Garden* opens in April. During summers of 1933 and 1934 works on *Yerma.* In September travels to Argentina for productions of *Blood Wedding, Mariana Pineda,* and *The Shoemaker's Prodigious Wife.* Delivers lecture on the aesthetic theory of *duende* and "How a City Sings From November to November."

1934   *Mariana Pineda* premieres in Buenos Aires in January. Lectures in Uruguay. Returns to Spain from Buenos Aires in March. *Yerma* premieres in December in Madrid.

1935   *Six Galician Poems* and *Lament for Ignacio Sánchez Mejías* published. *Blood Wedding* is staged in English at the Neighborhood Playhouse in New York with the title *Bitter Oleander. In the Frame of Don Cristóbal: A Puppet Farce* is produced. Writes *Sonnets [of Dark Love].* Doña

Rosita, the Spinster or the Language of the Flowers premieres in Barcelona in December.

1936   Finishes *The House of Bernarda Alba,* which is staged in 1945 in Buenos Aires and in 1950 in Madrid. Travels to Granada 14 July; Nationalists rebel against the Republic 17 July. Arrested 16 August, murdered 18 or 19 August.

ABBREVIATIONS

CP	*Collected Poems*
DS	*Deep Song and Other Prose*
FP	*Five Plays: Comedies and Tragicomedies*
FPP	*Four Puppet Plays, Play Without a Title, The Divan Poems and Other Poems, Prose Poems and Dramatic Pieces*
IL	*Impressions and Landscapes*
MP	*Mariana Pineda*
OC	*Obras completas*
OFYP	*Once Five Years Pass and Other Dramatic Works*
PP	*The Public and Play Without a Title*
SL	*Selected Letters*
TT	*Three Tragedies: Blood Wedding, Yerma, Bernarda Alba*

Understanding
FEDERICO GARCÍA LORCA

Introduction: Lorca, His Country and Times

Spain is a country of contrasting images, where, as evidenced in art, architecture, music, folklore, and history, Western and Arabic and Jewish elements fuse. Nowhere is that fusion more visible than in the southern region of Andalusia, where, near the city of Granada, Federico García Lorca was born on 5 June 1898. Poet, playwright, lecturer, musician, stage director, this versatile artist continues to attract critical attention and assert his central position in twentieth-century letters.[1]

Lorca's work has often been considered by literary critics to be the expression of the Spanish essence.[2] His friend, the Nobel-laureate and poet Vicente Aleixandre (1898–1984), described Lorca as firmly rooted in the land of Spain, in search of its profound wisdom. For another poet friend, Luis Cernuda (1902–1963), he embodied the inspired voice of the Spanish people, a voice possessed by a tragic sense of life and infused by its two essential passions, love and death. While Lorca referred to himself as "wholly Spanish," he professed to "execrate the man who sacrifices himself for an abstract nationalist ideal, loving his country with a blindfold on his eyes."[3] He felt Spain in his marrow, as he put it, but more importantly, he described himself as "a man of the world, the brother of all," a nonbeliever in political frontiers (*DS* 130). His works, devoid of facile local color, probe more deeply into the tragic feeling, the *pena* (pain, sorrow) hidden beneath the happy exterior of his country's colorful folklore, that of his native Granada in particular.

Granada's fertile *vega* (watered valley between hills), where Lorca's native village of Fuente Vaqueros is located, owes its abundance of water to the irrigation systems built by the Arabs who occupied Andalusia for over eight centuries. Their presence had an impact on the life and culture of the Iberian peninsula that no other European country experienced. Their expulsion in 1492 by the Spanish Catholic monarchs Isabel and Ferdinand reunified the territory politically. Spain then began its emergence as an energetic state, becoming by the seventeenth century the most powerful European empire, with control over the newly discovered American territories as well as much of Western Europe. Lorca often commented on how the Christian conquest of the Arabs destroyed a brilliant civilization, leaving Granada, the last Arabic kingdom to be reconquered, a poor and frightened city with the "worst bourgeoisie" of all Spain (*DS* 130). Public declarations of this sort only intensified the hatred the Right (composed of the most conservative groups, including the army, the Church, and the quasi-fascist political party the Falange) already felt for Lorca and other liberal intellectuals and ultimately contributed to his assassination in 1936, soon after the Spanish Civil War broke out.

Granada, the last stronghold of Arab rule, was for Lorca a fragmented city, with its Arabic and Jewish past and its Christian present, its thirst for adventure and lack of initiative, its calm exterior and hidden frustration and torment.[4] The divided identity of Granada is a constant presence in Lorca's life and works. In a 1929 speech he declared his artistic debt to the city that had opened its lyrical secrets to him, secrets that gave form to his poetic vision.[5]

Federico García Rodríguez, the poet's father, was a wealthy landowner whose extended family liked to gather to play music and sing. This love of music, as well as Lorca's paternal grandmother's liking for reading out loud, was inherited by the poet. Lorca's first artistic interest was in the piano, which he played with great talent. Music is thus a major presence in the images of his early writings and in the structure of some of his plays, such as *Bodas de sangre*, 1933 (*Blood Wedding*). Throughout his life, Lorca enjoyed reciting his poems and reading his plays in public or for small gatherings of friends. For that reason, he has often been characterized as the quintessential modern bard.[6] This direct contact of Lorca with his audience nurtured the communication between artist and public that he always felt to be an essential part of his art.

In 1897, three years after the death of his first wife, Federico García Rodríguez married the future mother of the poet, Vicenta Lorca Romero, a teacher. Although the use of both parents' last names is customary in Spain, in the case of Federico García Lorca the last name is commonly abbreviated to just the mother's, *Lorca,* which is more distinctive than the ubiquitous García. After Federico, the couple had four children: two sons, Luis (who died at the age of two) and Francisco, and two daughters, Concha and Isabel. The year 1898, when Lorca was born, marked the Spanish defeat in the war with the United States. The loss of Cuba, the Philippines, and Puerto Rico, the last colonies of the Spanish empire, was the culmination of an increasing national pessimism and general inertia stemming from an inept political system. This climate of discouragement was the central concern of the so-called Generation of 1898, a group of writers whose works addressed the critical situation of their country. In 1916 and 1917, during some of the study trips he took while enrolled at the University of Granada, Lorca met two members of this literary group: Miguel de Unamuno (1864–1936), philosopher, poet, novelist, essayist, professor, and chancellor of the University of Salamanca (one of Spain's leading institutions dating from the thirteenth century); and the poet and essayist Antonio Machado (1874–1947). The influence of these men is visible in Lorca's early works.

Since childhood, Lorca showed a great sensitivity and love for the land around him that remained a constant throughout his life and writings (*DS* 133). A primary source of his poetic imagery was this lifelong close connection with nature. In the Vega of Zujaira, some three miles away from Fuente Vaqueros, where his father owned land and where the family moved around 1907, Lorca wrote many of the early poems later collected in his *Libro de poemas,* 1921 (*Book of Poems*). As late as 1934 he declared that his childhood emotions were still integral to his art (*DS* 132–35).

Childhood is not just a theme for Lorca, but also a vital attitude and vision. Those who knew him personally attribute the fascination that his presence and personality evoked, as well as his power to communicate and seduce, to his intuitive and sympathetic connection with the mystery of the most elementary aspects of his surroundings.[7] Lorca's writings attest to his acute sensitivity to the voice of creation, which he attempted to capture with the amazement, faith, and pure emotion of a child:

> I love the land. All my emotions tie me to it. My most distant childhood memories have the taste of earth. The earth, the countryside, have wrought great things in my life. Bugs and animals and country people are suggestive to only a few people. My spirit can capture their suggestiveness the same as when I was a child. (*DS* 132–33)

His writings are fused with experience artistically re-created.

Lorca's theatrical vocation was stirred by the Catholic liturgical ceremonies he attended with his mother, which he reproduced in the backyard of his house in a game he called "saying Mass." Relatives and maids were asked to attend, and to weep after the child's emotional homilies. This theatrical altar later gave way to a puppet theater his mother bought for him after his enthusiastic response to one that traveled to Fuente Vaqueros for the annual fair. Lorca was then seven or eight years old. His love for the theater of puppets stayed with him. This type of theatrical production sought to communicate with its audience in ways that Lorca considered essential in his own plays. Gibson indicates how in his work as director of La Barraca (The Booth), a theater company sponsored by the Spanish Republic during the 1930s, Lorca accomplished some of the goals he perceived as intrinsic to puppet theater: an itinerant spectacle designed to take theater to the people, even in the most remote areas, and to

3

establish communication with the audience.[8] Moreover, unlike the actors of the time, whom Lorca criticized for their excessive mannerisms and their mere pretense of realism, the puppet itself, and the genre of puppet theater, made for a medium openly displaying its artificial, artistic nature, consciously loosening mimetic links with reality.

Lorca's rural childhood ended when the family moved to Granada in 1909, even though they continued to spend summers in the countryside until 1925, after which the family moved into the Huerta de San Vicente house in Granada. Young Lorca's preference and talent for music were far greater than his interest in school work. Francisco, Lorca's brother, states that Lorca was able to sing before he began to speak.[9] He later compiled and harmonized popular and traditional songs from different regions in Spain and studied the *cancioneros,* or collections of popular songs, that were published by scholars. Yet the first ballads he learned came from his native region, mainly from house servants. Lorca later recognized the nourishing role servants played in exposing the children of affluent families to the traditions of their country (*DS* 10). Many of Lorca's writings acquire meaning through the dialogue they establish with those popular songs and traditions.

Despite Lorca's gift for music, and for the piano in particular, his parents were determined that he prepare for a traditional career. Consequently, he registered in 1914 in the College of Liberal Arts and Law School at the University of Granada. Despite the stagnant atmosphere of the university at the time, Lorca was fortunate to have teachers such as Fernando de los Ríos Urruti (1879–1949), professor of political and comparative law, founder of the Granadine branch of the Socialist party, and president of the Center of Arts and Literature to which Lorca belonged during his early student years. During the Second Republic in the 1930s, de los Ríos held the position of minister of justice and then of education. He was influenced by the spirit of the Institución Libre de Enseñanza (Free Teaching Institution), founded in 1876. This institution opposed the impractical and authoritarian educational methods of the Catholic church, which had a monopoly on the schools; the Free Teaching Institution postulated instead closer contact with students through the tutorial system as the means to form Spanish youth for the intellectual rebirth of the country. Lorca recognized de los Ríos's mentorship from the outset, maintaining with him a lifelong friendship.

In this same educational spirit, and as a student at the University of Granada, Lorca went on four study trips around Andalusia and to Castile, Leon, and Galicia. The fruit of these experiences was reflected in his prose book, *Impresiones y paisajes,* 1918 (*Impressions and Landscapes*). Its publication came as a surprise to Lorca's friends, who viewed him as a musician, not as a writer. The death in 1916 of Antonio Mesa Segura, Lorca's piano teacher, greatly influenced his decision to choose writing over music, a career everyone assumed he would follow in view of his musical talent. The year 1916 thus marks the beginning of Lorca's writing, as his brother confirms.[10] During these learning years Lorca was part of an unorthodox group, consisting of some seventeen regular members, who called themselves El Rinconcillo (The Little Corner), a reference to their regular gathering place between 1915 and 1922, a corner of the Café Alameda in Granada. The *rinconcillistas* made their mark in the Granadine society through various functions, such as a ceremony honoring seventeenth-century baroque Granadine author Pedro Soto de Rojas (1584–1658), on whom Lorca later lectured. They disapproved of Spanish society, and of the provincial Granada middle class in particular. Young Lorca found great friends and advocates in this group during years when he felt internally fragmented, as expressed in his early writings and in his correspondence. The Catholic education he had received was being challenged by urgent demands of the heart. The figure of God the Father and his established church, as well as norms prescribed by society, represented for the young artist a set of inhibitions of the open expression of his feelings, including a budding homosexuality that was totally unacceptable in his religious and social milieu.

In the fall of 1919 Lorca went to Madrid on a journey his parents viewed as motivated by literary interests, due to the capital's prestige as a cultural center. He lived in the Residencia de Estudiantes (Students' Residence), or Resi, as it was familiarly called, an offshoot of the Free Teaching Institution. With some five hundred members, the Resi was a cultural center where eminent intellectuals lectured: Albert Einstein, Marie Curie, Andrés Segovia, Igor Stravinsky, and Maurice Ravel, among others. There Lorca befriended Luis Buñuel and Salvador Dalí, also living at the Resi. He was exposed to the Spanish avant-garde movement called *ultraísmo* (ultraism); even though he did not get directly involved with it, its artistic tenets—such as the emphasis on the poetic image, rejection of sentimentality, affirmation of the spirit of the machine age— influenced his poetry. Lorca was soon in the center of the artistic and intellectual life at the Resi, a brilliant member of what became a most dazzling group of twentieth-century Spanish artists in all areas, especially in poetry—the poetic generation of 1927.

In March 1920, Lorca's play *El maleficio de la mariposa* (*The Butterfly's Evil Spell*) was staged in Madrid. The poetic depth of the play was overlooked by a public unable to accept beetles and scorpions as characters, and the venture was a crashing failure. In 1921 Lorca published his *Book of Poems,* a collection in which sentimentality and melancholy are fused with powerful images articulating the young author's religious and sexual crises. Similar preoccupations, but in a more stylized poetic language, are expressed in *Suites,* on which Lorca worked from 1921 until 1923 but which were not published until 1983. Like the seventeenth and eighteenth centuries dance suites composed in related keys, *Suites* is comprised of sequences of poems related in theme.

During the fall of 1919, Lorca had begun his friendship with musician and composer Manuel de Falla (1876–1946). The two artists collaborated on various projects, especially the Festival of Deep Song in 1922, a competition aimed at revitalizing this old Gypsy art. Deep Song (Cante Jondo), a musical form of the Spanish Gypsies from the southern region of Andalusia often considered more genuine than popular flamenco, expresses the *pena* hidden by the gay exterior of the Andalusian; it is a visceral premonition of unredeemable death. This deep existential anguish wells up in the voice of the *cantaor,* or flamenco singer, impelled by the force of the *duende,* a type of Dionysian inspiration coming from the subconscious. Lorca defined the *duende* as "not a question of ability, but of true, living style, of blood, of the most ancient culture, of spontaneous creation" (*DS* 43). The *duende* inspiration dwells on the borderline where life and death meet and from where art emerges.

Lorca considered Deep Song to be one of the greatest creations of the Spanish people, the expression of the most profound aspect of the Andalusian soul and a source of pure poetry. Inspired by it, Lorca wrote a series of poems collected in *Poema del Cante Jondo* (*Poem of the Deep Song*), which he intended to publish for the festival but which did not appear until 1931. He also worked on his lecture "Cante Jondo. El primitivo canto andaluz" ("Deep Song: Primitive Andalusian Song"), which he delivered at the festival. The simplicity, conciseness, and musicality of the compositions in *Poem of the Deep Song* also characterize those in *Canciones,* 1927 (*Songs*), a collection he wrote between 1921 and 1926.

The repressive military dictatorship imposed by General Miguel Primo de Rivera (1870–1930; dictator 1923–1930) after his successful coup d'état in September 1923 forms the backdrop against which Lorca began work on his play *Mariana Pineda.* Based on the story of a Granadine woman executed in 1831 by the absolutist monarchy for having embroidered a flag in support of the liberal opposition, the play was produced very successfully in 1927 in Barcelona, with designs by Dalí.

In the line of the Deep Song poems of 1921 is *Romancero gitano,* 1928 (*The Gypsy Ballads*). Andalusia, represented mainly by Granada, and *pena* are the main themes of these eighteen poems written between 1921 and 1927.

Their success was so resounding that Lorca instantly became the most famous Spanish author of his time. However, this success proved to be a source of concern for the poet, as expressed in a letter to his friend Jorge Guillén:

> This gypsy *myth of mine* annoys me a little. They confuse my life and character. This isn't what I want at all. The gypsies are a theme. And nothing more. . . . Besides, this gypsyism gives me the appearance of an uncultured, ignorant and *primitive poet* that you know very well I'm not. I don't want to be typecast. I feel as if they're chaining me down. NO.[11]

In fact, in 1931, after returning from New York, Lorca told an interviewer that *The Gypsy Ballads* belonged to the past and that his poetry was now infused with a more precise and objective pathos (*OC* 2:892).

Lorca spent Easter 1925 at the homes of Dalí in Figueras and Cadaqués, on the Mediterranean coast. The intimate relationship that developed between the artists had a great impact on both. The years 1926 to 1929 are considered Dalí's "Lorcan period," from the obsessive presence of the poet's head in his paintings. The experience left a similarly important mark in Lorca's work.[12] During the summer of 1925 he wrote a series of prose dialogues in a style quite different from his previous work. Of special interest is *El paseo de Buster Keaton* (*Buster Keaton's Outing*), which reflects Lorca's great familiarity, and that of his generation, with American films and film actors. The style of these dialogues paved the way for later works in which Lorca's voice is less attuned to the Andalusian, traditional, and popular echoes characteristic of his earlier writings.

In February 1926, in Granada, Lorca delivered his lecture "La imagen poética de Don Luis de Góngora" ("The Poetic Image of Don Luis de Góngora"). The objectivity and distancing from reality so characteristic of the Cordoban baroque poet Góngora (1561–1627) seemed to make his artistic tenets coincide with the search of young poets for a type of pure art. Lorca remained faithful to the Gongorine aesthetics of structure and form long after the fashion for the seventeenth-century author had passed. The search for objectivity and the absence of sentimentality, hallmarks of Góngora's poetry, were also crucial to Dalí's early aesthetics, as Lorca elaborated on in his *Oda a Salvador Dalí* (*Ode to Salvador Dalí*), published in April 1926. In this composition, which continues the aesthetic direction outlined in the lecture on Góngora, Lorca recognizes the impact of his friend Dalí's paintings on contemporary art.

The year 1927 signaled the tercentenary of Góngora's death; it also proved to be a successful year for Lorca. His play *Mariana Pineda* was enjoying general acclaim in Barcelona; also in the Catalan capital, twenty-four of his drawings were exhibited at the Josep Dalmau Gallery of Modern Art; and his book *Songs* was reviewed very positively. His genius also reflected that of an extraordinary generation of young poets that included Jorge Guillén (1893–1984), Vicente Aleixandre (1898–1984), Rafael Alberti (1902–), Luis Cernuda (1902–1963), Pedro Salinas (1892–1951), Emilio Prados (1899–1962), and Manuel Altolaguirre (1905–1959). They formed a group united by friendship and based on shared artistic objectives.

This aesthetic unity was expressed most clearly in the commemoration of Góngora's tercentenary in Seville in 1927, leading to the group's denomination as the 1927 poetic generation. The invitation to this celebration came from Ignacio Sánchez Mejías (1891–1934), a bullfighter and author interested in flamenco, literature, and theater. During the celebrations Lorca and Alberti recited together a section from Góngora's *Primera Soledad* (*First Solitude,* 1627), and Lorca recited some of his own Gypsy ballads.[13] This public testament of Góngora's pure poetry soon gave way, however, to a poetry more concerned with social issues and human emotions. Thus, in an interview in 1928, Lorca responded to a question concerning his theoretical position by calling for a return to inspiration, passion, and instinct, leaving behind logical poetry (*OC* 2:889). Góngora's lesson had been learned, and it was time to move on.

In the spring of 1927 Lorca visited Catalonia again. These were months of intense intellectual discussions with Catalan intellectuals Lorca met in Barcelona, including Dalí, about surrealism and its program of unexpected juxtapositions and combinations in art stemming from the subconscious and dreams. Lorca had read about the movement, and the cultural atmosphere was receptive to it. Lorca's drawings included in the exhibition at the Dalmau Gallery reveal Dalí's influence on Lorca's aesthetic concerns at the time. When he returned to Granada Lorca continued to draw, finding great pleasure in making these "lineal metaphors," "pure poetry, or pure plasticity," as he called them (*SL* 119, 121). During 1927 and 1928 Lorca worked on the avant-garde review *gallo* (rooster), aimed at renewing the provincial, stagnant atmosphere of Granada (*OC* 1:1123). The publication, in the second issue of *gallo*, of the Catalan "El Manifest groc" (The Yellow Manifesto; in Spanish, "Manifiesto antiartístico" [The Manifesto Against Art]), proclaiming the end of old art in favor of the technological advances of the new world, outraged the city's bourgeoisie. *Gallo* did not survive beyond this issue, however, as Lorca soon became involved with other projects in Madrid.

Alongside his many professional successes Lorca was going through a difficult period artistically as well as emotionally, as expressed in his correspondence. In his letters to Catalan friends during the summer of 1927 Lorca was careful to insist on the independence of his aesthetic position from surrealism: "I HAVE AND I FEEL I HAVE MY FEET FIRMLY ON THE GROUND IN ART. I FEAR the abyss and the dreams in the reality of my life, in love, in the daily encounter with others" (*SL* 117). At the end of the summer and during the fall of 1928 he wrote about being enmeshed in serious sentimental conflicts, "afflicted by passions" that can be attributed to several circumstances, but mainly to his physical and aesthetic separation from his friend Dalí (*SL* 134, 143). Luis Buñuel seemed to belittle Lorca's surrealistic works in the presence of Dalí, and Dalí himself had strongly criticized *The Gypsy Ballads* as too traditional. Withdrawing from Dalí, Lorca had clearly chosen his own artistic path, which he described as "my new *spiritualist* manner, pure disembodied emotion, detached from logical control but—careful! careful!—with a tremendous poetic logic. It is not surrealism—careful!—the clearest self-awareness illuminates them [his poems]" (*SL* 135).

His relationship with Emilio Aladrén (1906–1944), a handsome young sculptor and womanizer, was also a source of jealousy and pain for Lorca. This relationship, and the growing distance between Lorca and Dalí, greatly contributed to Lorca's depression. This situation was exacerbated by General Miguel Primo de Rivera's dictatorship and his opposition to the intelligentsia. Lorca's play *Amor de Don Perlimplín con Belisa en su jardín,* 1933 (*The Love of Don Perlimplín and Belisa in the Garden*) was suppressed by government censors in 1929. Together with other writers, Lorca signed a document protesting the repressive political situation. All these factors gave Lorca the impetus to do what he had been saying for some time he would: leave Spain.

On 12 June 1929 Lorca left for America with Fernando de los Ríos Urruti. After a brief stay in Paris and London they arrived in New York on 25 June. There Lorca enrolled in English classes at Columbia University. Although Lorca never learned to speak English, his personality and musical talent helped him overcome linguistic barriers, as he dazzled people at parties with his singing and piano playing. Through American journalist Mildred Adams (1894–1980), whom Lorca had met in Granada in 1928, the poet was introduced to Henry Herschell Brickell (1889–1952), a literary critic for the *New York Herald* who had visited Spain and knew of Lorca's successful *The Gypsy Ballads.* He and his wife introduced Lorca to many friends at parties held at their apartment. In his visits to Harlem, Lorca was able to appreciate black-American music and to respond sensitively to the plight of blacks in American society. In 1931 he told an interviewer that his coming from Granada facilitated his sympathetic understanding of all persecuted groups, of the Gypsy, black, Jew that all people carry inside themselves (*OC* 2:891).

Lorca spent part of the summer at Lake Eden, in Vermont, at the home of Philip Cummings, an American student and poet whom he had met at the Resi in 1928. There he and Cummings worked on the English translation of *Songs.* Lorca also stayed at the home of Spanish friends, professors at Columbia, in the Catskill mountains near Shandaken, and in Newburgh, New York. When he returned to Manhattan in September he moved to John Jay Hall on the Columbia campus, where he resided until January 1930. Early in 1930 Lorca was invited by the Hispano-Cuban Cultural Institution to travel to Cuba. During this time Lorca composed poems that would later be part of *Poeta en Nueva York,* 1940 (*Poet in New York*).

Lorca witnessed the 1929 economic crash, as he wrote in letters to his family, and his anticapitalistic feelings deepened at the sight of human beings destroyed by what he perceived to be a cruel economic system. In an interview from 1933 he described Wall Street as a place where death and gold coexisted with a total absence of spirit (*OC* 2:904). For him New York was a mixture of inhuman architecture and anguish. Only blacks, whom Lorca described as the most spiritual element of North American culture, escaped the inhumanity of that world because they still had faith and hope (*OC* 2:902–3). He also expressed his fascination with the new "talking pictures," although his only screenplay, *Viaje a la luna* (*Trip to the Moon*), written in 1929 and published posthumously in 1980, originated as a silent film project and was never produced. He was also interested in off-Broadway fringe theaters like the Theater Guild and the Neighborhood Playhouse, where *Blood Wedding* would be produced in 1935 under the title *Bitter Oleander.* He felt New York was an ideal place to witness the new type of theater he was increasingly committed to creating for the revival of the Spanish stage (*OC* 2:891).

In March 1930 Lorca arrived in Havana and was received as one of the most famous Spanish writers of the time. Afro-Cuban music attracted him as much as jazz, particularly the type called *son,* a musical and dance form popular in Cuba in the 1920s and 1930s, especially in the province of Santiago.[14] In Cuba, Lorca lectured very successfully and wrote most of the play *El público,* 1976 (*The Public*). A commentary on contemporary theater, as well as a way of dealing with the question of sexual freedom, this play reflects how Lorca's state of mind continued to be tormented by personal questions and artistic concerns. In June 1930 he returned to Spain.

In December that same year *La zapatera prodigiosa* (*The Shoemaker's Prodigious Wife*) premiered in Madrid with great success, even though Lorca stressed that the play no longer reflected his current views on theater. From then on Lorca alternated his poetry writing with the production and direction of his own plays. His intense dedication to the theater in the decade of the 1930s sprang from his conviction that the genre was the instrument best suited to communicate with the public and to bring about change. He was acutely aware of the social nature of theater and of its aesthetic and didactic influence.[15] He often denounced the superficiality of bourgeois plays, which were enjoying great success on the Spanish stage. At the same time, he remarked that the experimental plays he was working on while in New York and afterward were unperformable, not only because of their innovative stage requirements, but more importantly because they dealt with themes the audience did not want to confront and because they denounced established hypocrisy. In 1935 he declared that the present times required the poet to open up his veins for others (*OC* 2:978), attesting to his belief in a theater committed to the human cause, that art for art's sake had become an untenable option for any authentic artist (*DS* 128).

Changes were also occurring in the government. Primo de Rivera resigned early in 1930. A provisional government was then established and elections were announced for April 1931. The victory of the Second Republic in these elections marked a new period for the country. The coming to power of the Republic announced the beginning of a democratic government open to social reforms. The intellectual and liberal middle class that favored the Republic set out to write a constitution that they believed would remedy the long-standing political, economic, and social ills of the country. However, the Republic's plans to take away the church's monopoly on education and its influence on society and to implement an agrarian reform were soon opposed by the traditional oligarchy (Church, nobility, army, landowners).[16] Lorca publicly aligned himself with the Republic, rejecting bourgeois values as he had since his early years in Granada. His well-known position as a leftist intellectual would prove to be fatal when the Civil War broke out and the Right took control of Granada.

In August 1931 Lorca finished the play *Así que pasen cinco años,* first performed in English in 1945 (*Once Five Years Pass*), which reflects his concerns about sterility and frustration. These themes permeate Lorca's production from *Book of Poems* to such later works as *Yerma* (1934) and *Doña Rosita, the Spinster* (1935). He also became involved in the creation and direction of the itinerant university theater La Barraca, a project of the Republic whose goal, in the new democratic spirit, was to present plays from Spanish classical authors from the sixteenth and seventeenth centuries to the people in rural areas of the country. This project fulfilled Lorca's belief that theater was especially suited to educational purposes (*OC* 2:906).

Under the sponsorship of the Committees for Intellectual Cooperation, founded in February 1932 and aimed at promoting educational exchanges, Lorca delivered a series of lectures around the country during March, April, and May 1932. One of these trips took him to Galicia, in northwestern Spain. This trip resulted in *Seis Poemas Galegos,* 1935 (*Six Galician Poems*), written in the Galician language. In the summer of 1932 Lorca finished his play *Blood Wedding.* The premiere of this play in 1933 at the Beatriz Theater in Madrid led to Lorca's first box-office success and thus provided him some financial independence. *The Love of Don Perlimplín and Belisa in the Garden* premiered at the Español Theater in Madrid in April 1933.

Meanwhile, Spanish fascism was advancing, encouraged by Hitler's rise to power in Germany in 1933. That year's Spanish elections brought victory to the Rightist electoral coalition CEDA (Spanish Confederation of Autonomous Right-Wing Groups) and to its leader José María Gil Robles (1898–1980), also head of the Catholic party.[17] Lorca had already shown his opposition to the right by joining the Association of Friends of the Soviet Union and by participating in a protest, held during the 1 May workers celebration, against Hitler's brutality. In September 1933 Lorca left for Buenos Aires, where he lectured and where his plays were widely acclaimed and financially successful. *Blood Wedding* premiered in Buenos Aires in October 1933; in December *The Shoemaker's Prodigious Wife* premiered in Argentina, in a much more elaborate, more musical mise-en-scène than the 1930 production; and in January 1934 *Mariana Pineda* premiered in Buenos Aires. Lorca traveled to Uruguay to lecture early in 1934, and then returned to Spain from Buenos Aires in April.

By this time the Right was becoming increasingly militant. José Antonio Primo de Rivera (1903–1936), the founder of the Spanish Fascist party in 1933, was imitating the brutal strategies of the German Nazis. Lorca responded to this violence by publicly aligning himself with "those who have nothing," and by espousing the need for intellectuals like himself "to sacrifice" (*OC* 2:973; translation mine). When Gil Robles became minister of war in May 1935 he appointed General Francisco Franco (1892–1975; dictator 1936–1975) head of his general staff, and all of the reforms implemented by the Republic in its early period were scaled back. The polarization between Republicans (supporters of the Republic and democracy) and the Right (conservatives and supporters of the Catholic church) was becoming sharply defined.

The death of Lorca's friend, the bullfighter Ignacio Sánchez Mejías, who was gored by a bull in August 1934, inspired his *Lamento por Ignacio Sánchez Mejías* (*Lament for Ignacio Sánchez Mejías*), published in May 1935. The premiere of his play *Yerma* in December 1934 polarized the press with enthusiastic reviews from left-wing newspapers and condemnation from those in the Right. *Blood Wedding* opened in New York in February 1935. That same year, *Doña Rosita, la soltera* (*Doña Rosita, the Spinster*), a play set in the provincial atmosphere of Granada, premiered in Catalonia; it deals with thematic concerns present in Lorca's work since his early poems: frustration and social restraints to personal fulfillment.

The February 1936 elections were preceded by general unrest among the working classes protesting against the increasing repression from the Right. The violent tactics used by General Franco agains workers' uprisings in Asturias, a Northern coal-mining province, wiped out the workers' revolts but did not eliminate the revolutionary fervor. The rising Fascists' attempt to return to the old order convinced the Left of the need to form a coalition of workers and trade unions, the Popular Front, aimed at returning to the policies of the first two years of the Republic. The Right was confident that it could repeat its 1933 victory by emerging as a united program of conservative parties. Before the February 1936 elections, Lorca read in public a statement in support of the Popular Front. This statement was later published, with Lorca's name prominently displayed, in the Communist paper *Mundo Obrero* (Worker's World). The Right failed to offer a solid and united program and the victory of the Popular Front caused the upper classes to fear a possible Marxist revolution. When Gil Robles lost, the followers of CEDA allied themselves with Primo de Rivera's fascist party. The polarization was now clearly defined, with fascist and right-wing groups on one side and communist and socialist youth associations on the other. At this time Lorca broadened his political activities by joining the Association of Friends of South America and the Friends of Portugal. These groups were devoted to fighting dictatorial regimes, such as those in Cuba and Brazil, and the one in Portugal under Antonio de Oliveira Salazar (1889–1970, dictatorial prime minister 1932–1968).[18]

In June 1936 Lorca finished the play *La casa de Bernarda Alba* (*The House of Bernarda Alba*). The cruelty of Bernarda Alba toward her daughters, her intolerance and intransigence toward anything or anyone who dared to contradict her beliefs, made her a metaphorical premonition of the tragic situation that existed in the country after the Civil War erupted in July 1936. (Before leaving Madrid for Granada, where he was assassinated in August, Lorca read *The House of Bernarda Alba* to a gathering of friends).

Lorca returned to Granada on 14 July 1936. On 17 July the Nationalist rebels, and their so-called National Movement with General Francisco Franco, revolted against the Republic in Spanish Morocco. It did not take long for these anti-Republican forces to take control of Granada. On 16 August Manuel Fernández Montesinos, Lorca's brother-in-law and Granada's socialist mayor, was murdered, and Lorca was arrested. After being detained for two or three days he was executed by order of the rebel governor, José Valdés Guzmán.[19] The murder took place on the outskirts of Granada, at dawn on 18 or 19 August. To justify the crime allegations were made that Lorca had been acting as an agent of the Soviet Union. Although Lorca was never a militant in any particular political party, his public declarations and friendship with individuals such as Fernando de los Ríos, minister of justice and later of public education for the Republic, identified him with the liberal leftist mentality and with the democratic and socialistic views the Right despised.

Critical analysis of Lorca's work was initially subsumed by the myths surrounding his death. Under Franco, discussion of Lorca's death was at first silenced. Later, it was attributed to confusion and error during the first moments of the rebellion. Numerous articles and books have been written about the circumstances and reasons surrounding the event. For some, Lorca's death resulted from a vendetta among Granada homosexuals, with no political motivations.[20] For others it was the result of the machine of terror deployed by the military, the fascists, and the extreme rightist forces that took over Granada during the first months of the rebellion.[21] According to Ramón Ruiz Alonso, a member of CEDA, the poet "had done more damage with his pen" than others were capable of with guns.[22]

From the beginning of his career Lorca had denounced the hypocrisy of the bourgeoisie and its conviction in the righteousness of its beliefs. He also had contempt for the insensitivity of the Catholic church toward the needs of the people. The uncompromising values of these two groups, church and bourgeoisie, clashed with the desire for freedom and civil rights defended by intellectuals and the working classes. Lorca had upheld the rights of the dispossessed and the freedom to express one's love in any form. He was able to tap into the common tradition of his people, one in which the most deeply felt hopes and expectations were free of political, religious, or social boundaries. He was, however, ultimately a victim of the violent frictions between those very boundaries. Lorca's assassination is still a subject of research because of the confusion surrounding it, but it is no longer the reason his writings continue to attract critical attention. Essays, books, anthologies, critical editions, festivals, and symposia analyzing his writings reveal an author with a profound understanding of his country's traditions, and a great artist far ahead of his time in his aesthetic tenets.

Notes

1. This brief introductory biographical account owes much to Ian Gibson's biography *Federico García Lorca: A Life* (New York: Pantheon, 1989). Of interest for Lorca's early years is the book by his brother, Francisco García Lorca, *In The Green Morning: Memories of Federico,* trans. Christopher Maurer (New York: New Directions, 1986).

2. Spanish poet and philologist Dámaso Alonso (1898–1990), a member of Lorca's generation, writes about the poet as the expression of the Spanish essence in *Poetas españoles contemporáneos* (Contemporary Spanish Poets) (Madrid: Gredos, 1958).

3. "Conversation with Bagaría," an interview from 1936, is included in Federico García Lorca, *Deep Song and Other Prose,* trans. and ed. Christopher Maurer (New York: New Directions, 1980) 130. Further references to this translation throughout the present study are cited parenthetically, abbreviated as *DS.*

4. For a lyrical evocation of Granada, see Lorca's lecture *How a City Sings from November to November,* trans. and ed. Christopher Maurer (San Francisco: Cadmus, 1984). Before the political and religious reunification of the Peninsular territory in 1492 under the Catholic Monarchs, the Iberian Peninsula was shared by Arabs, Christians, and Jews. Their harmonious coexistence is well documented; for example, in the major cultural center of Toledo intellectuals from each of the three groups worked together at the School of Translators under King Alphonse X (1221–1284). As main players in the money market, Jews determined the conditions for lending and credit to all sectors of society. Their financial preeminence made Jews the target of hatred and resentment that culminated in their expulsion from the Iberian Peninsula in the fifteenth century.

5. See *Obras Completas* (Complete Works), ed. Arturo del Hoyo, 18th ed., 2 vols. (Madrid: Aguilar, 1973) 1:1154. Subsequent references to this work, abbreviated *OC,* are cited parenthetically.

6. The poet Jorge Guillén (1893–1984), a friend and frequent correspondent, offers a telling account of García Lorca's magnetism and personal charm in "Federico en persona" (Federico in Person), the prologue to *OC,* volume 1 (xv–lxxxi; see esp. xv–xviii, xliii).

7. Guillén, "Federico en persona" (xv–xviii).

8. See Gibson, *A Life* 15–16, 17–18.

9. Francisco García Lorca, *In The Green Morning* 45.

10. "Primeros escritos de Federico" (First Writings by Federico) 160, a section in Francisco García Lorca's *Federico y su mundo* (Federico and His World), ed. Mario Hernández (Madrid: Alianza, 1980) 158–73 that was not included in the English translation, *In the Green Morning.*

11. See Federico García Lorca, *Selected Letters,* ed. and trans. David Gershator (New York; New Directions, 1983) 94. Subsequent references to this work are cited

parenthetically, abbreviated *S.L.* with the page number.

12. See Rafael Santos Torroella, *La miel es más dulce que la sangre. Las épocas lorquiana y freudiana de Salvador Dalí* (Honey Is Sweeter Than Blood. The Lorcan and Freudian Periods of Salvador Dalí) (Barcelona: Seix Barral, 1984) 18, 85.

13. See Gibson, *A Life* 197–99.

14. Alejo Carpentier, *La música en Cuba* (Music in Cuba) (México: Fondo de Cultura Económica, 1946) 242.

15. In public statements and interviews through the 1930s Lorca stressed the social nature of theater, the artist's need to communicate with the public, and his solidarity with the dispossessed and marginalized (see *OC* 2:895, 2:906, 2:973, 2:978, 2:1019–20).

16. For background information concerning the Second Spanish Republic and the Civil War, see Gabriel Jackson, *The Spanish Republic and the Civil War, 1931–1939* (Princeton, N.J.: Princeton UP, 1972), and Gerald Brenan, *The Spanish Labyrinth: An Account of the Social and Political Background of the Civil War* (Cambridge, Eng.: Cambridge UP, 1974).

17. See Gibson, *A Life* 366.

18. See Gibson, *A Life* 430.

19. Valdés Guzmán had been a member of the Fascist party and was the son of a general in the Civil Guard (a paramilitary police force founded in the mid-nineteenth century to secure rural areas from bandits; confrontations were perennial between the Civil Guard and working classes and Gypsies). See Ian Gibson, *Granada en 1936 y el asesinato de Federico García Lorca* (Granada in 1936 and the Assassination of Federico García Lorca) (Barcelona: Editorial Crítica, 1979) 63.

20. See Louis Schonberg, *Federico García Lorca. L'homme. L'oeuvre* (Federico García Lorca: The Man, His Works) (Paris: Plon, 1956) 115–35.

21. See Gibson, *A Life* 446–70; Gibson, *Granada en 1936*, esp. chapters 5, 6, 12.

22. Cited in Gibson, *A Life* 458; see also 455–59.

CHAPTER 1

The Major Poetry

This chapter deals with Lorca's three major poetry collections: *Poem of the Deep Song, The Gypsy Ballads,* and *Poet in New York.* The discussion of selected poems from these books will illustrate Lorca's thematic and aesthetic concerns in the decade of the 1920s.

In Lorca's poetry, images and symbols are inextricably woven together and function as vehicles for major themes recurring throughout his oeuvre. The moon, blood, and the color green, for example, are some well-known Lorcan symbols expressing the all-pervasive themes of life and death, vitality and decay, desire and frustration. Within this symbolic structure Lorca's poetry attests to the author's continuous reflection upon the nature of poetic language. Lorca's metaphoric transformations achieve the freedom of artistic autonomy together with the awareness of the irretrievable distance between the word and the world, between art and reality. The impossibility of reenacting the original, mythic fusion of word and object, of the name with the thing it designates, explains the tone of failed desire that pervades Lorca's poetics and accounts for the poet's awareness of the artificiality of language, of poetry as a construct.

As Russian critic Roman Jakobson states, the distinctive feature of poetry "is present when the word is felt as a word and not a mere representation of the object being named or an outburst of emotion."[1] My critical reading will address Lorca's writings as texts that reflect on language itself, texts that often comment upon writing as a theme and upon their own linguistic construction, not only within the poems themselves but also in relation to other literary genres. Poetic language functions as a tool allowing the artistic expression of the world but hindering direct apprehension of it. Lorca's art faces both the enabling and limiting aspects of poetic language, that is, language is a self-contradictory tool but the only one available to the artist.

Poetry occupied Lorca throughout his life and permeates his dramatic works. His first collection, *Book of Poems* (1921), follows Symbolist and Romantic poetic traditions also evident in his first staged play, *The Butterfly's Evil Spell* (1920). Romantic overtones can be heard in later works, as in the play *Mariana Pineda* (on which Lorca began work in the 1920s); however, we also see at this point an infusion of irony and an obvious concern with formal structure. The themes of childhood, nature, sexual and religious crisis, imagination versus reality, together with pressing questions about the creative process itself, appear in poems as well as in dramatic works. In addition to *Mariana Pineda,* the plays *The Shoemaker's Prodigious Wife* and *The Love of Don Perlimplín and Belisa in the Garden* (on which Lorca also began work in the 1920s, although they were not produced until 1930 and 1933, respectively) are stylized versions of the conflict between imagination and reality, a theme that receives differing elaborations throughout Lorca's writings.

While in Madrid in the 1920s, Lorca came into contact with the avant-garde movements. Some of the aesthetic tenets of these movements (emphasis on the image and humor, and elimination of narrative and sentimental elements) had an impact on the poetry collections Lorca was then writing, *Poem of the Deep Song, Suites, Songs,* and *The Gypsy Ballads.* Another major influence in this period was the Spanish baroque poet Luis de Góngora, whose tercentenary was commemorated by Lorca and his generation in 1927. Gongorine aesthetics relies on the imagination to discover unexpected relations in the world that are then expressed in startling metaphors, as exemplified by Lorca in *The Gypsy Ballads.* The year 1928, when that collection was published, marks a crucial new direction in Lorca's aesthetics. The poet moves from advocating the transformation of reality by the imagination to affirming the realm of inspiration, where poetry is detached from logical connections with the world. Inspiration leads to the *hecho poético* (poetic fact or event), an image freed from analogical constraints and thus endowed with its own poetic logic. These aesthetic concerns imbue Lorca's writings during his American experience (1929–1930), from which came *Poet in New York* (1940) as well as innovative dramatic works such as *The Public* (1930) and *Once Five Years Pass* (1931). During the last six years of his life, Lorca continued to write poetry, including the works published posthumously in *The Divan at Tamarit* (1940) and *Sonnets [of Dark Love]* (1984). Themes of time, the beloved's absence, fertility versus sterility, and desire versus societal restrictions permeate both poetic and dramatic works from these last years, such as the trilogy, *Blood Wedding, Yerma,* and *The House of Bernarda Alba.*

Deep Song

The Festival of the Deep Song, held in June 1922, was promoted by Spanish musician and composer Manuel de Falla and by Lorca. Both artists viewed Deep Song as the most authentic musical expression of southern Spain and were worried about its adulteration. In order to help preserve the purity of this ancient music, Falla and Lorca planned the festival competition. As one of the events leading up to the festival, in February 1922, Lorca delivered his lecture "Cante Jondo. El primitivo canto andaluz" ("Deep Song: Primitive Andalusian Song"). Some aspects of Deep Song discussed in this lecture must be understood in preparation for the reading of *Poem of the Deep Song*.

Lorca based his lecture on Falla's research on Deep Song. In the lecture, he differentiates this musical form (the most ancient primitive music in Europe, originating in songs of India), from its modern popularized version, flamenco. Although Deep Song is associated with Gypsies, they did not originate it. When Gypsies arrived in Spain in the middle of the fifteenth century they found in Andalusia an indigenous musical tradition consisting of Arabic and Hebrew elements which they fused with their own music. To it they added elements similar to those found in Hindu chant, such as enharmonic modulation and the reiterative use of one sustained note. The resulting combination is what is known today as Deep Song. Deep Song is a complex musical form voicing the anguish and despair pervading the human condition. These compositions, traditionally sung in a coarse voice, are difficult to interpret. In contrast to the colorful flamenco, where histrionics are emphasized for popular consumption, Deep Song succeeds only when emotion comes through the voice of the *cantaor* (singer) and the *duende* appears.

Lorca developed his theory on the *duende* in his lecture "Juego y teoría del duende" ("Play and Theory of the *Duende*"), delivered in Argentina in 1933. *Duende* is a power that comes not from artistic virtuosity or technical competence but from the unconscious. The *duende* of Deep Song is not controlled by reason or analogy—as is the case with inspiration coming from the muse—but arises from the dark and liminal areas of being where passionately personal experience attempts to burst all bounds and life struggles against death. That is why the substance of Deep Song is the experience of *pena negra* (dark sorrow). *Duende,* sorrow, and their expression in Deep Song spring from a desire that forever strives but is never fulfilled.[2]

Poem of the Deep Song (1931)

Lorca learned much from Deep Song that benefited his poetry. The despair characteristic of this *duende*-inspired music and the conciseness of its form echoed Lorca's existential concerns and offered him a paradigm for artistic exploration. Far from imitating Deep Song, Lorca merges his own inspiration with these popular sources, resulting in a highly stylized new artistic creation. In *Poem of the Deep Song,* Lorca creates meaning by infusing intense emotionalism within carefully set formal structures.

The book opens with an introductory poem, "Baladilla de los tres ríos" ("Ballad of the Three Rivers"). The book is then organized around the three main forms of Deep Song: *siguiriya, soleá, saeta,* plus a fourth section on the *petenera.* The *petenera* is a song intended to be danced. It is thus considered less pure than the other three, where the emphasis lies solely on the guitar and the voice. The *petenera* section is followed by four less unified sections on various topics related to flamenco, including the capriccios. The book closes with two dramatic dialogues.

In addition to their connection with music, Lorca's poems also draw upon pictorial traditions to portray various aspects of the world of Deep Song. Like scenes from a *retablo* (altarpiece), the poems paint different scenes of a story or event. The three main types of songs (*siguiriya, soleá,* and *saeta*), as well as Lorca's references to the cities of Granada, Córdoba, and Seville, correspond to the tripartite structure of the altarpiece so common in Spanish churches. Other aspects, such as the *petenera,* the flamenco vignettes, and the capriccios, are elements added to the essential core of Deep Song. The *retablo* model allows Lorca to present the story told in Deep Song as the expression of the history of the Gypsies and of Andalusia, and in a form that, like the pictorial images in an altarpiece, expresses the maximum of pathos with the minimum of verbal narration.

The introductory "Ballad of the Three Rivers" paints a stylized picture of a polarized Andalusia. At one pole is an Andalusia characterized by its desire for life and love, which is symbolized by the dynamic Guadalquivir River and the seaboard region of Seville. At the other extremity is the region's frustration in death or unfulfillment, represented by the humble Darro and Genil rivers of Granada and the interior regions of Andalusia. The polarity Lorca envisions in Andalusia is one he confronts in his own art between passion and its expression in a poetic construct that, by shaping emotion, constrains it within formal boundaries.

This polarized perspective, as it illustrates the ever-present conflict between content and expression, is continued in the *siguiriya* section of the book, entitled "Poema de la Siguiriya gitana" ("Poem of the Gypsy Siguiriya"). The *siguiriya* is a form of Deep Song considered by Lorca the prototype of that art. Dating probably from the fourteenth or fifteenth centuries, the *siguiriya* is imbued with the tragedy of the Gypsies, who sing it when their pain becomes unbearable. Lorca's poetic rendition of the *siguiriya* is entitled

"El paso de la Siguiriya" ("Passage of the Siguiriya"; *CP* 102–3):

> A girl of dark skin
> among black butterflies,
> next to a serpent of mist,
> a serpent of white.
>
> Sky of earth,
> *earth of light.*
>
> Walking chained to the trembling
> of a rhythm that never arrives,
> a heart of silver in her breast,
> a dagger in her right.
>
> *Siguiriya,* where are you taking
> your rhythm headless and blind?
> What moon will harvest
> your sorrow of rosebay and lime?
>
> *Sky of earth,*
> *earth of light.*

The personification of the *siguiriya* as a dark girl is a mythic embodiment of the song's feeling and of its particular attributes. The butterfly is a symbol traditionally associated with the soul and with poetry, while the serpent represents evil or some type of dark or terrestrial wisdom. The butterflies' blackness makes the spirit of the *siguiriya* seem disturbing, while the whiteness of the serpent of mist points to the confusion or lack of clear definition in this song's coilings. This disarray in the order of things is reiterated in the chorus, with the dialogue between earth and sky, darkness (of earth) and light (of sky). The references to silver and the dagger associate this musical expression with metals, which in Lorca are often identified with the moon (as both cold and silvery). Silver, dagger, and the moon form a symbolic constellation for the premonition of danger and death.

The *siguiriya* begins traditionally with an anguish-filled scream and continues with a series of vocal inflections with no distinct beginnings or ends. The sorrow of this song is left unresolved because it stems from the existential awareness of death. Lorca objectifies this sorrow in the images of rosebay and lime, common plants in the Andalusian landscape and symbols of sterility and death in his symbolic language. This poem illustrates the tragic fate of the *siguiriya* as an expression of human suffering. The anguish articulated in this song is not resolved, for it remains trapped in the structural boundaries of the very voice and guitar expressing it.

The ten compositions of the *soleá* section, entitled "Poema de la soleá" ("Poem of the Soleá"), (*soleá* is an Andalusian pronunciation of the word *soledad,* meaning solitude or loneliness) depict the landscape of interior Andalusia, a dry, quiet, old land of sorrow. Several poems reiterate the analogy between a plowshare entering the ground and a dagger stabbing a chest ("Puñal/Dagger," *CP* 108–9). Consequently, the harvest of sorrow from that land is compared to the sorrow of the human heart, conveyed through Deep Song as an ever present, existential pain. The *soleá* is thus a faltering voice better articulated in the scream, the "Ay!" that comes from the land pervaded by sorrow and thus provides the title for the following poem (*CP* 110–11):

> The scream leaves
> on the wind
> its shadow of cypress.
>
> (Leave me in these fields,
> leave me here crying.)
>
> All has broken in the world.
> Nothing remains but silence.
>
> (Leave me in these fields,
> leave me here crying.)
>
> Bitten by bonfires,
> lightless horizons.
>
> (Leave me, I tell you,
> in these fields here, crying.)

The careful structuring of this poem establishes a seesaw movement between the three- and two-line groupings and the intercalated lines for chorus, placed in parentheses. While the line groupings locate the sorrow in the landscape, the chorus refers it back to the subjectivity of the poetic speaker. The first three lines associate the scream with death through the image of the cypress, a tree endowed with funereal connotations since the age of Greek myths. Death has destroyed all hope of cosmic harmony: "All has broken in the world." The remaining silence represents the failure of the *soleá,* for its voice is uttered in the void. The lightless horizon (lines 10–11) holds no hope or future promise; it appears dark because its light has been consumed in the bonfires of time. In the chorus's lines, the speaker demands that any consolation be considered impossible and therefore rejected; he uses the command form, repeats deictic words ("these fields, "here") and addresses the reader directly ("I tell you").

The "Poema de la saeta" ("Poem of the Saeta") section consists of eight compositions evoking the atmosphere of the *saeta,* a plaintive melody sung to the sculptures of Christ and the Virgin as they are carried on *pasos,* or floats, by penitents during Easter processions. *Saeta* means arrow, connoting the piercing character of this song, which wounds with its sorrow. While the *saeta* is sung the procession stops, not resuming until the song is finished. Night is the time for this song, illuminated by the candles and oil lamps of floats and penitents in the processions, by the lampposts in the streets and fireflies in the air. The center stage for the *saeta* parade is Seville, identified with the famous Giralda tower in the cathedral built by the Arabs in the twelfth century that still stands on the banks of the Guadalquivir. "Sevilla/Seville" is the title of the following poem (*CP* 118–21):

> Seville is a tower
> full of bowmen so fine.
>
> *Seville for wounding.*
> *Córdoba for dying.*
>
> A city lying in wait
> to coil up long rhythms
> like burning vine tendrils
> or winding labyrinths.
>
> *Seville for wounding!*
>
> Over her clear plain
> beneath the bow of her sky,
> she lets her river's
> constant arrow take flight.

Córdoba for dying!

And crazed with horizon,
she mingles in her wine
the perfection of Dionysus
and the bitterness of Don Juan.

Seville for wounding.
Seville, always, for wounding!

Even more pointedly than the *siguiriya* and the *soleá,* the *saeta* depicts the movement of desire. Its meanderings and coilings mirror those of the word projecting itself forward in search of fusion with the world. The *saeta* articulates the search more than the fulfillment of it, the coilings of the word and desire in a movement without fulfillment. Seville is for Lorca the scene where desire is displayed. By contrast, Córdoba, like Granada in the introductory poem, is the interior of Andalusia, which Lorca associates with frustration and death. Seville is the symbol and target for the *saeta:* the vertical structure of its Giralda tower and its river traversing the landscape replicate the *saeta* shooting its song of desire toward the city, where its long rhythms will coil up in the city's winding streets (*CP* 119). The whole city resonates with the song, with the sky and plain forming the bow itself. Lorca finds in the geography of Seville the poetic articulation of the wound of desire that the *saeta* melody expresses. Hence Seville's wine, or passion, is a mixture of Dionysus and Don Juan (*CP* 121). It is a perfect orgiastic and Dionysian celebration, for it allows the open expression of desire. It is also bitter like Don Juan's passion, a Sevillian himself, because its quest for the object of desire is never fulfilled.

The eight poems in the "Gráfico de la Petenera" ("Graphic of the Petenera") section refer to the *petenera,* a dance. In "Danza" ("Dance," *CP* 126–29) the *petenera* is represented by six Gypsy girls dancing in the garden, limned against the darkness of the night. The graphic nature of the poem is clear in the insistence on the whiteness of the girls contrasting with the black of night. "In the night of the garden, / dressed in white, / dance six gypsy girls." These six girls are creatures of the moon in "Las seis cuerdas" ("Six Strings," *CP* 126–27), another poem in this section, in which the role of the six girls is given to the strings of the guitar:

> The guitar
> makes dreams cry.
> The sobbing of lost souls
> escapes
> its round mouth.
> And like the tarantula
> it weaves a great star
> to ensnare sighs floating
> in its black
> cistern of wood.

The strings are depicted as a tarantula weaving in its music the same message of fatalism that Lorca perceives in the "great star" of the moon. Beginning in his early poetry, the moon is associated with the cyclical passage of time; its beams make it look like a tarantula in the sky weaving the threads of time and frustration into the fabric of human existence. These poems create a constellation of images where the girls/strings—the tarantula of the guitar—replicate in their music the same message of death that the poetic speaker perceives in the tarantula/moon.[3] As it captures that message, the guitar music echoes the striving of language to voice human suffering within and beyond verbal boundaries.

The section entitled "Viñetas flamencas" ("Flamenco Vignettes") depicts major figures in flamenco (Silverio Franconetti and Juan Breva) and various aspects of this art. The "Seis caprichos" ("Six Capriccios") section, which also deals with various elements of the world of Deep Song (the oil lamp, the castanet), illustrates a concern with images that is reminiscent of Góngora and the *ultraísmo* avant-garde movement. The next section, entitled "Adivinanza de la guitarra" ("Riddle of the Guitar," *CP* 146–47) presents the guitar as a crossroad where six maidens, represented by the strings, are dancing. They would like to fall into a reverie of the past, but golden Polyphemus (the cyclops in Homer's *Odyssey*), with its one eye (the middle hole), an image for the guitar, holds them in his embrace. This poem can be seen as encapsulating a view on aesthetics. The six strings are the "words" of the guitar, since they modulate its voice. They want to sing nostalgic, dreamy songs (a possible allusion to a type of Romantic and symbolist poetry), but are kept prisoner by the guitar itself, that is, by the constraints of the instrument. Similarly, the word, actualizing the potential in language, cannot be reduced to a mere reflection of feelings, since it has to fulfill the demands of language as a system with its own norms.

The book closes with two dramatic dialogues written in 1925, "Escena del teniente coronel de la Guardia Civil" ("Scene of the Lieutenant Colonel of the

Civil Guard," *CP* 152–57) and "Diálogo del Amargo ("Dialogue of Amargo, the Bitter One," *CP* 156–63). Just as Lorca objectifies feelings through personification, he uses dramatization to give concrete shape to basic emotions. These dialogues, which include stage directions, offer a distinct contrast between the direct, almost schematic language of the characters and the lyrical tone of the directions. The characters' "realistic" language also contrasts with their qualities as creatures of myth, while the stage directions, traditionally just a convenient tool, become an arena for lyrical expression. This reversal illustrates Lorca's constant experimentation with the expressive means offered by different genres. In "Dialogue of Amargo" the main character, the bitter one, is one of three young men on the road to Granada. Left behind, alone, Amargo meets a rider (a familiar Lorcan image of the premonition of death) from Malaga whose family sells extraordinary knives of gold and silver. The gold knives, reminiscent of the sun, go straight to the heart when used to attack people; those of silver, a possible allusion to the moon, cut the throat like a blade of grass. Amargo ends up accepting the man's invitation to ride with him when the fat serpent of the south, the full moon, comes out. The moon/serpent is the central image of the Lorcan conception of life and death as a cycle in which humans are trapped. The sun bleeds its vitality at sunset, when it is neutralized by the white moon. This bled vigor and spilled passion, caused by the wound of frustration, are absorbed by the moon in its ceaseless phases of time and death. *Poem of the Deep Song* thus ends with Amargo as a possible paradigm for the human condition, as well as for Lorca's reflection on the nature of art and its tenuous link with the world that it purports to re-create.

Lorca was attracted to Deep Song as the artistic expression of a despair that went deeper "than the present heart that creates it or the voice that sings it, because it is almost infinite" (*DS* 30). The works included in *Poem of the Deep Song* are made to express profound emotions but do not contain or possess them; they are artistic constructs pointing to timeless feelings. Lorca described Deep Song as an expression "withdrawn into itself" (*DS* 33), a characterization that echoes the artist's conflict with the poetic word. In this book Lorca tries to express profound emotions within the tight formal constraints of the poem. However, in the same moment as articulating these emotions, the word constrains them within its own limitations as a verbal construct. Deep Song is the musical articulation of human despair because, as in the conflict with poetic language, it strives for release, or a recipient or object of fulfillment, which remains elusive.

The Gypsy Ballads (1928)

Most of the eighteen compositions that comprise *The Gypsy Ballads* were written between 1921 and 1927. The book was published in 1928 under the title *Primer romancero gitano* (*First Gypsy Ballad-Book*), commonly abbreviated to *The Gypsy Ballads*. It won instant fame for Lorca. The ballad is the most distinctive traditional Spanish verse form, consisting of a series of eight-syllable lines that rhyme assonantly (similar vowel sounds) in the even-numbered lines. Developed orally between 1250 and 1500, and still alive in the oral and popular tradition, ballads were later compiled in collections, or *romanceros*. This poetic tradition had been familiar to Lorca since childhood. Most of his Gypsy ballads were included in letters and published in periodicals. They were also recited for friends, thus following a transmission reminiscent of that of the old ballads sung by minstrels.

Lorca described this book as "a retable (portrait) of Andalusia," a land where mysticism and vagueness, coming from its Arabic and Jewish background, are fused with the order, precision, and reason attributed to its Roman past. He chose to call it Gypsy because he considered the Gypsy to be "the loftiest, most profound and aristocratic element" of Spain (*DS* 105). However, Lorca's Gypsy does not have much to do with the real Gypsy living in Andalusia. As the author repeatedly insisted, Gypsies "are a theme" like any other (*SL* 94). They are chosen as the means to re-create a myth of a primitive, natural ideal of life. In this ideal, imagination, creativity, and freedom prevail over the restraints that modern society, through law, reason, and order, places on vital human desires.[4] The great presence in *The Gypsy Ballads* is the Andalusian *pena* (pain) that the Gypsy so faithfully embodies and that Lorca identifies with Granada as the essence of Andalusia.

Lorca emphasized the mythic character of this collection. The Gypsy is presented as the keeper of the "alphabet of Andalusian and universal truth," as the embodiment of a type of basic and primary life whose elements the different ballads portray (*DS* 105). The ballads can also be read as moments in an ongoing meditation on poetic language, and as various resolutions to conflicts facing the poet in his search for artistic expression. Poems in this Gypsy altarpiece have a more elaborate narrative than in *Poem of the Deep Song,* but the narrative is eclipsed by the lyrical and mythic projection of the language toward a hidden level, the other side of the story being narrated, where poetic mystery is never fully elucidated.

The image of the moon, present throughout the collection, is most significant in the first and last poems. The opening ballad, "Romance de la luna, luna" ("Ballad of the Moon, Moon," *CP* 518–21) is the best example:

> The moon came into the forge
> in her bustle of flowering nard.
> The little boy stares at her, stares.
> The boy is staring hard.
> In the shaken air
> the moon moves her arms,
> and shows, lubricious and pure,
> her breasts of hard tin.
> "Moon, moon, moon, run!
> If the gypsies come
> they will use your heart
> to make white necklaces and rings."
> "Let me dance, my little one.
> When the gypsies come,
> they'll find you on the anvil
> with your lively eyes closed tight."
> . . . .
>
> Closer comes the horseman,
> drumming on the plain.
> The boy is in the forge;
> his eyes are closed.
> . . . .
>
> Oh, how the night owl calls,
> calling, calling from its tree!
> The moon is climbing through the sky
> with the child by the hand.
>
> They are crying in the forge,
> all the gypsies, shouting, crying.
> The air is viewing all, views all.
> The air is at the viewing.

The reflection of the moonbeams/arms on the anvil creates a dance-like vision mixing sexual connotations with a feeling of detachment ("lubricious and pure"). The ambiguity of the moon is a constant in this heavenly body as symbol. Located between the heavens and the earth, the moon is celestial, but in its various phases it partakes of the human destiny of birth, maturity, and death. Closely associated with the fertility rhythms of nature (in some countries agricultural work is still organized around the phases of the moon), the moon for many early cultures (Orphic and Pythagorean sects, the Vedas, the Romans, for example) is also the place to which all dead return.[5] Lorca has captured the ambivalence of the moon as a cold star full of romantic implications and suggestions of mystery, danger, death. Blacksmithing, a common activity among Gypsies, is here depicted as the way Gypsies transform metals into beautiful artifacts. In the context of artistic creation, the forge corresponds to the act of poetry writing that Lorca is himself performing.[6] Thus, the boy could be viewed as the young poet, strongly attracted by an inspiration in the form of a feminine figure who embodies a mixture of passion and detachment, seductive mystery and danger. His verbal resistance ("Moon, moon, moon, run!") shows an instinctive suspicion of the danger entailed in falling prey to the moon's enticement.

In his critical study of this collection Herbert Ramsden mentions the popular superstition that the moon was the messenger of death for children who stared at it.[7] The ballad is also reminiscent of the Greek myth of Endymion, a beautiful young man who was seduced into eternal sleep by moon goddess Selene. At the end of the ballad, the moon wins, absorbing into her cold whiteness the open-eyed stare of the child, representing the inspiration for creative writing. Thus, this book could be read as the direct result of the inspiration by the moon. Her light shines over the Gypsy vignettes depicted in the various poems, bringing forth the latent side of reality that plumbs the depths of these mysteries. This is the realm, repressed in broad daylight, from which come creativity as well as the danger of daring to delve into forbidden territories. The moonlight thus symbolizes the inspiration coming from the subconscious, from the realm of instincts. While the Gypsy boy has been engulfed in that realm by the moon, the adult Gypsies are able to transform the moonlight into works of art ("white necklaces and rings," *CP* 519). Paralleling the workings of the primitive mind, the Gypsies rely on their imagination to shape the mystery of natural phenomena into more intelligible forms. However, their final lament indicates how irreducible that mystery remains (lines 25–28). Their crying is the elegiac pain that Lorca identified as the dominant presence of this collection. They cry for the boy who has disappeared, who represents the creative impulse. He has been swallowed up by a realm of mystery that remains elusive to the Gypsies' artistic transformations. Their elegy laments the failed desire, the failed attempt to link with a surrounding world.

"Romance sonámbulo" ("Sleepwalking Ballad," *CP* 526–31) has provoked a great number of commentaries about the many possible avenues it opens to the imagination. Its somnambulant atmosphere places the reader in the realm of the unconscious, in a context similar to the one created by the moon's dance in the forge:

> Green oh how I love you green.
> Green wind. Green boughs. . . .
> With waist of shadow,
> she dreams at her rail,
> green flesh, hair green,
> and her eyes, cold silver.
> Green oh how I love you green.
> Beneath the gypsy moon
> things are looking at her,
> and she can't look at them.
> . . . .
>
> "Compadre, I want to trade
> my stallion for your house,
> my saddle for your mirror,
> my knife for your blanket.
> Compadre, I have come here bleeding,
> from the Cabra Pass."
> "If I could, I would, lad.
> Your offer would be taken.
> But I am me no more,
> nor is my house my own. . . ."
> "Let me go at least
> to the high rails of the house. . . .
> Great railings of the moon,
> where the water roars."
> . . . .
>
> Over the face of the rain-well
> rocked the gypsy girl.
> Green flesh, hair green,
> and her eyes, cold silver.
> An icicle of moonlight
> holds her on the water.
> . . . .

> Drunken Civil Guardsmen
> were beating on the door.
> Green oh how I love you green.
> . . . .

The color green connotes here not only vegetative life and fertility but also the color of rotten flesh: life as fatally bound to the terrestrial cycle of life and death.[8] Green is also associated with the ambivalent color of the moonlight (whitish, silvery, greenish) and with sterility and frustration (Lorca again makes the moon the dominant presence in the scene).[9] The moonlight exerts its fatal power over the Gypsy woman dreamily waiting for someone on her balcony at night. She ends up drowning in the well and is thus found by the other two characters involved in the narrative: a wounded man, possibly a smuggler, who arrives at dawn from the mountains, and his comrade, who apparently lives in the same house as the Gypsy girl.[10] The somnambulant atmosphere in this ballad would permit reading the three characters as projections of the speaker and the ballad as a commentary upon the act of poetic writing. The smuggler's illegality could correspond to the speaker in his half-conscious state, escaping from the law and order of reason. He is desperately seeking a "normal" life in love and marriage with the Gypsy girl, who represents the speaker's desire for a fruitful life and for vital poetry. This wish is mixed with the speaker's forceful expression of the desire for green, which voices the ambivalence of his passion/ poetry. Thus, the girl appears steeped in the green light of the moon, alienated from her surroundings. Things look at her but she cannot return their gaze; she, as the embodiment of the speaker's desire, is unable to establish a link with outside reality. The comrade suggests a father or authority figure to whom the younger man appeals for help. The comrade's alienation ("But I am me no more, / nor is my house my own") suggests the loss of any rational resource for the smuggler, who is therefore fatally bound to existential suffering and unfulfilled passion.

The ascent of both male characters to the high green railings of the moon (the reflection of the moonlight on the balcony), where the Gypsy woman awaits, could be read as the ascent of the speaker toward a climactic confrontation with the frustration of his desire. The moon railing is described as the terminus of their upward journey, symbolic of a moment of truth in the speaker's life, a head-on confrontation with the nature of his existence. In Lorca's writings the impulses of love/desire and poetry are closely intertwined; the ballad's upward journey could then also represent a critical point in the speaker's poetic writing, the center of the moon's realm from which that writing emanates. Lorca frequently uses images of cisterns, pools, and wells of stagnant water, where moon rays exert their hypnotizing effect on the victims who sit at their edge in meditation and reverie. The reiteration of this poetic topos, or common place, calls attention to its importance in Lorca's writings, for it also symbolizes the poet's struggle with his craft. The poet desires to make the word create the worlds of meaning that will bring fulfillment, yet his desire is frustrated by the reflective nature of language. Word and object keep playing a game of reflections with no resolution; the attempt to cause their fusion—or to follow the path of desire— brings death, as represented in the drowning of the Gypsy girl. In the end, the smuggler faces the drunken civil guards violently pounding against the door as they pursue him. They interrupt the sleepwalking atmosphere that has allowed the writing of the poem. The repetition of the first quartet at the end of the poem reiterates the fatality of this green of life, inevitably bound to death.

In contrast to "Sleepwalking Ballad," "La casada infiel" ("The Unfaithful Wife," *CP* 532–37) does indeed depict sexual fulfillment, but under false pretenses, as the woman hides her married status from the Gypsy with whom she makes love. He takes her to the river, a place commonly associated with sexual and other amorous encounters, under the impression that he would be the privileged recipient of her virginity, a highly prized gift in the Gypsy world. The undressing of both protagonists is a process of gradual liberation from social constraints, culminating in the freedom of the sexual act:

> That night the road I ran
> was the finest of them all,
> without a bridle or stirrup
> on a filly made of pearl.
>
> (*CP* 535)

However, the freedom lasts only as long as the sexual encounter. Afterward, they both have to face the reality of their social situation: she as a dissatisfied married woman and he as a "legitimate" Gypsy (as he describes himself later in the ballad). As such, he has to disregard the satisfaction of the adventure and view the woman as a common prostitute, for she allowed herself to have this illicit adventure despite being married.[11] Sexual freedom is thus soon censured by societal norms.

The Gypsy Ballads, as a whole, maintains a tight association between two dichotomies: sexual fulfillment and repression, and artistic achievement and frustration. In "The Unfaithful Wife" the moment of sexual climax is also the peak of poetic achievement. Coldness and passion, as described in the woman's thighs ("one half filled with fire, / the other half with cold," *CP* 535), are perfectly juxtaposed, and the couple performs a dance in which strict form and instinct are in harmony. All restrictions have been discarded, and the narrator abandons himself fully to his sexual and artistic adventure. However, the story is narrated from the male's point of view and as already in the past. Although there are indications that the woman was the seducer, the narrator wants the reader/listener to believe that he complied as a favor to the woman, who was unable to resist his sexual charms. Because the event occurred in the past, the adventure is framed by "the light of understanding" that has come over the Gypsy after the fact and that causes him to be "more discreet" in his telling of the episode (*CP* 535). The fulfillment of the adventure is inhibited at the level of reality by being told or described. Thus the telling, or language, which shapes the adventure into a coherent story simultaneously limits its vitality. This ballad, possibly the most popular of the whole book, presents a conception of language that, although allowing the creation of fictional worlds, implies a distancing of language from external reality. The poet/Gypsy is here a braggart who, by telling his adventure, inspires the admiration of his peers but also realizes how far he remains from the actual experience.[12]

The next three ballads in the collection form a triptych dedicated to three angels: Saint Michael, associated with Granada; Saint Raphael, associated with Córdoba; and Saint Gabriel, associated with Seville. "San Miguel (Granada)" ("St. Michael [Granada]," *CP* 538–43) opens with a depiction of a pilgrimage to the angel's chapel, which is a shrine of popular devotion, on the feast of St. Michael (29 September). The statue of the angel is described as being swathed in lace and surrounded by lanterns. It was customary in Spain for unmarried women to dress the statues of saints, an activity that was conventionally viewed as vicariously compensating for their sexual frustration. In Lorca's ballad St. Michael is an emasculated archangel, the prototype of an artificial and rancid religiosity, who in his alcove remains distant from the people who come to see his shrine.

The poetic speaker indicates that St. Michael "sings in the glass" and that his petticoats are encrusted "with lace and fine brocade" (*CP* 541, 543). The Spanish is "espejitos y entredoses"; *espejitos* is the diminutive of *espejo* (mirror) and connotes a type of rhinestone used to decorate the angel's apparel. The saint thus becomes a reflecting surface. These reflecting spaces, which appear in other ballads under various guises, function as metapoetic images where the text refers to the act of poetic creation, to the poet's world of appearances as he engages in the activity of writing. The rhinestones on St. Michael's petticoats reflect the voice or temperament of Granada. It is with the preciosity of such detailed and minute areas that the city diffuses and tames its passion. St. Michael voices the desire Granada represses under the guise of delightful and exquisite details. The angel represents the fusion of "shouts and miradors" (glassed-in balconies) that Granada was for Lorca, a city closed within itself, hiding its frustration behind the protective glass of its miradors and the walls of its secluded gardens.[13]

In "San Rafael (Córdoba)" ("St. Raphael [Córdoba]," *CP* 542–45), the statue of the angel protector of Córdoba, the native city of Góngora, stands between the Roman bridge and the mosque, and marks the border between the mysterious context of the water—the Guadalquivir River—and the stone of the statue, mosque, and bridge. The angel's foot, which is compared to a fish, is the point uniting the two Cordoba's that Ramsden identifies as the Arabic Cordoba of reeds and the Cordoba of Roman architecture:[14]

> Only one fish in the water,
> joining two Córdobas:
> soft Córdoba of reeds,
> Córdoba of architecture.
> (*CP* 545)

The image of the angel's foot is a synecdoche which refers to the whole statue: "a marble foot affirms / its radiance, chaste and spare" (*CP* 545). The mediating character of the angel makes him an image of the balance between the order and reason of the Roman past, and the vital, sensual values that Lorca attributes to the Arabic world. Another polarity is that between religion/mythology (St. Raphael/Neptune) and the crass reality of the vendors, sneering boys, and tin cans at the river's edge. The surface where these polarities unite is the river Guadalquivir, a representation of the space where the poetic transformation takes place. Just as the solidity of the Roman monuments breaks up in the reflective surface of the rippling waters to become the "Córdoba broken into gushers," the poem fuses emotion and form, reality and art. But the young boys defy and tease St. Raphael's claim to unite both Córdobas (*CP* 543). They represent the commentators on the artistic project of harmony, thus reminding one of the artificiality of the fusion, of its creation by art. However, the angel's image insists on the Gongorine equilibrium of opposites, which, as Ramsden remarks, is one Lorca sought in his own art.[15]

"San Gabriel (Sevilla)" ("St. Gabriel [Seville]," *CP* 546–49) is a retelling of the Annunciation of the Virgin. In this ballad, Gabriel is the picture of grace and sensuality walking down the streets of the Andalusian city. Annunciation of the Kings is the name of the Gypsy woman on whom Gabriel will bestow his gift of life. As the bearer of the Word, Gabriel is associated with light: he is a "star" whose radiance "opens jasmines" on Annunciation's face and brings forth an outpouring of sound and vitality (*CP* 547, 549). Annunciation is associated with the moon (like the Virgin Mary, of whom she is a representation), and thus the recipient of Gabriel's sun-like radiance. The result is the birth of the child. This ballad offers an example of fulfillment, but it is not free from dark premonitions. As St. Gabriel walks down the street, his patent leather shoes crush "the dahlias of the wind / with two cadences that sing / in brief celestial mourning" (*CP* 547). The rhythm of this angel's walk and his message of sexual fulfillment are already marked by frustration in death. The same foreboding reappears in connection with the child, who, as Gabriel prophesies, will bear "a dark spot and three wounds" (*CP* 549). The three wounds are an allusion to the three nails in Christ's Crucifixion, and the dark spot (in Spanish, *lunar,* from *luna,* moon), connects the child with Annunciation "rich in moons" (*CP* 549), signaling his tragic destiny. As the fusion of suffering and love, life and death, Christ exemplifies the tragedy implicit in human fate.

The last three poems in *The Gypsy Ballads* are grouped under the heading "Tres romances históricos" ("Three Historical Ballads"). The first, "Martirio de Santa Olalla ("Martyrdom of St. Eulalia," *CP* 570–75), depicts St. Eulalia, a virgin and patroness of Mérida, a city in western Spain where she was martyred in 304. The saint's martyrdom and glorious transformation are described in the second and third parts of the ballad:

> II
> *The Martyrdom*
> A gusher of green veins
> blossoms from her throat.
> . . . .
>
> In the crimson holes
> where her breasts were,
> rivers of white milk
> and miniature heavens are seen.
> A thousand tiny trees of blood
> spread across her back,
> their damp trunks holding off
> the scalpel of the flames.
> . . . .

III
Inferno and Glory
   Undulating snow lies still.
Eulalia hangs from the tree.
The carbon of her nakedness
smears the freezing wind.
Night pulls taut and gleams.
Eulalia, dead in the tree.
The inkwells of the cities
slowly spill their ink.
. . . .

   A golden Shrine of Christ
shines in burned-out skies,
from gorges in the hills
to nightingales in branches.
Bits of stained glass leap.
Eulalia white on white.
The Angels and the Seraphim
sing: Holy, Holy, Holy.

The martyrdom is depicted with images of spring blossoms ("green veins," "trees of blood"), as though the saint's sacrificed body became an image of life budding against death. When hanging dead from the tree, Eulalia's burnt body contrasts sharply with the snow-covered landscape in the background. Its blackness is connected with the ink and inkwells (lines 17–18) and, consequently, with the act of poetic writing itself. Starting with Lorca's early poetry, ink imagery alludes to the smudge that separates language from a direct union with the world it represents. Eulalia's burned body stands out against the white page of the landscape, like the printed word on the page. When it becomes white against white (line 24), the body is "silenced" (like removing the word from the page) by dissolving its mark into the background. It becomes the equivalent of the monstrance, with it a symbol of purity made equal to silence. The sublimation of the body's desire coincides with the elimination of writing, of the word as the inscription of desire. Hence, at the end, the angels sing in praise of the fullness of being that the saint has achieved.

"Burla de Don Pedro a caballo. (Romance con lagunas)" ("Joke about Don Pedro on Horseback [Ballad with Lacunae and Lagoons]," *CP* 574–79) is perhaps one of the most puzzling poems in *The Gypsy Ballads*. The fact that it is called a historical ballad has led critics to identify the Don Pedro in the title with the Castilian king Pedro the Cruel (1334–1369), the baroque playwright Pedro Calderón de la Barca (1600–1681), or, less plausibly, with Pedro Soto de Rojas (1584–1658), on whose work Lorca commented. Don Pedro has also been identified as Peter the Apostle.[16] He could also represent the average man making the existential journey. He is depicted as traveling along a trail, weeping inconsolably while he seeks love and daily bread. This reference to the Lord's Prayer indicates that Don Pedro seeks the love and salvation promised by the bread of the Eucharist. The three lacunae in the ballad are groups of verses that vary in length and interrupt the narrative, thus functioning as lapses in the flow of words. The lacunae also allude to lagoons as masses of water, for they describe the watery surface under which words remain or continue. These lacunae are thus spaces where the ballad refers to the act of poetic creation. The waters in them hide life's mystery by covering the words under their surface:

Under the water
the words continue.
On top of the water
a round moon.

(*CP* 575)

The water's surface, like the text, offers a whimsical interplay of representation and creation, of what is directly stated and what is only suggested, thus diverting the reader from a facile understanding of the message. The narrative proceeds, and Don Pedro has now reached a golden city among cedars. He wonders if it is Bethlehem. We later learn that Don Pedro's somber steed has been found dead, and the city is in flames. A man goes inland, weeping. Perhaps this is Don Pedro, now totally reduced to his unredeemable loneliness.

In the last lacuna, words and their meaning continue to hide under the waters, but on the surface the forgotten Don Pedro is playing with the frogs (*CP* 579). Starting in Lorca's early poetry, frogs are associated with death and faithlessness. Both toads and frogs point to dark, dangerous sexuality. They could also refer to some kind of onanistic sexual game to which Don Pedro is ridiculously reduced, impotent to achieve any expression in love or poetry. The *burla,* or joke, to which the title alludes is played on Don Pedro. Hoping to find love and bread, sexual fulfillment, life, and artistic achievement, he finds only emptiness and death. It is thus a *burla* played on the speaker himself, of whom the protagonist is a projection. The *burla* is also directed at the reader, since Don Pedro, exemplar of the human condition, depicts the situation of humankind.[17]

The Gypsy Ballads concludes with "Thamar y Amnón" ("Thamar and

Amnon," *CP* 578–85), a biblical story of incest described in 2 Samuel 13. The collection begins with the moon as a mother/seductress performing an ambiguous dance in front of a Gypsy boy and ends with incest between brother and sister. The narrative of "Thamar and Amnon" is also presided over by the moon, whirling through the sky over dry lands. The season is a torrid summer turning the earth into a body full of scarred wounds and burns. On the terrace, Thamar's naked body shines with the cold whiteness of the moon, while the body of her brother Amnon is pure "burning flesh." As images of the polarity between sun and moon, the incestuous passion of sister and brother acquires a cosmic projection, representing the cycles of the sun and moon, day and night. These opposites complement one another: the sun's "bleeding" at dusk is absorbed by the moon, which, in turn, dissolves in the light of the new day. This symbolic cosmic incest is a recurring Lorcan image of the inescapable cycle of time, a continuous, serpent-like movement with no fruitful outcome. When the seduction begins, King David's horses neigh in the courtyard, representing the fulfillment of sexual desire. While snow-white cloths are reddened inside the chambers, Amnon flees upon his mare, and when only the echo of the hooves is heard, the father, David "took a scissors / and cut the strings of his harp"(*CP* 585). The song is thus ended (as is the altarpiece of Andalusia that this book represents for Lorca) by the hand of David, a poet.

The concluding triptych of historical ballads offers three different outcomes for the sexual and artistic expression of desire that correspond to those in the triptych of the angels. If St. Michael represents a kind of rancid religiosity that sublimates desire through attention to trivial detail, Eulalia represents the religious path of sublimating desire by denying the body and transforming it into a symbol of a higher life. Thus her ballad ends with poetry transformed into the voice of angels and seraphim singing "Holy, Holy, Holy." The failure of Don Pedro's hope and faith in the message of Bethlehem forces his desire to turn upon itself. His presumed onanism implies an inability to direct his desire toward another person and alludes to the solipsistic activity of the artist playing with words that can no longer establish a link with the world. The joke of which Don Pedro is the victim recalls the boys by the river edge who teased the statue of St. Raphael for claiming to effect an equilibrium between opposites. When desire is fulfilled, as with Thamar and Amnon or with St. Gabriel and Annunciation, it is of a forbidden nature and has painful effects.

Like the symbolic bleeding of the sun at dusk, and its absorption by the moon at night (the background for Amargo's death at the end of *Poem of the Deep Song*), the incestuous union of Amnon and Thamar—representations of the sun and moon— delineates the image of the *ouroboros,* or serpent, biting its own tail. The moon-serpent bites the "tail," or end, of the day at dusk, and only releases it at dawn in a continuous cycle. As a central symbolic configuration in Lorca's writings, the *ouroboros* does not connote the continuity of time and of eternal return, as it is traditionally interpreted, but time as a self-consuming, repetitive cycle with no outlet. The moon-serpent is also an image of the self-reflexive nature of language, of expression consumed within its own verbal boundaries. The fulfillment of desire implies destruction or dissolution. Poetry is maintained by the desire or nostalgia for something whose nature remains elusive. Sexual fulfillment, or achieving the right blending of words in a poem, is a temporary release that cannot stop desire, which by its own nature must remain unfulfilled. As objectifications of desire and of the creative impulse, these ballads also indicate that although inspiration may be patterned in the poem, it is never totally captured there.

The Gypsy Ballads is a brilliant display of the Gongorine aesthetics of the metaphor and the imagination. Its own artistry, however, reveals these ballads to be perfectly constructed artifacts irrevocably distanced from the desire they articulate. As they proclaim the success of their metaphoric transformations, these ballads also point to the dependence of their images on reality. Through inspiration (and not imagination, as Lorca was careful to differentiate in his 1928 lecture "Imaginación, inspiración, evasión" (Imagination, Inspiration, Evasion) the poet is able to discover new and unexpected combinations with no correlative in objective reality, since they point to a different realm, that of poetic truth and its articulation in the poetic fact or event. The poetic fact voices the realm of poetic truth, a context of mysterious and intense emotions, of passions and instincts beyond reason or logic. *The Gypsy Ballads* probe into areas where what is mysterious and dreamlike challenge logic, but the poetic articulation of that realm is left to later works, such as *Poet in New York.*

Poet in New York (1940)

Lorca's death prevented him from assigning to his New York poems a final configuration. An editorial controversy raged between two groups: those who contend that the poems are correctly organized as one work and those who believe Lorca intended to collect them in two books, *Poet in New York* and *Tierra y luna* (*Earth and Moon*).[18]

The critic García-Posada, as well as others, sees two major aspects in this collection, the sociological and the personal.[19] Some poems present Lorca's reaction to the socioeconomic conditions he witnessed in New York, while others express more personal concerns, such as lost childhood and faith, failure in love, and artistic frustration. Lorca's correspondence before his departure for New York shows he was depressed. His friendship with Dalí was declining at both the personal and the aesthetic levels and his close relationship with the young sculptor Emilio Aladrén was also collapsing. In the artistic realm, Lorca was trying to maintain a balance between the pressure to accept the latest tenets of surrealism and his need to remain faithful to his aesthetic premises.[20] The success achieved by *The Gypsy Ballads* was becoming a nuisance, as was expressed in Lorca's letters, because the artistic value of his work was being overshadowed by its "popular" appeal (*SL* 94). Artistic frustration and Lorca's feeling of emotional abandonment by his two closest friends intensified the need to get away from Spain that he had felt for some time. Lorca described his stay in New York as "the most useful experience of my life" ("Lecture: A Poet in New York" 197). In New York he became acquainted with a society entirely different from the one he had known in Spain. This new setting inspired a new poetic voice that, although not inspired by New York alone, received a vital impulse from the experience Lorca had there. His American stay also developed his strong interest in social issues. Upon his return to Spain in 1930 Lorca devoted most of his efforts to the theater, which he thought provided the most effective means of communication in order to provoke a change in social consciousness.

The New York poetry is not a drastic break from Lorca's previous work. His *Songs* and *The Gypsy Ballads,* as well as the narrations *Nadadora sumergida (Submerged Swimmer)* and *Suicidio en Alejandría (Suicide in Alexandria)*, probably written in the summer of 1928 while he was in Catalonia with Dalí's family and published later that year, herald the so-called surrealist poetry from the New York period. Also in 1928 Lorca promoted the avant-garde magazine *gallo* in Granada. His friendship with Dalí directed him toward surrealism as well. However, Lorca avoided the automatism favored by surrealists, and was careful to qualify his new style of writing as "detached from logical control," but not surrealistic, because it was endowed "with a tremendous poetic logic" (*SL* 135). In *Poet in New York* Lorca moved in the realm of what he called the *hecho poético* (poetic fact or event). In his lecture "Imaginación, inspiración, evasión" (Imagination, Inspiration, Evasion, *OC* 1:1034–40), delivered on several occasions in 1928 and 1930, he states that the *hecho poético* emerges directly from the realm of inspiration. Contrary to the dependence on reality from which any poetry of the imagination necessarily originates, the *hecho poético* frees itself from reality, thus allowing for the incursion into the realm of the poetic inspired by the *duende*. As Lorca indicated in "Lecture: A Poet in New York" (185), a major objective in *Poet in New York* is to get beyond the superficial gaiety of New York to reveal what civilization represses with its established religion and accepted attitudes. Frequently, these poems reverse well-known romantic images conventional in such genres as the ode, the nocturne, or the love poem. Contrary to the Gongorine aesthetics of distance, objectivity, and detachment, this book's poetic speaker calls attention to himself as the subject engaged in the activity of writing by using devices such as deictic words (showing or pointing out directly with terms such as *here, this*), and apostrophe (the addressing of an absent person or personified thing). Other frequent devices, such as enumeration and anaphora (repetition of a word or phrase at the beginning of two or more verses), call attention to the speaker's voice, which urgently seeks to provoke an effect through repetition. Language, however, cannot reenact the original link with the world. Instead of objectifying this alienation through various musical expressions or Gypsy types, as in the two previous collections, *Poet in New York* expresses the crisis through the speaker's subjectivity, thus acquiring increased urgency.

The poems are grouped in ten sections with different titles. The first section, "Poemas de la soledad en Columbia University" ("Poems of Solitude at Columbia University," 4–21), addresses the speaker's alienation in New York, which evokes memories of his childhood as a world of dreams forever lost. The first poem in this section, "Vuelta de paseo" ("After a Walk," 6–7), sets the tone for the rest of the collection:

> Cut down by the sky.
> Between shapes moving toward the serpent
> and crystal-craving shapes,
> I'll let my hair grow.
>
> With the amputated tree that doesn't sing
> and the child with the blank face of an egg.
>
> With the little animals whose skulls are cracked
> and the water, dressed in rags, but with dry feet.
>
> With all the bone-tired, deaf-and-dumb things
> and a butterfly drowned in the inkwell.
>
> Bumping into my own face, different each day.
> Cut down by the sky!

(7)

The *I* of the speaker occupies a central position here, as in other poems, conveying the neo-Romantic, confessional tone of the collection. The repetition of the same verse at the opening and conclusion calls attention to the polarity of city and sky, and to the alienation from the transcendent realm: New York is a fallen world. The opening lines elaborate on the speaker's fragmentation through the image of "shapes." Shapes and forms, equivalent of the word, occupy a central role in this book, representing attempts to impose some form on the surrounding chaos. In addition to connoting the biblical fall, the serpent's undulating movement represents for Lorca the existential cycle without escape or transcendence. Because of its transparency, the crystal suggests a more transcendent reality. It is also a possible reference to water or to some type of a reflective surface mirroring the poetic text, where the artistic transformation and sublimation could occur. The poet/speaker is confronting an artistic and existential choice: to express the shapes that constitute this world or to escape into evasive art. He articulates his sense of loss and confusion when he states: "I'll let my hair grow."

In his pain the speaker finds solidarity with nature, animals and humans crushed by modern technology ("the amputated tree," "the child with the blank face of an egg," "the little animals whose skulls are cracked"). In the city, water, and other natural elements, loses all majesty and appropriate functions and seems to incorporate the poverty of the humans who wade barefoot in it (line 8). Moreover the butterfly—a traditional symbol of life, idealism, and poetry—drowns in the inkwell of all poets, who, distanced from nature, are unable to articulate beauty. The city is also an inkwell where nature's programs and language have been smudged, their crystal transparency lost by technology's designs, pollution, and bureaucratic excesses. Besides the obvious social commentary, these images point to the literary activity itself, to the depressed state of the poet's inspiration and to his inability to effect any real changes in the situation. The result is the loss of identity. The speaker's social mask does not coincide with his true being, therefore, he does not know who he is ("Bumping into my own face, different each day").

This first poem succinctly addresses some of the main themes of the book: alienation and loss of identity. It also presents some of its main characters (children, nature, animals) and points to major polarities around which meaning is organized, such as, earth/sky, nature/civilization, salvation/fall, word/void, mask/truth. Some of the most common rhetorical devices in the book are announced here: the apostrophic and exclamatory tone is conveyed with the repetition of the opening verse at the end; and the cumulative reality of poverty and destruction is expressed through the parallel structure of the intermediary lines with the anaphora (*with*) and polysyndeton (repetition of conjunctions, *and*).

Perception is the key term in "1910 (Intermedio)" ("1910 [Intermezzo]," 8–9), one of three poems dedicated to lost childhood in this first section. This composition is set at the time when Lorca was twelve years old, on the border between childhood and adolescence. From the viewpoint of the attic—where, as a child, the speaker used to daydream and fantasize—the poem's imaginative transformation takes place:

> Attic where the ancient dust assembles statues and moss.
> Boxes that keep the silence of devoured crabs.
> In the place where the dream was colliding with its
>   reality.
> My little eyes are there.

(9)

Through poetic transformation the empty boxes become crabs whose meat, or life, has been devoured in the process of time. Words, like those boxes in the attic that contained all possible meanings for the child, are now emptied. Like the backward walk of the crabs, the poet has gone back in time, only to discover that in the attic, where as a child he thought all dreams could be fulfilled, those dreams now collide with the reality of emptiness:

> Don't ask me any questions. I've seen how things
> that seek their way find their void instead.
> There are spaces that ache in the uninhabited air
> and in my eyes, completely dressed creatures—no one
>   naked there!

The image of the hole—emptiness—is pervasive in this collection, pointing to the poet's crisis.[21] The attempt to connect with the world is thwarted by an emptiness, the void of lost identity. This existential realization also applies to the speaker's attitude toward his own writing. The words he uses are like the "completely dressed creatures" he locates in his eyes, that is, in his perception of reality. Those words find their way into the poetic text, where they seek to represent reality but, instead, are confronted with the emptiness of their own artificiality. The subtitle, "Intermezzo," refers to the transitory place in the speaker's childhood "where the dream was colliding with its reality," the point where word and referent no longer coincide.

The second section of *Poet in New York* is entitled "Los negros" ("The Blacks," 22–41). Lorca spoke of blacks as the only group that in the uprooted world of New York had remained in touch with nature. The poet confessed that he wanted to write "*the* poem of the black race in North America, and to show the pain the blacks feel to be black in a contrary world" ("Lecture: A Poet in New York" 187). Their African beginnings is contrasted with the standards of technology and inhuman science North American society imposes on them in "Norma y paraíso de los negros" ("Standards and Paradise of the Blacks," 24–27). In "El rey de Harlem" ("The King of Harlem," 28–37), the speaker sees a uniformed black doorman as the representation of the African king he could have been. All the natural vitality associated with blacks is oppressed by a civilization that imprisons their king in the uniform of a doorman. Through repeated apostrophes the speaker calls on blacks and Harlem to shed their mask of conformity:

> Ay, Harlem! Ay, Harlem! Ay, Harlem!
> There is no anguish like that of your oppressed reds,
> or your blood shuddering with rage inside the dark
>   eclipse,
> or your garnet violence, deaf and dumb in the
>   penumbra,
> or your grand king a prisoner in the uniform of a
>   doorman.
>
> (31)

Modern civilization not only crushes life through poverty and abusive working conditions but also represses natural tendencies by imposing societal norms. Thus Lorca appeals to the red and garnet of vital blood, the hidden side identified with nature or the knowledge of the trees that is representative of the paradise of blacks. There, in that paradise, "the coral absorbs the ink's desperation." The redness of coral (blood), love, and passion will counteract the black ink flowing over the page in the desperate act of writing. In the paradise of blacks, life will take over any other supplementary activity. Thus, in "The King of Harlem," the speaker expresses the need to cross bridges, those in the city as well as those bridges leading beyond conventional reason, in order to reach the other side or realm of passion and instinctual life. When allowed to flow freely, this blood will surge over rooftops, and the forest's marrow, symbolic equivalent of the blood, will slip through the cracks of civilization. These two poems are a revolutionary appeal to awaken and reveal the "black murmuring," the "dark eclipse," the "deaf and dumb violence" of blacks in order to reestablish the link with nature. Without the revolution, Harlem will have to keep hiding its true identity as demanded by white civilization.

The word *doble* in the title "Poema doble del lago Eden" ("Double Poem of Lake Eden," 80–83), in section 4, directs the reader to approach this poem with the idea of duplicity intruding into the paradisiacal setting of Lake Eden, a duplicity that is implied in the reflection in the lake near which the poetic meditation takes place.[22] The poem is double because the speaker refers to his old childhood voice, which is ignorant of bitterness:

> Ay, my love's ancient voice,
> ay, voice of my truth,
> ay, voice of my open side,
> when all the roses spilled from my tongue
> and the grass hadn't felt the horse's impassable teeth!
>
> (81)

These lines recall a prelapsarian time when word and object fully coincided. What the speaker finds in the present is the rupture between his voice and a context where nature has been replaced by aluminum, and harmony by the voices of drunkards. The word cannot link with a world where all elements are disjointed; the personal and social crisis is an artistic one as well. This is a double poem because, standing by the mirror surface of the lake, the speaker confronts the emptiness of his own words. He wants to go beyond the surface to circle "the things of the other side," to the inner truth that society forcefully represses:

> I want to cry saying my name,
> rose, child, and fir on the shore of this lake,
> to speak truly as a man of blood
> killing in myself the mockery and the suggestive power
> of the word.
>
> (83)

Looking into his reflection in the water, the speaker, like Narcissus, longs to reunite with his true voice, the one that by saying the word enacted its referent. This longing for a primordial language coincides with the desire to recover the true identity that hypocritical societal norms repress for its sexual "deviance." The same desire is expressed in "Cielo vivo" ("Living Sky," 84–87), where only under the roots, that is, underneath and behind appearances, is it possible to learn the truth about those things that, according to the norms of logic and reason, appear wrong. This meditation ends on a note of hope mixed with desperation: "I stumble sleepily through eternity's fixed hardness / and love at the end without dawn. Love. Visible love!" (87). Love devoid of dawn would entail eliminating the cycle of time, prolonging the fusion of desire and object. Hence, by overcoming that endless game of reflection, love could be apprehended in its fullness.

"Nueva York (Oficina y denuncia)" ("New York [Office and Denuncia-tion]," 130–35) offers a good illustration of rhetorical devices, images, and themes characteristic of *Poet in New York:*

> Under the multiplications,
> a drop of duck's blood;
> under the divisions,
> a drop of sailor's blood;
> under the additions, a river of tender blood.
> A river that sings and flows
> past bedrooms in the boroughs—
> and it's money, cement, wind
> in New York's counterfeit dawn.
>
> (131)

The unexpected juxtaposition of elements from the world of mathematics and finances with those from the animal world, highlighted through anaphoric repetition, such as of the phrase *under the,* offers the other, or hidden, side of appearances. This revelation is a major objective of Lorca in this collection, as in his play *The Public.* The sudden contrast of sizes, as "a drop of blood" with "a river," elicits emotions of endearment for the minute, insignificant animals sacrificed on the altar of modern civilization, as well as a feeling of horror at the scope of the destruction. Metamorphosis is also a major motif in this col-lection. The river of blood, comprising all the workers coming to New York from the boroughs, is transformed through their labor into "money, cement, or wind"; their humanity is expended for the maintenance of the city. Poetic signs, such as the duck (or any animal), or the sailor, recur to connote the world of nature or freedom versus civilization and oppression. The marginalized bor-oughs define their inhabitants as outsiders to the center of power. New York is associated with death, since that is where the river of blood, or life from the boroughs, ends.

The *I* of the poetic speaker occupies a central position here, as in other poems, emerging from the midst of the urban destruction:

> I know the mountains exist.
> And wisdom's eyeglasses,
> too. But I didn't come to see the sky.
> I'm here to see the clouded blood,
> the blood that sweeps machines over waterfalls
> and the soul toward the cobra's tongue.

(131)

The verb *to see,* the eyes—perception in general—are important in this book, as elsewhere in Lorca's aesthetics. Lecturing about Góngora ("The Poetic Image of Don Luis de Góngora," *DS* 64), Lorca characterized the poet as the professor of the five senses, sight being the first. Sight is the ability to capture reality in visual metaphors, whereby semantically disparate elements are unexpectedly fused. However, the speaker has not come to New York to see (or simply observe) the scenery, but to witness what lies beneath the apparent progress of technology. He knows there are mountains, or nature in general, to which he could choose to retire and live peacefully, or which he could make the topic of his poetry. He also knows that there is the world of study and intellect, which he alludes to with "wisdom's eyeglasses." However, the speaker confesses to have come to witness the constraints on nature and the human spirit imposed by modern civilization, as the last three verses indicate.

In order to express the scope of the destruction, the poem resorts to hyperbolic enumeration and polysyndeton. For New York to function daily, four million ducks, five million hogs, two thousand pigeons, one million cows, one million lambs, and two million chickens have to be killed. Throughout the night, trucks carry into the city milk from "cows wrung dry," "manacled roses" to be turned into perfume for the rich, and all the innocent animals killed to feed the urban monster. Witnessing this, the speaker feels denunciation is justified:

> I denounce everyone
> who ignores the other half,
> the half that can't be redeemed,
>
> . . . .
> I spit in all your faces.
> The other half hears me,
> devouring, pissing, flying in their purity,

> like the supers' children in lobbies
> who carry fragile twigs
> to the emptied spaces where
> the insect antennae are rusting.
>
> (133)

The other half, or other side, is what is hidden behind the glitter and surface gaiety of modern civilization, and that which the speaker identifies with purity, as opposed to the corruption of the city. That purity is expressed through natural bodily functions and through the children playing with dead insects that so much mirror the children's own opaque lives. Negation is used to reinforce the horror of the affirmative: "This is not hell, but the street. / Not death, but the fruit stand," and immense things are contrasted with small, symbolizing how life and aspirations are frustrated by the big designs of civilization:

> There is a world of tamed rivers and distances just
> beyond our grasp
> in the cat's paw smashed by a car,
> and I hear the earthworm's song
> in the hearts of many girls.
>
> (133)

The speaker foregrounds life in its most minute forms, represented by earth as the basic element of human nature that modern technology has forgotten. In this light, a question is raised at the end about the poetic project:

> What shall I do now? Set the landscapes in order?
> Order the loves that soon become photographs,
> that soon become pieces of wood and mouthfuls of
>   blood?
> No, no: I denounce it all.
> I denounce the conspiracy
> of these deserted offices
> that radiate no agony,
> that erase the forest's plans,
> and I offer myself as food for the cows wrung dry
> when their bellowing fills the valley
> where the Hudson gets drunk on oil.

(135)

"Set things in order" and "denounce" are posited as two different choices. The first alludes to a type of writing in which elements are structured in harmonious but lifeless forms. Denunciation, as public proclamation, is the chosen form of expression, for Lorca's intention is to unmask seeming order and progress even if he thereby necessarily creates much disorder. Hence he will bring out the agony, not only of life in the inhuman offices, but also the contradictory tension implicit in life, the agony caused by conflicting impulses that technological uniformity cancels or ignores. The Hudson Valley is thus a vale of tears, the reverse of the pastoral topos.

Section 8 of *Poet in New York* is entitled "Dos odas" ("Two Odes") and comprises "Grito hacia Roma (Desde la torre del Chrysler Building)" ("Cry to Rome [From the Tower of the Chrysler Building]," 148–53) and "Oda a Walt Whitman" ("Ode to Walt Whitman," 154–63). The ode is a markedly formal lyric poem expressing lofty ideas. Lorca's odes address two "lofty" topics: Rome, where the Vatican is located, and a great literary figure, Walt Whitman. However, their content subverts expectations, thus joining the project of the book: to address what is not apparent because it is repressed or silenced by the order of reality. Hence, behind the Vatican as the symbol of the Christian faith, the poet discloses corruption and betrayal; and behind Whitman's official identity as the prototype of the poet, Lorca finds the epitome of homosexuality.

"Cry to Rome" has been interpreted as the speaker's protest of the Lateran Treaty between Pope Pius XI (1857–1939) and Italian fascist leader Benito Mussolini (1883–1945). In February 1929 this treaty reconciled the Papal State and the Italian government after sixty years of nonrelations. Thanks to this treaty, the Pope was recognized as the sole ruler in the Vatican, while the fascist dictatorship of Mussolini received the seal of approval at an international level.[23] The poem is a strong indictment of the Catholic church and of its betrayal of the people. It begins by enumerating a series of calamities that will befall the Holy See, which misuses the sacred oil of holy sacraments to anoint the military powers and where a man, the Pope, pisses on the dove of the Holy Ghost.

While "there is no one to bestow the bread or the wine," a consciously exaggerated number appear to denounce the enormity of destruction:

> There are only a million blacksmiths
> who forge chains for tomorrow's children.
> Only a million carpenters

49

who make coffins with no cross.
Only a crowd of laments
unbuttoning their clothes, waiting for the bullets.

(149)

The man who scorns the dove (the Pope) should shed tears in which to dissolve his rings and diamond telephones. Instead, he ignores the mystery of the ear of wheat, the Eucharist. He gives the lamb's blood, which is a clear reference to Christ as the prototype of innocent victim, to the "pheasant's idiot beak," a reference to Mussolini and to political power, or worldly vanity (151). The speaker exhorts the oppressed to scream in protest. He addresses his call to blacks removing spittoons, boys trembling beneath the authority of executives, women drowning their fertility in the pollution of a technologized society, and the multitudes of workers (hammers), artists (violins), or dreamers (clouds) that have been relegated to the fringes by urban society for their lack of practical value (151, 153). They should all scream, even if their brains were then bashed against the wall, to demand their daily bread, so that the will of the earth, which offers its fruit to everyone, shall be done. The socialist tone and content of this poem is evident. *Poet in New York* appeals to all voices to join in the denunciation of injustice.

It is likely that Lorca arrived in New York with a set of preconceived ideas about the urban paradigm of modern civilization. New York filled Lorca with fascination and horror, as it did many other artists who went to the city in the first half of the century: Georgia O'Keefe, Hart Crane, T. S. Eliot, and others. The failure behind the bright exterior of modern civilization was shown in Fritz Lang's *Metropolis* (1926), a movie that had a great impact on Lorca's generation. Like the terrible struggle of New York's sharp-edged buildings against heaven ("Lecture: A Poet in New York" 185), Lorca's American poetry depicts a struggle with form, a confrontation with the emptiness of the word in view of a world gone mad. Poetic signs constantly refer to void spaces and to physiological evacuation. In accordance with Lorca's frequent association of the creative process with the physiology of blood and veins, this book is an outpouring. Words emerge like fluids running through the page, mostly voicing their inability to retain forms. The more those words accumulate, the more their material presence proclaims their emptiness.

The never-ending cycle of life and death, embodied in the image of the moon and its constant phases, is ever present. As in previous books the moon is still the empty and cold Diana, whose light presides over the false landscape of the urban context. The poet opts for the earth, removed from the multiple masks of civilization.24 He thus affirms his solidarity with the suffering of the help-less and dispossessed. This commitment to the earth took an important direc-tion after Lorca's return to Spain in 1930. The American experience had reaf-firmed his conviction that theater, through its direct contact with the audience, offered the best means to effect social and artistic change. During the 1930s Lorca's poetry was augmented with feverish activity in theater and lecturing.

Notes

1. Roman Jakobson, "What Is Poetry?," *Semiotics of Art: Prague School Contributions,* ed. Ladislav Matejka and Irwin R. Titunik (Cambridge, Mass., and London: MIT Press, 1976) 174.

2. Lorca's lectures on Deep Song and *duende* come from *DS* 23–41, 42–53. For the background of Deep Song, see Norman C. Miller, *García Lorca's Poema del Cante Jondo* (London: Tamesis, 1978), and Edward F. Stanton, *The Tragic Myth: Lorca and Cante Jondo* (Lexington: UP of Kentucky, 1978). These studies also provide detailed commentaries on Gypsies and Lorca's *Poem of the Deep Song.* References to *Poem of the Deep Song* and to *The Gypsy Ballads* are taken from *Collected Poems* (New York: Farrar, Straus & Giroux, 1991), vol. 2 of *The Poetical Works of Federico García Lorca,* ed. Christopher Maurer, trans. David K. Loughran and Will Kirkland, henceforth cited parenthetically in the text, abbreviated as *CP.*

3. See David K. Loughran, *Federico García Lorca: The Poetry of Limits* (London: Tamesis, 1978) 77. For the image of the spider-moon, see Javier Herrero, "The Spider-Moon: The Origin of Lorca's Lunar Myth," *Studies in Honor of Bruce W. Wardropper,* ed. Dian Fox, Harry Siebert, Robert TerHorst (Newark, Del.: Juan de la Cuesta, 1989) 147–62.

4. See Lorca's *Romancero Gitano: A Ballad Translation and Critical Study,* trans. Carl W. Cobb (Jackson: UP of Mississippi, 1983) 52–53, 59. The lecture-recital "On the Gypsy Ballads" is found in *DS* 104–22.

5. For the symbolic meaning of the moon, see Juan Eduardo Cirlot, *A Dictionary of Symbols,* trans. Jack Sage (New York: Philosophical Library, 1962) 204–6.

6. For the image of the forge in Lorca, see Javier Herrero, "'La luna vino a la fragua': Lorca's Mythic Forge," *De los romances-villancicos a la poesía de Claudio Rodríguez: 22 ensayos sobre las literaturas española e hispanoamericana en homenaje a Gustav Siebenmann,* eds. José Manuel López de Abiada and Agusta López Bernasocchi (Madrid: José Esteban, 1984) 175–97.

7. Herbert Ramsden, *Lorca's "Romancero gitano": Eighteen Commentaries* (Manchester and New York: Manchester UP, 1988) 1.

8. Rupert Allen, "An Analysis of Narrative and Symbol in Lorca's 'Romance sonámbulo'," *Hispanic Review* 36.4 (1968): 346–49.

9. J. M. Aguirre, "El sonambulismo de Federico García Lorca" (Sonambulism

in Federico García Lorca), *Bulletin of Hispanic Studies* 44.4 (1967): 271–73.

10. The narrative of this ballad has received different interpretations (see, for example, Beverly J. DeLong-Tonelli, "The Lyric Dimension in Lorca's 'Romance sonámbulo'," *Romance Notes* 12.2 [1971]: 289–95, and Allen, "An Analysis of Narrative and Symbol in Lorca's 'Romance sonámbulo' " 338–52). Some critics believe the Gypsy woman commits suicide in view of the imminent capture and death of her lover. The time of her death is also debated: some believe the woman to be dead from the poem's beginning, others believe she dies later. Carl W. Cobb, in *Romancero Gitano,* offers a somewhat psychoanalytic reading. In "'Romance sonámbulo,' An Archetypal Drama," *Hispanic Journal* 7.2 (1986): 17–24, Norman C. Miller considers this poem "a miniature play with a clearly defined introduction or prologue, two distinct acts, [and] an epilogue" (17). Miller views the various characters as Jungian archetypes: the Gypsy girl would be the anima figure with "no objective reality outside of the young Gypsy smuggler's psyche" (19); the father would be the Wise Old Man (20). Both archetypal projections are "unconsciously evoked by the Gypsy in an attempt to find a way to retain his hold on life and to reorient himself toward a better, more harmonious balance between unconscious and conscious mental functioning" (23).

11. See Christoph Eich, *Federico García Lorca, poeta de la intensidad* (Federico García Lorca, Poet of Intensity) (Madrid: Gredos, 1976) 34–35.

12. See Ramsden, *Lorca's "Romancero gitano"* 43.

13. In "Granada (Paraiso cerrado para muchos)" (Granada [Closed Paradise for Many] *OC* 1: 936–40), Lorca elaborates on the aesthetics of the diminutive that characterize Granada's taste for reduced dimensions and for detail in art and architecture (see chapter 5 of the present study).

14. See Herbert Ramsden, "Round Perspective and Lyric Tension in *Romancero gitano,*" *"Cuando yo me muera . . .": Essays in Memory of Federico García Lorca,* ed. C. Brian Morris (Lanham, New York and London: UP of America, 1988) 99.

15. Ramsden, "Round Perspective" 99.

16. See Eutimio Martín, "Hacia una lectura de 'Burla de Don Pedro a caballo'" (Toward a Reading of 'Joke about Don Pedro on Horseback" by Federico García Lorca), *Hommage/Homenaje a Federico García Lorca* (Toulouse: Université de Toulouse-Le-Mirail, 1982) 180, and Charles Marcilly, *La burla de Don Pedro a caballo de Federico García Lorca* ("The Joke about Don Pedro on Horseback" by Federico García Lorca) (Paris: Librairie des Editions Espagnoles, 1957) 7. Marcilly points out the religious connotations in this ballad, while Doris M. Glasser, in "Lorca's 'Burla de Don Pedro a caballo'," *Hispania* 47.2 (1964): 295–301, elaborates on its debt to an old Spanish popular song which has inspired several poetic and dramatic works, such as *El caballero de Olmedo (The Knight of Olmedo),* a play by Spanish Golden Age author Lope de Vega (1562–1635).

17. For a reading of the *burla,* see Martin, "Hacia una lectura" 187.

18. See "Notes on the Poems," *Poet in New York,* trans. Greg Simon and Steven F. White (New York: Farrar, Straus & Giroux, 1988) 260–67, vol. 1 of *The Poetical*

Works of Federico García Lorca, ed. Christopher Maurer, 2 vols. Page references to individual poems are keyed to this edition. Maurer translated "Lecture: A Poet in New York," also included in this edition of *Poet in New York.* Henceforth, all references to the lecture are cited parenthetically.

The polemic centers on the authority of the two editions of this book published almost simultaneously in 1940: the Seneca edition published in Mexico under the directorship of Lorca's friend, the poet José Bergamín (*Poeta en Nueva York. Con cuatro dibujos originales. Poema de Antonio Machado* [Poet in New York. With Four Original Drawings. Poem by Antonio Machado], and the Norton bilingual edition, translated by Rolfe Humphries, published in New York (*The Poet in New York and Other Poems of Federico García Lorca*). Bergamín, who received the manuscript from Lorca himself, took some editorial liberties concerning accents, commas, and placement of poems. The Norton edition, based on a copy given to Humphries by Bergamín, seems more faithful to the original. Part of the argument for a division of the manuscript into two books is based on the assertion that the group "properly" entitled "Poet in New York" is of a descriptive nature, presenting the poet as a traveler arriving in the city, staying, and then departing, while those constituting "Earth and Moon" are abstract and introspective, dealing with death and dissolution. The textual basis for grouping the poems in two collections is a list, handwritten by Lorca, of seventeen titles of poems destined for the collection called "Earth and Moon." Of those, three were included in *The Divan at Tamarit, 1940,* three were never collected, and the remaining eleven were published as part of *Poet in New York.* It seems Lorca intended to publish the book illustrated with photographs of various scenes, including the Statue of Liberty, a burned black man, male students dancing in women's clothing, blacks dressed in tuxedos, Wall Street, Broadway in 1830, a street with serpents and wild animals, and the stock market (see Miguel Garcia-Posada, *Lorca: Interpretacion de Poeta en Nueva York* (Lorca: An Interpretation of *Poet in New York*) [Madrid: Akal, 1981] 19, 21, 33). Maurer ("Notes on the Poems," *Poet in New York* 265–66) indicates the untenability of the two-book theory due to recent contributions to the debate. Contrary to the supporters of the two-book theory, Andrew A. Anderson ("Poeta en Nueva York una y otra vez," *El Crotalón. Anuario de Filología Española* 2 [1985] 37–51), views the Seneca and Norton editions as far from provisional. Anderson argues that these editions are very likely based on two copies of an "original" which the poet had asked his secretary to type. By paying close attention to Lorca's comments and letters in the final years of his life (1935–36), Anderson is able to conclude that Lorca thought of the New York poems as a unified whole. Also, there is enough evidence to support the idea that there were plans to publish the book that were thwarted by the outbreak of the war. For in-depth critical readings of the published collection, see Richard L. Predmore, *Lorca's New York Poetry: Social Injustice, Dark Love, Lost Faith* (Durham: Duke UP, 1980), and Betty J. Craige, *Lorca's Poet in New York: The Fall Into Consciousness* (Lexington: UP of Kentucky, 1977).

19. *Lorca: Interpretacion de Poeta en Nueva York* 63.

20. For an elaboration on Lorca's crisis, see Ian Gibson, *Federico García Lorca: A*

Life (New York: Pantheon, 1989) 228–33.

21. See Miguel García-Posada, 111.

22. I want to thank Christopher Maurer for bringing to my attention the reflection of the waters of Lake Eden implicit in the word *doble*.

23. See Juan Cano Ballesta, "Historia y poesía: Interpretaciones y sentido de 'Grito hacia Roma'" (History and Poetry: Interpretations and Meaning of "Cry to Rome"), *Revista Hispánica Moderna* 39.4 (1976–1977): 210–14. On the other hand, John K. Walsh, in "The Social and Sexual Geography of *Poeta en Nueva York*," *"Cuando yo me muera . . .": Essays in Memory of Federico García Lorca,* ed. C. Brian Morris (Lanham, New York and London: UP of America, 1988) 113–14, does not think the poem refers to something so far away from the poet's experience at the time, and reads it as a protest against the Pope's failure to help during the Cristeros' (militant Catholics') rebellion in Mexico. The confrontation between Catholics and the Mexican government came to a head in 1926 when Catholics resorted to violence against the anticatholic laws in some Mexican states. The religious struggle continued in 1927 and 1928, with many priests being deported or incarcerated. In June 1929 the Pope issued a call for the Cristeros' capitulation. Father Pedroza, the leader of the Cristeros' cause, was subsequently killed by the federalist army (*Enciclopedia Universal Ilustrada Europeo-Americana.* Apéndice VII [Madrid: Espasa Calpe, 1932] 296–300). According to Walsh, Lorca must have been aware of the protest of his friends in New York who were interested in Mexican politics.

24. In "Blind Panorama of New York" Lorca writes: "Only the Earth exists / here. / The Earth and its timeless doors / which lead to the blush of the fruit" (75). See also García-Posada 241.

CHAPTER 2

The Major Plays

In the 1920s, when Lorca started his career as a playwright, Spanish theaters were enjoying great success producing bourgeois conventional plays that featured realistic settings and characters whose beliefs and expectations faithfully echoed those of the audience. Although some directors were experimenting with unconventional repertoires and innovative theatrical techniques,[1] the Spanish stage was dominated by comedies of manners in the style of Jacinto Benavente (1866–1954) and the Alvarez Quintero brothers (Serafín [1871–1938] and Joaquín [1873–1944]), while the theater of such dramatists as Henrik Ibsen, Anton Chekhov, Bertolt Brecht, and Luigi Pirandello, then triumphing in Europe, was disregarded. Lorca criticized the shallowness, the absence of real art in the Spanish theater (*OC* 2:906), its excessive use of mannerisms, and its backwardness in relation to the latest stage developments. As he stated in "Charla sobre teatro" ("A Talk about Theater," 1935, *DS* 123–26) theater was crucial "for the edification of a country" and its people; it could not be just a pastime, because a function of theater was to show the audience the limitations of their beliefs and to exemplify "the eternal norms" of the heart and human feelings (*DS* 124).

Lorca's dedication to the theater throughout his career, most intensely toward the end of his life, was based on the belief that this art form offered the best means to achieve a more direct contact with a much wider audience (*OC* 2:978) than could ever be reached with the more intimate genre of lyric poetry. Even if the public did not always want to be confronted with serious questions, Lorca recognized the integral role of such questioning in legitimate theater (*OC* 2:973). The Spanish theater had lost its authority by seeking only to please the public; the time had come to make it the instrument that would elevate the audience to higher levels of understanding (*OC* 2:918). Starting with his first staged production, *The Butterfly's Evil Spell,* Lorca's theater reveals a conscious exploration of different styles as means of expression aimed at communicating with the audience without compromising aesthetic values, and the awareness that this communication is achieved through the play as an artistic construct fully aware of its formal requirements.

Lorca's work with the itinerant university theater La Barraca attests to his commitment to artistic theater as a means to educate people and achieve social awareness. Originating in November 1931 this project was conceived by a group of students from the University of Madrid. Their main motives were their dissatisfaction with the official theater of the time and their enthusiasm for the ideals of the Republic. The initial project proposed the installation of one permanent theater, a type of *barraca* (a large stall or fairground tent used for vaudeville acts)[2] in a strategic place in Madrid as well as a traveling one that would go throughout the country presenting plays during summer and holidays.[3] La Barraca's production expenses were covered by the Republic, but the actors, directors, and crew were not paid (*OC* 2:894–96). Members of La Barraca, mostly university students, volunteered their time and talent to the task of revitalizing and popularizing Spain's classical repertory of works by Cervantes (1547–1616), Calderón de la Barca (1600–81), and Lope de Vega (1562–1635). As Lorca indicated in a 1931 interview, they were moved by a great political idea, understanding "political" in the broad sense of education of the people.[4] By doing so, they were contributing to the creation of a new, democratic Spain. This project was clearly aimed at the people, and in the eyes of the Right, La Barraca had a definite leftist agenda. Lorca was happy to accept the directorship and was fully involved with the company during the period 1932–1935. The project fitted his desire to take the theater to the people and make it accessible to everyone.

The so-called rural trilogy—*Blood Wedding, Yerma,* and *The House of Bernarda Alba*—has been traditionally appraised as the culmination of Lorca's dramatic production. According to this critical view, his earlier plays are more or less successful exercises, and those he wrote almost simultaneously with the trilogy (*Once Five Years Pass, The Public,* and *Play Without a Title*) are experiments in which Lorca somehow lost his true direction. *The House of Bernarda Alba* would thus be the peak of Lorca's dramatic output, as evidenced in its decreased reliance on poetry as compared with *Blood Wedding*—a change usually identified with Lorca's gradual mastery of his dramatic talent.[5] This critical evaluation has been reappraised as scholarly work and study of Lorca's more experimental plays has progressed (see chapter 4 of the present study). Poetic imagery in Lorca's plays, far from being discarded as a mere adornment, is recognized as an intrinsic part of the dramatic action. Regarding the more experimental plays, Lorca himself claimed them as his true voice. Although the theater at the time may have been unprepared for such a different dramatic orientation as those plays represent, they are presently achieving increasing recognition in critical studies and stage performances.[6]

A thread that unites these three plays is the central role played by language as the means either to express passion and desire or to repress them with the institutionalized discourse of social and religious power. Some characters embody the opposite discourses of either desire or repression; others find themselves caught in the contradictions between passion and its frustration. Dialogues often develop on the fringes between the expression of passions and the need to repress it. The force of desire is so powerful that the mere act of naming or talking about it often leads to destruction and tragedy. Its voice expresses the inner truth, speaks the language of freedom, which often goes against all reason, pulling characters to sure danger and tragedy. However, the alternative is also tragic, since to repress desire leads to an unfulfilled life, a living death. This trilogy centers around the dynamic of expression/repression, which also corresponds to the inner/outer polarity that permeates Lorca's writings.

The symbolic order of the patriarchal culture, as categorized by French psychoanalyst Jacques Lacan, proves useful for describing the system that underlies Lorca's trilogy. This system is a diacritical movement between the symbolic order of representation—which Lacan defines as the order of judgment, of the norm and of immovable truth—and the personal order of desire. The discourse of repression frames the symbolic order, governing and regulating desire. It is spatialized within the four walls of the house, where characters, especially women, are expected to remain in order to protect their honor from other's gossip. Embroidering and sewing, laces, silks, and linens, become images of a way of life where instincts are repressed and desire is sublimated through the refinement of those activities. The outside world determines the social and religious rules that regulate all aspects of human behavior, permitting men much more freedom than women.

Blood Wedding (1933)

Blood Wedding, completed in 1932, premiered in 1933 in Madrid. In 1935, translated as *Bitter Oleander,* it opened in New York at the Neighborhood Playhouse with little success, largely due to the difficulty of rendering Lorca's lyricism into English.[7] However, it became his most-staged play during Lorca's life, allowing him, for the first time, to become financially independent from his family.

Many of Lorca's poetic and dramatic creations originated in real events. *Blood Wedding* was inspired by a news story Lorca had read in the papers four years earlier. In 1928, in Almería (a southern Spanish province), a woman about to marry had eloped with another man the day before the wedding. The bride's prospective brother-in-law killed the lover, and the bride was almost strangled by her own sister.[8] From this incident Lorca developed his own play after a long gestation period during which the reality of the event was stylized and recreated. The poet's brother remarks that this play "only took a week to write; but in maturing it took years."[9] In Lorca's play the elopement occurs during the celebrations following the wedding ceremony. The Bride leaves with Leonardo, with whom she had been emotionally involved sometime before and who is now married to one of her cousins. The news story is artistically transformed into a play paradigmatic of basic human emotions and situations. Most of the characters are identified by a generic name (Mother, Bride, Groom) indicating their archetypal or exemplary nature. Supernatural characters such as the Moon and Death overstep the "realistic" boundaries traditionally respected by bourgeois plays. Objective reality is thus overshadowed by other realms of existence implicated in human destiny and beyond the control of reason and logic.

In act 1 the Groom's mother still remembers the loss of her husband and eldest son. Both were killed by members of the Félix clan, to which Leonardo belongs. The Mother's recollections of the past dwell on the disparity between the vitality of her husband and son and the smallness of the knife that killed them. She is thus apprehensive about the Groom's going out alone in the fields—he is her only living son—and about the previous relationship of the Bride and Leonardo, a Félix, even though he was only a child when the murders occurred. These initial forebodings are fulfilled in the last act, in which the couple is chased down by the Groom and his clan. With the cooperation of the Moon and Death, personified as a young Woodcutter and an Old Beggar Woman, respectively, Leonardo and the Groom kill each other. The play ends with the Mother, Leonardo's wife, and the Bride, accompanied by other women neighbors and friends, lamenting the death of the two men by the ominous knife the Mother had so feared from the outset.

Lorca's theater is a multi-media work, a *Gesamtkunstwerk,* in which prose is intertwined with poetry, music, movement, and rhythm. Poetic images are no mere adornment, but woven into the fabric of the characters and the action, thus creating a symbolic world with its own internal consistency. In act 1 the Groom is associated with vital colors, with the green of the vineyards, where he goes to work, and with the red in the wine and the grapes he is going to eat.[10] The Mother associates men with wheat (*TT* 36), and later the Groom and Leonardo are referred to as "the golden flower" (*TT* 94). In act 1, scene 2, Leonardo's wife and mother-in-law are singing a lullaby to the baby, whom they call "carnation" and "rose" (*TT* 42). Through this color imagery, Lorca creates a series of associations that provide a metaphorical level to the plot. The baby and the

Groom/Leonardo (as two sides or aspects of the same character) are representations of the son (or of the means to achieve the son) as an image for love and hope. They are associated with the gold of the sun, which will later be stained by the red of blood (like the symbolic death of the sun at dusk) in the Groom's and Leonardo's death and, figuratively, in the child's abandonment by his father. The obvious allusions to the wine/blood of the Eucharist prefigure the ultimate sacrifice of Christ, the Son of man, a sacrifice that for Lorca had failed, since the world did not pay heed to it. This network of symbolic references projects the action onto a cosmic scale—the cyclical passage of time in which day expiring at sunset is engulfed by the moon and reemerges at dawn. This cycle perpetuates for Lorca the frustration of life, since desire is constantly thwarted by time and death. The son/child image is associated with the creative process throughout Lorca's writings and in this trilogy in particular. The son is not only the fruit in which life and love should culminate; he is also artistic expression, the poem, in which the author seeks to articulate form with desire, the inner discourse with the outer language of objectivity. Since the characters' desire is obstructed by death—since time is woven into the texture of life—the failure of the son is Lorca's representation of the tragedy of the human condition. It also represents his view of language as the means available to the artist to articulate a world of meaning. The artist seeks to express his truth but is inevitably constrained by the norms of a verbal system that alienates the truth it purports to articulate.[11]

At the very beginning of the play Lorca presents the knife that the Groom requests "to cut the grapes" (*TT* 34). The Mother refers to the knife as a "serpent" (*TT* 35), introducing its connotation of fatal sexuality, like its biblical counterpart, in the initial scene of harmonious life between the Mother and the Son/Groom. The moon-serpent image is re-created as the moonbeams, which, like the silvery blade of the knife, will fall onto the warm chest of both Leonardo and the Groom so that death will enter, just as the serpent entered the garden heralding human mortality. Solar and lunar mythologies, and a sense of the dissolution of life, are evoked through the images, establishing the basic conflict of this play and of the lyrical language Lorca created for it; that is, the inextricable fusion of opposite forces at the basis of human life.

The lullaby in act 1, scene 2 is a fine example of Lorca's integration of poetry into the dramatic action. Aware that Leonardo spends his nights furiously riding his horse to the Bride's house, the Wife and mother-in-law express their apprehensions through the poetic images of the lullaby. In the lecture on lullabies he delivered in 1928, "Añada. Arrolo. Nana. Vou Veri Vou. Canciones de Cuna españolas" ("On Lullabies," *DS* 7–22), Lorca referred to these songs in general as an "initiation into poetic adventure" (*DS* 14); the mother takes the child into an imaginary world from which he returns tired and sleepy. In this play's lullaby, the baby is carried to a land where a big horse does not want to drink the water. The horse is male sexuality, as well as creative impulse, reminiscent of Pegasus, the winged horse symbolic of poetic talent.[12] As a funerary image, the horse can also be a representation of death.[13] Water is a symbol of life and fertility; it also connotes the continuous passage of time. However, the lullaby's water is black, which explains the horse's refusal to drink it (*TT* 42). The water that could satiate the horse's erotic thirst is tainted with premonitions of death.

The horse is also the main protagonist in the child's poetic world as described by Lorca in his lecture on lullabies. The child moves in a poetic realm of faith still free from reason, a place where "a snow-white horse, half nickel and half smoke, falls suddenly injured, a swarm of furious bees at its eyes" (*DS* 15). (The horse in *Blood Wedding*'s lullaby is also injured by a silvery dagger stuck in his eyes.) Bees are a well-known image for laboriousness and for the creative process, and are commonly associated with the diurnal order (the sun implied in golden honey); the silvery dagger is often associated with moonbeams and night. The horse (or erotic and creative impulse) is thus attacked by reason and organized work (bees), and by forces from the subconscious. The fusion of these various symbolic meanings suggests that the sexual and artistic impulse moves in a liminal area full of danger. The big horse in the lullaby is an allusion to Leonardo, whose name (meaning "lion") also endows him with the sexual and erotic impulses commonly associated with the image of the horse. For Gustavo Correa, this lullaby anticipates and summarizes in a lyrical form the dramatic events that are to occur.[14] Leonardo and his horse are moving on the borderline between the symbolic social order and the realm of passions, where the danger of death prevails. The impending convergence of these two planes is evident at the closing of act 1, when the Groom and Mother depart from the Bride's house after all the wedding arrangements have been made. The Bride and her servant are looking at the wedding presents the Groom has brought when Leonardo's horse is heard lurking outside.

In act 2 the first guest to arrive on the wedding day is Leonardo, who has come by himself on his horse. A conversation between him and the Bride reveals that their passion is still very much alive. The difference in wealth is mentioned as the reason their marriage did not take place. Material possessions and societal norms hindered the free expression of love, a theme that runs through the trilogy. Since Leonardo is now married, the Bride consents to marry the Groom to avoid the temptation Leonardo presents. In marriage she hopes to find the peace she cannot have with Leonardo tempting her.

Leonardo lets her know that keeping things bottled up inside, as she plans to do in her marriage, only brings trouble: "To burn with desire and keep quiet about it is the greatest punishment we can bring on ourselves" (*TT* 60). Although the Bride refuses to listen, she feels herself drawn by his voice and its message pulling her like the strong current of a river—the water of passion tainted by death that the horse in the lullaby refused to drink. While this charged exchange is taking place, the appearance of order is maintained by the house servants making arrangements for the wedding. The epithalamium, or wedding song, is sung; it is an invitation to a circle dance: "Awake, O Bride, awaken, / . . . / sing round and dance round" (*TT* 61). The circle connotes life's plenitude in its everlasting cycle, which is echoed by the round orange-blossom wreath worn by the Bride and reiterated in the song the servant sings (act 2, scene 2) while preparing the tables for the guests: "A-turning, / the wheel was a-turning / and the water was flowing, / for the wedding night comes" (*TT* 67). These lines reflect the cyclical passage of time correlated to water flowing. Alongside these wishes for union, fertility, and happiness there is the undercurrent of disaster, already suggested by Leonardo's presence as the first wedding guest and his conversation with the Bride. When the Father sees him, he comments: "That one's looking for trouble. He's not of good blood" (*TT* 68). Good blood here entails knowing how to behave according to rules and conventions. Those who dare threaten the established order go against the blood, that is, familial and societal conventions. Leonardo represents instincts challenging the calm and restrained Groom and the official order of the wedding celebrations.[15]

The danger of letting the discourse of desire prevail is that blood could be spilled, destroying patterns that have taken many years to establish. Thus the Mother says: "it's so terrible to see one's own blood spilled out on the ground. A fountain that spurts for a minute, but costs us years" (*TT* 69–70). The Mother would do everything possible to keep things within the limits of convention. However, the play dramatizes the existence of other impulses opposed to the desires for tranquility and normalcy expressed by the Mother, urges that can take over, disrupting the established symbolic order. These impulses do not necessarily come from outside the characters but are integral parts of their nature, in the texture of life and being. The opposition of these two forces is what creates tragic human fate. Hence the Bride, acknowledging the force of her desires, feels as though she had been "struck on the head" (*TT* 75). All her intentions of locking herself in the house with her husband are not going to prevail. When the Bride's absence from the wedding party is first noticed, the

Father says: "She must have gone up to the railing" (*TT* 76). As in "Sleepwalking Ballad," the railing is associated with the moon, since its light is reflected there at night. The Bride thus enters the realm of the moon, or the order of instincts, whose fatal influence will be pervasive in the last act.[16]

Act 3 scene 1 takes place in the forest at night, a setting traditionally identified with the dark region of the mind, with poetic imagination and fantasy. It is reminiscent of Shakespeare's *A Midsummer's Night Dream,* a work that strongly influenced Lorca, who perceived the love of Titania for the ass as an example of the unpredictability of love.[17] A lyrical exchange takes place between three Woodcutters about the Bride's and Leonardo's elopement. In this setting of primordial emotions, the Woodcutters represent the popular belief that nature, the moon, and cosmic elements participate directly in human destiny. Hence, the first Woodcutter predicts that their pursuers will not fail to see them when the moon comes out. Their fate has already been sealed, as was already suggested by the silvery dagger in the eyes of the lullaby's horse. However, the second Woodcutter believes Leonardo and the Bride did the right thing by following their passion, "the path of [their] blood," as the first Woodcutter adds (*TT* 79). Here, to follow the path of your blood entails following one's instincts. But choosing that path also creates problems. In this play, the image of blood is the central symbol of desire constrained within well-defined boundaries by societal norms. However, when those boundaries are crossed, when blood is spilled in violent death, or desire is permitted to run freely in the sexual encounter, the traces of the blood dissolve in the earth in the existential pattern of death and decay. Ironically, that blood becomes the fertilizing liquid from which new life emerges, repeating the cycle of life and death that Lorca perceives as inescapable. Lorca's characters reflect this tragic view, for they are caught between desire and the outside order, with no escape. If they follow the path of desire, they risk losing themselves, while if they negate it, they find themselves rotting inside.[18] Desire cannot be reconciled with the demands of the symbolic order of culture; these are contradictory forces.

The Moon is personified as a young Woodcutter with a white face. In early mythology and religion, the moon is hermaphroditic. As the opposite of the day/sun, the moon connotes the realm of the subconscious, of death, but also of creativity, since true art requires contact with the darkest areas of being.[19] The moon complains of extreme cold and asks to be let in (*TT* 81). However, s/he is convinced that that night there will be red blood for her cheeks. The death that the moon heralds is fused with erotic connotations; the moonbeams—like knife blades piercing the scene—yearn "to be blood's pain" (*TT* 81). Thanatos and eros—as the impulses for death and love—are fused in the path of desire marked by the moon. Hence, the next character to appear is Death, personified as an Old Woman. A dialogue between her and the Moon ensues. The Moon's light will illuminate the men's chests so that death can enter through the knife.

By the time Leonardo and the Bride appear on stage, their fate has already been decided by the agreement between the Moon and Death. The man and woman have an intensely passionate dialogue. Leonardo confesses the impossibility of resisting his attraction for her. Without an outlet, his desire "was choking" his flesh "with its poisoned weeds" (*TT* 87). Similarly, the Bride confesses to being drawn to Leonardo: "Nails of moonlight have fused / my waist and your chains" (*TT* 89).[20] In the final scene white predominates in the set, which, according to Lorca's instructions, "should have the monumental feeling of a church" (*TT* 90). The whiteness of the setting and the archetypical nature of the characters indicate that the play depicts fundamental human emotions and the human condition. The only characters on stage are women, the recipients and protectors of life, lamenting its destruction. In the group, the weaving girls are reminiscent of the Parcae (or Greek fates, divine spinners of the thread of life and destiny). It is significant that the first girl is weaving with red wool, the color of blood, whose "thread" has woven the tragic fate of the characters, suggesting that death is intertwined with life's daily passage. The round, woven wedding wreath of orange blossoms has been transformed on the metaphorical plane into the blood wedding.

The Beggar Woman appears at the door and announces the arrival of the two corpses, Leonardo's and the Groom's. Both men are identified as united in their death. As embodiments of two possible directions for desire—to keep it within the parameters marked by the outside order (the Groom) or to follow it without restraint (Leonardo)—their deaths indicate the failure of any attempt to harmonize those directions. The Bride, who has been directly caught between them, also returns, her skirt and hair stained with blood (*TT* 94). Her whiteness has been tainted with the spilled blood, but ironically, neither the marriage nor the passionate escapade with Leonardo have been consummated. As she explains to her mother-in-law: "I was a woman burning with desire, . . . and your son was a little bit of water from which I hoped for children, land, health . . . but the other one's arm dragged me along like a pull of the sea. . . ." (*TT* 96). This character embodies the hopeless impasse that constitutes Lorca's tragic view, for she, as Bride, remains filled with desire. Recalling the opening scene, the play ends with the Mother's soliloquy about the knife, the tiny knife that killed both

Leonardo and the Groom, the knife

> . . . that slides in clean
> . . . .
> and stops at the place
> where trembles, enmeshed,
> the dark root of a scream.

(TT 98)

The cold knife, which the Moon used to help Death's task, has finally warmed up in the innermost place of the human chest, at the root of the scream which, like in Deep Song, voices the tragic existential fate. The Groom and Leonardo are two sides of the same figure, both sons exemplifying the failed fusion of instincts with the public language of reason and order. This final scene with the knife echoes the lullaby's horse with the silvery dagger in his eyes. It also recalls Lorca's own search for the work of art, "the poem that pierces the heart like a sword" (*SL* 85). These images objectify Lorca's tragic sense of the nature of life and art. If neither of the available existential options is viable, a similar situation applies to art. For Lorca, art resides in tension, for it cannot be reduced to a perfectly designed formal construct or to mere emotions. Rather, it has to pierce the heart by articulating the impossible tension between emotion and form, instincts and reason.

Yerma (1934)

Yerma, written between the summer of 1933 and the summer of 1934, premiered on December 1934 in Madrid. Right-wing newspapers were offended by the immorality they perceived in the play, while Republican and left-wing publications acclaimed it as a great work. This split in public opinion placed Lorca on the Left; the Right later identified him as an enemy of their political objectives and views, and killed him for it. *Blood Wedding* continued to be a great success, and with *Yerma* Lorca finally became financially successful.[21]

The word *yerma* means "barren," as in "barren earth." In the play it is the name of a woman whose only wish is to conceive a child. Nowhere it is said that she is sterile, and she seems to believe that the lack of enthusiasm in her husband's lovemaking is responsible for her not becoming pregnant. Yerma has been married to her peasant husband Juan for two years when the play begins. Her patience is running out as time goes by and she gradually realizes she is being excluded from the fertility cycle that nature displays all around her. Her religious upbringing and sense of honor do not permit her to have extramarital relations, as a village Old Woman suggests she do when Yerma admits to the perfunctoriness of her sexual relations with her husband. As a last resort Yerma goes on a pilgrimage to a shrine of popular religious devotion to pray for her womb to be blessed with a child. In the orgiastic atmosphere of the celebrations, Juan finally admits that he is not interested in having a child. Yerma is forced to face the denial of her wish and the unbridgeable distance between her and her husband. Therefore, when at the end Juan makes a sexual advance at her, Yerma kills him. She is unable to participate in a sexual relationship devoid of meaning since it is no longer intended to conceive a child.

Yerma's sexuality is inhibited; she cannot openly enjoy intercourse with her husband because of a traditional education that has instilled in her the belief that sex has to be for procreation. For his part, Juan, as a man, has also been conditioned by tradition to view sex as an activity for a man's satisfaction, often with no regard for the woman's. He is thus unable or unwilling to give Yerma pleasure. Both are victims of an upbringing inhibiting pleasure and the open enjoyment of each other on equal terms.

Subtitled "a tragic poem," this play can also be viewed as a commentary on Lorca's relationship to the act of poetic creation. In order to write, it is necessary to let oneself go, to sing openly, as the Old Woman tells Yerma she did when she conceived. When sexual, religious, social, and moral prescriptions are constraining, the creative impulse cannot flow, and the poet is thwarted. Socially hemmed in because of his own sexuality, Lorca must have felt, like his heroine, the restraint on his sexuality/creativity. Moreover, the success of conventional, bourgeois plays on the Spanish stage presented a real obstacle to the writing of more daring and authentic plays. In *Yerma* erotic games—or their equivalent, writing—are always associated with the child/poem. Those who can sing freely harvest the desired fruit.[22] Neither Yerma nor Juan are free singers: Yerma wants to sing in order to give birth to a child, but Juan is not willing to collaborate in that creation and is interested only in satisfying his momentary need. He does not see nor care about any (pro-)creative point to lovemaking. They cannot unite and produce the child/poem because they are singing different tunes. By killing Juan, Yerma confirms her status as a victim of the barrenness brought about by her subjection to the social and religious norms of the symbolic order. To repress sexuality and its free expression for the sake of morality or honor is for Lorca equivalent to castration (physical and poetic).

In act 1, scene 1, Yerma is asleep. Her dream is made visible on stage by the figure of a shepherd leading by the hand a child dressed in white. The son image in *Blood Wedding* makes its appearance here at the very outset. The Shepherd is the projection of Victor, a village shepherd with whom it is suggested Yerma had a brief sentimental relationship when she was fourteen. It is also intimated that Victor is the only one with whom she could have felt the love that would engender the desired child. Hence, the child in white led by the shepherd is the child Yerma desires, unconsciously associated with Victor. The dream has allowed Yerma to express her yearning freely, but, in waking reality, she has to face repression. That reality is embodied in her husband Juan, who appears on stage on his way to work in the fields. Still under the influence of her dream, Yerma wants her desire to fuse with her reality. Hence, she passionately declares her love for Juan, reminding him of her happiness on their wedding night: "Didn't I sing as I turned back the fine linen bedclothes?" (*TT* 104). As these words indicate, Yerma's initial happiness in marrying Juan has taken a different turn as time passes without their conceiving a child. Juan's only consolation is for Yerma to wait, be patient, and stay home, as honorable women do.

When María, a neighbor, announces her pregnancy to Yerma, she refers to her child as "a dove of fire" her husband slipped inside of her through her ear on their wedding night (*TT* 108), an allusion to the Holy Ghost blowing his breath of life through the Virgin's ear (Luke 1:38).[23] María's view of conception is that the flow of life and creativity fills her body. The same attitude toward sex is displayed by the First Old Woman, mother of nine children. To Yerma's question about what she ought to do to have children, the woman responds: "I laid down face up and began to sing. Children came like water" (*TT* 112). Singing, breath, voice, and flowing water are the images related to fertility and to creativity. These examples suggest the association of conception with the innocent and unreflective attitude of the participants. María and the Old Woman do not feel detached from the natural life surrounding them, for they do not seem to be directly affected by religious or societal constraints. Yerma, on the other hand, is a highly self-reflective character. Her unfruitful body becomes an obsession to the point that for her, she is the embodiment of sterility. If María and the Old Woman are in touch with the source of life, Yerma's self-awareness increases her alienation from nature. If she could, Yerma would like to conceive the child by herself. Yerma's fate suggests that a highly self-reflexive attitude in life and art leads to sterility, since it has no effect beyond its own boundaries.

Juan's energy, by contrast, is not directed toward sex, singing, creativity, or living life as an artistic enterprise, since his work in the fields consumes his strength and time. The couple's sterility results from societal and religious repression of human sexuality and, by implication, of creativity in general. As a consequence, neither one is able to establish a truthful and mutual relationship with the other or anyone else. As in *Blood Wedding,* repressing desire leads to sterility and death, as it is made evident in act 1, scene 2, in which a passionate exchange takes place between Victor and Yerma. Yerma compliments Victor on his voice, "a stream of water that fills your mouth" (*TT* 117) and confesses to having heard a child crying as though it were drowning close by. Within the network of images already established, that child's drowning is a poetic equivalent of the loss of the progeny/product (child/poetry), since Victor and Yerma cannot act on their hidden desires for one another. Ironically, Juan enters and tells Yerma he will not be home that night because he has to irrigate the fields, and since there is very little water left, he has to guard it from thieves. While all his energy is directed toward work, Yerma's field remains barren. Her empty breasts, whose milk cannot flow to nurse a child, are "two rhythms of a horse's gallop" (*TT* 131). The horse galloping with no direction implies unfulfilled desire, as in *Blood Wedding,* where Leonardo's wild rides to the Bride's house connote the frustration of his desire for her.

Yerma's increasing feeling of failure runs parallel with Juan's attempts to control her movements. In act 2, scene 1, while they wash by the riverside, a group of laundresses talk about how Juan asked his sisters to live in his house in order to keep an eye on his wife. The village is gossiping about Yerma, saying she stays out at night, and Juan wants to safeguard his honor. One laundress refers to Juan's sisters as "smeared with wax," as growing "inwards" (*TT* 121). Juan and his sisters embody repression encircling Yerma, making a prison from which there is no escape except in tragedy. The laundresses' scene, one of fertility, of free singing and flowing water, is contrasted in act 2, scene 2, by Juan's conversations with his sisters and with Yerma. The distance between the couple is becoming wider and more unbridgeable. Juan speaks a language of enclosing, locking up, accumulating property, safeguarding in the name of honor; while Yerma's speaks of anguish, of vital potential locked up inside of her with no hope for release. Her frustration makes Yerma say to María, "I'll end up believing I'm my own son" (*TT* 133). She feels as if she were becoming her own thwarted desire; her self-absorption is choking her. Victor's departure to other fields with his brothers seems to give Yerma the final reason to go to Dolores, the sorceress, in search of a remedy.

In act 3, scene 1, Yerma lets Dolores know that she and Juan engage regularly in lovemaking but without passion: "When he covers me, he's doing his duty, but I feel a waist cold as a corpse's" (*TT* 140). The problem, according to Yerma, is that Juan does not want children, therefore his passionless lovemaking does not bring the seed. She, by her own admission, hates "hot" women, that is, those women who freely engage in the pleasures of sex. Even though she now knows she does not love Juan, "By honor and by blood," he is her only salvation. Instinct, or love, thus contradicts honor and marriage. Yerma is caught between her marriage vows, as prescribed by the cultural symbolic order, and her desire. When Juan discovers that Yerma has visited Dolores, he accuses her of causing him dishonor with her comings and goings alone at night, and Yerma replies heatedly that he is the one she is looking for. Identifying Juan with the child she so much desires, she exclaims: "Look how I'm left alone! As if the moon searched for herself in the sky" (TT 142). Like the moon's endless cycle, Yerma's failed desire is making her turn in circles: "I'm entering the darkest part of the pit," she remarks (TT 143).

In act 3, scene 2, which concludes the play, the action takes place during a pilgrimage in the environs of a hermitage high in the mountains. The romería, or pilgrimage, evokes one held in Moclín, a small village north of the Vega of Granada. As a yearly event childless women go up to the chapel of the Christ of the Cloth, located on a hill, to pray that they may be made fertile. The supposed religiosity of these pilgrimages invariably turns into celebrations in which men and women behave much more freely than usual, so that women become pregnant for causes more natural than supernatural.[24] In Lorca's play two masks—male and female—begin the dance of desire. Lorca's stage directions indicate that they should not look grotesque, "but [be] of great beauty and with a feeling of pure earth" (TT 147). This dance of sexuality should thus appear truly beautiful to Yerma, who would witness and hopefully internalize its message, freeing herself from her inhibitions.

The female mask sings of a sad wife bathing, an allusion to the traditional theme of the bath of fertility.[25] Rising and shaking his horn, the male announces to the sorrowing wife that she will blossom when he "spreads out his cape" (TT 148). The dancing and singing evolves into an orgiastic praise of lovemaking. When the masks leave, the Old Woman offers her son to Yerma, who, obviously not having absorbed any of the sexual message of the dance, rejects the other in the name of her honor. It is not a matter of wanting another man with whom to conceive, for Yerma has come to realize the utter impossibility of fulfilling her desire.[26] Totally constrained by societal and religious norms, Yerma's desire is consuming her. The only outcome is to complete that process of self-consumption by destroying the object that could still maintain some hope of fulfillment: Juan.

At the celebration, when Juan kisses Yerma in an obvious sexual advance after openly admitting his lack of interest in a child, Yerma kills him in disgust.[27] But by killing him, Yerma is left alone, a moon figure reduced to her own sterility, revolving on her own axis in her own inescapable tragedy. It is not only that Yerma is sexually inhibited by her upbringing and social situation; Yerma is Lorca's embodiment of the frustration inherent in human desire. Her child, like her longing, is doomed never to be born and live. By strangling Juan, her only real possibility of bringing that child forth, Yerma acknowledges the limitations imposed on her desire and, by extension, on human desire in general. In the association of love and poetry that this play develops, Yerma's unconceived child is the song/poem that, even before its inception, is already marked by the limitations of language, by the impossibility to make the word coincide with the plenitude it purports to represent. Now she knows for sure that her body will be dry forever, and she exclaims: "I myself have killed my son!" (*TT* 153).

Throughout the play Juan has tried to silence Yerma, making her stay locked up in the house. He withholds his seed by his being obsessed with his work in the fields. Yerma, in turn, desires a child, but feels constrained by the norms imposed by honor and religion. Her repression precedes her marriage and is a consequence of her upbringing. In her character, Yerma reflects the distortions that a repressive system can inflict on vitality. For Lorca, growing up and entering the order of reason and restrictions meant the "withering" (*marchitarse*) of the flower of possibilities of childhood, the age when it was still possible to dream of a direct link with the world. His instincts and desires demanded his dedication to a type of life and creativity free from restrictions, but his reason and societal hobbles put limits on him and continually threatened to wither the flower of his poetry. Pressured to keep his creative flow within socially acceptable channels, he felt the constant danger of seeing his art, like Yerma's, wither.[28]

Victor the shepherd and Juan the laborer demarcate the land that is Yerma, the earth woman.[29] Victor sings a tune beyond the societal and religious boundaries demarcating the land; Juan sings—or expresses himself in a sexually creative manner—only occasionally and in a contrived manner. In the end, the earth remains barren within the boundaries imposed upon her and her desire. This situation echoes that of the Bride caught between the Groom and Leonardo in *Blood Wedding*. In both plays male desire has two irreconcilable urges that trap female desire when they collide. The female character can break away from societal and existential constraints only by some extreme act (Yerma strangling her husband, the Bride and Leonardo disrupting the wedding altogether). There are subtle references to the moon accompanying this moment, indicating its implication in the tragedy. In *Blood Wedding* the moon intervenes by brightening up the men's chest with its beams to guide the deadly knife. In *Yerma,* when Juan makes the fatal erotic move, he tells his wife that she looks beautiful in the moonlight (*TT* 153). In Lorca's poetic world, the spilling of blood (or the overflowing of desire) occurs in the realm of the moon, away from the reason and logic associated with the diurnal context, because it is in the lunar realm that the character faces his/her truth and acts upon it, no matter how extreme or dangerous it may be. Ironically, the red or blood of desire is consumed as it is expressed in the dissolving whiteness of the moon's temporal cycle. Similarly, art, as necessarily expressive of desire, is marked by the distance from direct experience imposed by the white page. The existential cycle incorporates desire and frustration, life and death, inscription and dissolution as two complementary opposites.

The House of Bernarda Alba (1945)

Lorca completed *The House of Bernarda Alba* in June 1936, shortly before his death, but it did not premiere until 1945 in Buenos Aires. The inspiration for this play appears to have been Frasquita Alba Sierra, a neighbor of Lorca's family in the village of Asquerosa (today, Valderrubio). She was a domineering woman, twice married and the mother of eight children, but not necessarily as tyrannical a mother as Bernarda of Lorca's play.[30] The setting of this play is inside Bernarda's house, behind the walls and demarcations that the Bride and Yerma were crossing. The action introduces the hypocrisy hidden behind the mask, or shell, of societal, religious, and honor norms.

Lorca subtitled this play "A Drama About Women in the Villages of Spain" and intended it to be a "photographic document." This intent reflects Lorca's interest in making the theater a vehicle of communication with his people, as he stated in 1935 "A Talk about Theater" (*DS* 123–26). Notwithstanding this documentary intention, poetic images are an intrinsic part of the dramatic action of *The House of Bernarda Alba,* as in *Blood Wedding* and *Yerma*. These images create a symbolic level of meaning that counterbalances the realistic claims of the plot.[31]

Stage directions for Act 1 indicate that the season is summer. A great silence dominates the stage, which depicts "a very white room" in Bernarda's house. The aseptic setting, resembling a prison or convent in the thickness and whiteness of the walls and the "heaviness" pervading the whole atmosphere, is contradicted or counterbalanced by the pictures of unrealistic scenes with nymphs and imaginary kings (*TT* 157) decorating the walls.[32] It is as though the two worlds of reality and fantasy—the symbolic order and desire—were in confrontation from the outset. Antonio María Benavides, Bernarda Alba's second husband, has just died, and his funeral is taking place at the church. Poncia, an old servant who has served the family for many years, and a younger servant, a maid, are preparing the house for the funeral gathering. Their comments clearly show their dislike for Bernarda, whom they describe as a violent "domineering old tyrant" (*TT* 157), obsessed with cleanliness, and hated by her husband's relatives. Class differences are also established: "All we have is our hands and a hole in God's earth" (*TT* 159), Poncia remarks. Yet, ironically, a clear hierarchical system of abuse has been established; when a beggar knocks, the servant treats her as poorly as Poncia treats that servant and as Bernarda treats Poncia.

We also learn that Antonio María Benavides sexually abused young lower-class women, whom he could easily control. Alone on stage, the servant expresses her feelings openly about the abuse she had to take from her master: "Take what's coming to you, Antonio María Benavides stiff in your broadcloth suit and your high boots. . . . You'll never again lift my skirts behind the corral door!" (*TT* 160). However, as soon as the funeral guests start to arrive, the servant's tone changes drastically, adopting the lamenting style required by the circumstances. This instance of hypocrisy shows at the outset the contradiction between seeming and being, between what is said and what is meant, the outer and inner languages around which the play is organized.

Bernarda's actions throughout the play are intended to repress all open expression of personal desires; thus her first word as she enters is "Silence!" (*TT* 161), as it will be her last. As she returns from church with the funeral party she makes the servant leave, since that is not her place: "The poor are like animals—they seem to be made of different stuff" (*TT* 161), Bernarda remarks. This prejudice about lower social classes, together with Bernarda's cruelty and violence, are contrasted with her seeming piety, which underscores the distance between appearance and reality. Religious feeling needs to be shown more than truly felt, Lorca is indicating, thus denouncing the hypocritical shell of societal and religious structures. This hypocrisy goes to the extreme of negating reality if reality does not conform with the norms prescribed by that code of behavior. So when a girl in the funeral party says to Angustias, the oldest of Bernarda's daughters from her first marriage, that Pepe el Romano, to whom Angustias will soon be engaged, was at the church, Bernarda denies it, even though Angustias admits to having seen Pepe there. Since a single girl is expected not to look at men, Bernarda denies the truth of her daughter's desire and natural curiosity, supporting the artificial code of social behavior. However, she is quick to point out to the girl that her aunt was seen very close to a widower, implying that the aunt behaved improperly.[33] Totally dominated by the social code, Bernarda is incapable of maintaining a fruitful, mutual, human relationship with other people, including her own daughters. When they control all aspects of human behavior, outside norms ultimately desensitize or even physically kill the people subject to them.

When the funeral is over Bernarda is happy to see the people leave and to be momentarily spared from their malevolent gossip. Bernarda's "tongue like a knife" is her defense against any other mordant tongue in the village that might attack her reputation and that of her house and daughters. As she puts it, this is a village of wells, where one drinks with the fear of being poisoned (*TT* 164). Nothing seems to flow, for it is a stagnated village of closed doors, of poisonous relationships from which there is no escape, as Bernarda's house itself illustrates. Instead of the three years customary for mourning, Bernarda imposes eight, during which her five daughters, who vary in age from twenty (Adela) to thirty-nine (Angustias), as well as her own mother of eighty, will remain locked up in the house. In accordance with prescribed social rules, and even going beyond them, Bernarda thus creates physically and literally the existential imprisonment that Yerma and the Bride experienced. Most of the daughters know that they will not marry, as one of them, Magdalena (age thirty), states, but they are forced to stay inside and embroider their sister Angustias' trousseau. To their complaints Bernarda retorts, "That's what a woman is for" (*TT* 165). A woman of their social status is not supposed to work outside, and is thus reduced to "needle and thread" (*TT* 165). When Poncia tries to tell Bernarda of the need her daughters have of a man, Bernarda denies it vehemently: her daughters do not need a man, simply because she says so. Bernarda's code, like the social order it represents, brings about the most extreme of reversals, for it denies natural needs in order to present itself as the natural norm. To Bernarda, no one in the village is worthy of her daughters, whom she is willing to sacrifice to a life of seclusion and frustration rather than allow them to marry someone socially beneath them. A case in point is Martirio, aged twenty-four; Bernarda forbade a young man from the village, Enrique Humanas, to court her because he belonged to a lower social class. Consequently, Martirio is doomed to a life of martyrdom (as her name suggests).

This situation occurs inside Bernarda's walls, but it also seems to reflect the larger society, as the conversation of Martirio and her twenty-seven-year-old sister Amelia indicates. The sisters talk about a common friend who, since becoming engaged, is not allowed by her fiancé even to go to the doorstep (*TT* 169). It is impossible to know whether it is better to have a beau or to remain inside the house, Amelia remarks, since men (and hence, society), impose such cruel norms on women. Besides, for men, marriage is a matter of gaining the material possessions of the future bride and of getting a submissive wife. Pepe el Romano fits the bill perfectly; even though he wants Adela, he becomes engaged to Angustias, who is much older and less attractive, because of her money.

Magdalena remembers past days when life was happier, when gossip was not as cruel, when they didn't have to lock themselves up inside for fear of what people might say (*TT* 170). Similarly, the house, an image of a container/womb filled with the women's vitality and desire, is rotting under the influences of religion, society, and honor.[34] Adela is the one who most openly challenges her mother's authority. In her search for ways to break through the walls of her mother's prison she defies the conventions for mourning by wearing a green dress that she received for her birthday, and goes to the corral to feed the chickens, the only witnesses of her beauty. Moreover, it appears that Pepe has been leaving the window (where it was customary for lovers to hold their rendezvous) at night much later than Angustias thinks. The possibility of his playing a double game (by staying longer to be with Adela after Angustias retires for bed) is thus subtly suggested, and it will be later confirmed when his relationship with Adela is discovered.

Signs that Bernarda's rule is going to be challenged come from her own mother, María Josefa. She loudly calls to be let out of her room because, in her demential fantasy, she wants to go to the seashore to marry a handsome young man. María Josefa represents the voice attempting to unlock the constraints of the symbolic cultural order. She articulates what all the others wish, but do not dare to express openly. Her name—which fuses the female and male figures (Mary and Joseph) of the prototypical family (Mary, Joseph, and Jesus)—plus her insistence to voice her desire, threaten the binary oppositions (male/female, reason/emotion, etc.) that secure the grounds of the symbolic order, of its "phallogocentric" beliefs.[35] Therefore, she is considered insane and kept locked up. When Poncia insists to Bernarda that her daughters have human needs, Bernarda replies by implying her total control over the situation. While her mother is crazy, she, Bernarda, has "her five senses" and knows what she is doing (*TT* 175). In the world of the play the opposition between craziness and "knowing what one is doing," or "having the five senses," acquires an ironic value. Bernarda's "rational" control of the situation is going to prove fatally weak, and the truth of her mother's "crazy" warnings about the daughters' frustration will be confirmed.[36] In the middle of this discussion María Josefa appears with flowers on her head and breast, in drastic contrast with Bernarda's black dress. Although Bernarda tries to silence her, María Josefa reiterates her wish to go to the seashore to marry a beautiful man (*TT* 175). The image of the seashore is thus contrasted with the village of wells and stagnant water, and the free-flowing water with imprisonment and inertness. In the language of the play, reason and common sense repress the free expression of desire, calling it crazy.

The "very white room" in act 1 changes to a "white room" in act 2, and while the walls were described as thick at the outset, suggesting seclusion and impenetrability, the stage directions here indicate that "the doors on the left lead to the bedrooms" (*TT* 177). A different perspective toward the depth or interior of Bernarda's house is thus created, as if, with the photographic camera, the spectator were allowed to penetrate farther into the characters' psyches. The focus shifts from the "physical" activity in act 1, with the characters' comings and goings, to their psychic activity. In the opening scene the sisters embroider while they talk. Angustias characterizes the house as "this hell" (*TT* 177) and says of Adela that "She's getting the look of a crazy woman" (*TT* 180). Poncia finds Adela "restless, trembling, frightened" (*TT* 177), to which Martirio adds: "There's nothing, more or less, wrong with her than there is with all of us" (*TT* 177). Something is corroding their minds, and salvation lies in getting out of the house. They increasingly complain about the heat, suggesting that they suffer not merely from the high temperatures but also from the growing intensity of the passion mounting inside each of them, making the situation inside the house doubly unbearable. Pepe, who has been coming to see Angustias, is not leaving at one or one-thirty in the morning, as she thinks, but at four, according to Poncia. When her sisters ask her what Pepe said to her the first time he came to her window, Angustias's answer shows Pepe's indifference to her: "'I need a good, well brought-up woman, and that's you—if it's agreeable'" (*TT* 179). It is evident that their union is based on a social arrangement of money and convention in which love and passion have no place.

Adela herself complains that her body aches (*TT* 181). Martirio's question "with a hidden meaning" as to how Adela slept the night before reinforces the suspicion that Pepe might be spending more time at the house with someone other than Angustias. When Martirio tries to hinder her movement, Adela responds by proclaiming her will to do whatever she chooses with her body. Adela identifies herself with her body as the expression of her true being. Her body is the target of the inquisition and control her sisters and mother impose in accordance with the outside order. Adela reveals to Poncia that she has been exposing her body at the window for Pepe to see. Poncia's advice is to let the marriage of Angustias and Pepe take place, since, as expected, Angustias's poor health will not permit her to take a pregnancy to term. She will die, and Pepe will then marry the youngest and prettiest of the sisters, Adela, as it is customary for widowers to do in that region (*TT* 182). Yet it is already too late for

Adela has been taken away by the force of her instinctive desire for Pepe. Like the Bride in *Blood Wedding* speaking about her desire for Leonardo, Adela confesses to Poncia: "Looking in his [Pepe's] eyes I seem to drink his blood slowly" (*TT* 183). Like the Moon in *Blood Wedding* searching for blood to warm up her pale and cold cheeks, Adela becomes a type of moon creature facing the truth of her consuming passion and voicing it as a desire to drink Pepe's blood, that is, his vitality.[37]

While the heat is becoming unbearable inside the house, outside the reapers are heard singing on their way to the fields. Poncia describes them as "forty or fifty handsome young men" (*TT* 184) who have come from the mountains, far from the stagnant atmosphere of the village. They are associated with wheat, nature, and sexuality, and with singing, an image of fertility as in *Yerma*. Adela would like to be one of them, as she exclaims, so that she could come and go as she pleased. The reapers' song asks for the village women to open their doors and windows, to open themselves to the coming of the seed of life, the opposite of the locking and closing in Bernarda's house.

The storm of passions is approaching when Angustias appears on stage looking for one of Pepe's pictures that has disappeared from her bedroom. Martirio comments, "But couldn't it have jumped out into the yard at midnight? Pepe likes to walk around in the moonlight" (*TT* 188). He likes to walk around with the moon, with which Adela has been clearly identified. The picture is finally found in Martirio's bed. This unexpected turn of events shows that the storm is even more threatening than was first suspected. Not only is Adela desperate for Pepe, but Martirio is as well. Bernarda realizes that Angustias must get married, not for the sake of her daughter's happiness, but to get Pepe away from the household. Poncia has been trying to warn her of the seriousness of the situation inside the house (*TT* 191), but Bernarda has refused to listen or to admit that her prison was not inescapable.

An episode involving an unmarried woman who murdered her illegitimate baby to hide her shame sheds light on the situation in the house. The villagers drag the woman through the streets and want to kill her. Like that woman, Adela has also been dragged by her sexual passion (*TT* 195). During this scene, Adela is described as holding her belly—suggesting that she may be pregnant by Pepe—as she vehemently opposes killing the woman, whom Bernarda is in favor of cruelly punishing: "Yes, . . . let them all come and kill her! . . . Finish her before the guards come! Hot coals in the place where she sinned!" (*TT* 195). For Bernarda, even homicide is justified in order to preserve society's demands for morality.

Act 3 opens with another scene change inside the house, to the interior patio, where the walls are "lightly washed in blue" (*TT* 196). The stark white of sterile purity is now shaded with a blue of unreality in consonance with pictures of nymphs, legendary kings, and fantastic landscapes that cover the walls. The intended photographic "realism" is revealing a situation whose claims to rationality and order verge on the irrational. The more the action moves into the core of the house, the more the picture shows the distortion caused by repression.

While Bernarda and her daughters have dinner, a heavy blow is heard from a stallion in the corral kicking against the walls. A clear reference to Pepe, the stallion appears in the middle of the corral, filling the darkness with its size and whiteness (*TT* 201). This huge, white beast, overpowering the darkness, contrasts sharply with the black of the night, heralding the storm of passions about to break. According to various reports, Pepe and his horse have been heard every night at different hours. The stallion now alerts the spectator to the presence of Pepe, or to the presence of the masculinity and sexual impulses this character connotes. As the stallion's blows become increasingly loud, Adela gets up to get a drink of water and to go for a walk as far as the gate (*TT* 199). The gate serves as a symbolic boundary, for Adela is now on the border between her mother's authority and outside freedom.

Amelia comments about the extreme darkness of the night, a good night for hiding and for thieves, as Martirio remarks alluding to Pepe's lurking outside (*TT* 201). The tragedy in the house, according to Poncia, is coming to a head on this ominous night, propitious for all kinds of clandestine activities. The façade Bernarda so fiercely defends is being threatened by dark forces that she has blinded herself to. Adela, who is interested in the spheres above the constraining walls of her mother's prison, who, according to Martirio, almost breaks her neck by looking up at the stars so much, will hang herself later for having dared to cross over the prescribed boundaries.[38] Here, as in other plays, Lorca aims the death blow at the neck as the site of the voice, which corresponds symbolically to the poem. That voice, the expression of desire in life and art, is thus choked off by societal or religious forces or existential limitations.

After the exchange between Amelia and Martirio, the sisters go to bed and Bernarda talks with Poncia about the servant's fears about something wrong happening in the house. Nothing is happening, Bernarda is convinced, because she is watching over everything (*TT* 202). Poncia is well aware of the distance separating the daughters' external appearance from the turmoil within them. Not even a mother can see "inside a person's heart" (*TT* 202), remarks Poncia. Ironically, just when Bernarda should be watching most closely, her stubbornness blinds her fully. That night, when the storm explodes, is precisely when she says she will sleep well. Poncia's remark is fitting: "When you're powerless against the sea, it's easier to turn your back on it and not look at it" (*TT* 203). Bernarda, the apparent epitome of power and control, is judged by the servant as powerless against the sea of erotic expression, freedom, and openness, the place where María Josefa wanted to escape to and marry a handsome young man. After having tried unsuccessfully to warn Bernarda, Poncia washes her hands of the whole situation.[39]

Suddenly, noises are heard and dogs begin to bark. The servant indicates that someone must have entered through the back door. Soon Adela enters to drink water. In the symbolic language of the play, her thirst is going to be quenched by Pepe, who is waiting for her in the corral, or who perhaps is leaving after having been with her. The dogs are going mad, sensing the restlessness in the inhabitants of the house. In the midst of all this, with the forces of the night and moon loose, María Josefa appears, singing to a lamb she holds in her arms as if it were her child. She wants to take her "child" to the seashore and "to the palms at Bethlehem's gate" (*TT* 205). Bethlehem is obviously the site of hope and new beginning; the place where love was incarnated to redeem the world. The theme of the son, as in *Blood Wedding* and *Yerma,* connotes here the Son, the Lamb of God, the epitome of love that the repressive house has crucified. Yet María Josefa will not be able to free her child, because Bernarda is watching.[40] Again the son will be sacrificed on the altar of order and reason.

Adela's comings and goings suggest that she has been with Pepe in the corral. Martirio warns her to leave Pepe alone, but Adela's reply expresses a decision to go beyond her mother's boundaries and try to satisfy her desire: "I've seen death under this roof and gone out to look for what was mine (*TT* 207). She is willing to go to any length to be with Pepe, now that she has tasted passion, even if it means to be marked with the "crown of thorns" (*TT* 208) given to women involved with married men. When Martirio tries to stop Adela, Bernarda enters. Adela takes hold of her mother's cane—a representation of the Phallus, rule of the symbolic order, of which Bernarda is the mouthpiece—and breaks it to declare her demand for freedom (*TT* 209). The other sisters enter, including Angustias, and Bernarda asks for a gun. Adela tries to escape, but Angustias, a subjugated victim of the social order, is not willing to let her go, to proclaim the triumph of her body. This insistence on the body offers the counterpart to the social and religious code that designed to negate it.

A shot is heard, the one Bernarda has fired to hit Pepe. Adela believes he has been shot, and she runs outside. Martirio knows the shot did not hit him, but chooses not to inform Adela—although she does tell Bernarda that she saw him leave on his horse. Adela's body is then found hanging. Bernarda, disregarding the truth as well as the tragedy of the situation, can only think of declaring, for the sake of appearances, that her daughter died a virgin. Bernarda's last word, *silence,* is aimed at repressing the pain, the tears, the truth. The "documentary" character of the play ironically focuses on a total reversal of reality, as the final scene illustrates: Bernarda, the paragon of social prescriptions, decides to negate reality—the reality of her daughter's tragedy—for the sake of preserving the demands of institutionalized repression and its claim to "reality."

In Lorca's theater, women endure the most acute conflict between nature and society, reality and imagination. In Adela's case, her rebellion leads her to total sterility in death; in the Bride and Yerma, to the same sterility in seclusion from society; in other characters, such as María Josefa, to madness. In Bernarda's case the control of the outside world makes her house a symbolic representation of her inner world or womb, a space where life is fatally oppressed. The child that Adela could have had, like the child in Lorca's works in general, is sacrificed in the perpetual cycle of repression against human nature perpetrated by societal and religious norms. Bernarda embodies what for Lorca means the loss of oneself: the denial of or opposition to human inclinations, the betrayal of one's desires. By consistently negating her instincts Bernarda has lost all contact with her true self. The norms that shape her life have nothing to do with who she really is. Therefore, she seems like a cardboard figure bereft of nuances. Just as the Bride, Yerma, and Adela never see their fruit materialize, the house/womb never blossoms, but rots inside, filled with lost hopes and frustrations.

Lorcan characters, and women in particular, are caught in the contradiction that opposes their inner desire with the outside order. The tragedy of their situation results from the impossibility of resolving this conflict. They can either conform to society and live a false life, denying their being, or they can follow their desire and end in physical or living death. Lorca is acutely aware of what feminist critics Carolyn Heilbrun and Catharine Stimpson term "the female experience of perception."[41] Recognizing the masculinization of prevailing theories of tragedy, these critics mark the difference in the tragic pattern for men and women. While for tragic male characters consciousness and action go hand in hand, for women "consciousness must outpace the possibilities of action," and "perception must pace within an iron cage."[42] Lorca denounces the repressive symbolic order that limits action for his female characters or that drives them to act out of despair with tragic consequences. Just as in his youthful prose work *Impressions and Landscapes* he denounced the absence of charity, of companionship with others in the life of Catholic convents (see chapter 5 of the present study), he maintained throughout his life that society and religion overdo their ordering role by imposing rules that hinder fruitful, mutual relationships with other human beings. The moon's realm is foregrounded in Lorca's writings, and in this trilogy in particular, because it is in the lunar sphere that the characters confront the truth of being. Ironically, self-affirmation runs parallel to dissolution or destruction. The tragic absurdity of this situation places Lorca's view in the forefront of the theater of his time, along with Brecht, Beckett, and Pirandello.[43]

The language and symbolism of *The House of Bernarda Alba* follow those of *Blood Wedding* and *Yerma,* showing progression in delineating the blossoming/withering of the child as the image for love and poetry. The sun/moon images parallel the discourses of reason and desire, the polarity between the outer and inner realms as two contradictory impulses that live together, and undermining each other's effects.

Notes

1. Spanish authors such as Miguel de Unamuno (1864–1936), in *El otro* (The Other), and José Martínez Ruiz (1873–1967), in *Lo invisible* (The Invisible), published under the pseudonym Azorín, were attempting new ways in playwriting. (See Gwynne Edwards, *Lorca: The Theater Beneath the Sand* [London: Marion Boyars, 1980] 10–26; also see chapter 1 of Luis Fernández Cifuentes, *García Lorca en el teatro: La norma y la diferencia* [García Lorca in the Theater: The Norm and the Difference] [Zaragoza: Prensas Universitarias, 1986]).

2. See Andrew A. Anderson, "Los primeros pasos de 'La Barraca': Una entrevista recuperada, con cronología y comentario" (The First Steps of "La Barraca": A Recovered Interview with Chronology and Commentary), *L'"imposible / posible" di Federico García Lorca,* ed. Laura Dolfi (Napoli: Edizioni Scientifiche Italiane, 1989) 194. I wish to thank Andrew Anderson for sending me his article on La Barraca, which substantially helped to clarify my own views of the subject.

3. See Ian Gibson, *Federico García Lorca: A Life* (New York: Pantheon, 1989) 320–22.

4. Anderson, "Los primeros pasos de 'La Barraca'," 188–89, 195.

5. Anderson challenges the "opinions concerning not only the 'representativeness' but also the 'centrality'" of the trilogy ("The Strategy of García Lorca's Dramatic Composition 1930–1936," *Romance Quarterly* 33.2 (1986): 212). Page references to these three plays are to the translations in *Three Tragedies: Blood Wedding, Yerma, Bernarda Alba,* trans. James Graham-Luján and Richard L. O'Connell (New York: New Directions, 1955). They will be cited parenthetically in the text, abbreviated *TT.*

6. *The Public* was staged in Milan in 1986, in Madrid in 1987, and in Paris in 1988, and was reviewed in the major Spanish newspapers. (See bibliography for critical studies on these experimental plays).

7. See Gibson, *A Life* 400.

8. Francisco García Lorca, Prologue, *Three Tragedies: Blood Wedding, Yerma, Bernarda Alba,* by Federico García Lorca, trans. James Graham-Luján and Richard L. O'Connell (New York: New Directions, 1955) 19; Gibson gives a slightly different account, *A Life* 335.

9. Francisco García Lorca, Prologue 20.

10. For an analysis of the use of poetic imagery in Lorca's plays, see Robert Barnes, "The Fusion of Poetry and Drama in *Blood Wedding," Modern Drama* 2.4 (1960): 395–402.

11. José Angel Valente studies the image of the dead or unborn child in Lorca's production in "Pez luna" (Moon Fish), *Trece de nieve* 2d series 1–2 (1976): 191–201.

12. Rupert C. Allen, *Psyche and Symbol in the Theater of Federico García Lorca. Perimplín, Yerma, Blood Wedding* (Austin and London: U of Texas P, 1974) 176.

13. Juan Eduardo Cirlot, *A Dictionary of Symbols,* trans. Jack Sage (New York: Philosophical Library, 1962) 144–45.

14. Gustavo Correa, *La poesía mítica de Federico García Lorca* (The Mythic Poetry of Federico Garcí (Eugene, Oregon: U of Oregon Publications, 1972) 72. See also Norman Miller, "Lorca's 'Nana del caballo grande': A Psychological Perspective," *Hispanófila* 3.93 (1980): 37–46; and Julian Palley, "Archetypal Symbols in *Bodas de sangre," Hispania* 50.1 (1967): 74–79.

15. For an elaboration on the image of blood, see Correa 69–71, Palley 78, Allen, *Psyche and Symbol* 210.

16. Carlos Feal points out this association in "El sacrificio de la hombría en *Bodas de saugre"* (The Sacrifice of Manhood in *Blood Wedding*), *Modern Language Notes* 99.2 (1984): 276.

17. In the prologue to *The Butterfly's Evil Spell* (1919; see chapter 3 of the present study), Lorca explains that the story related in that play was told to the writer by "An old wood sylph, escaped from one of the great Shakespeare's books" (*Five Plays: Comedies and Tragicomedies,* trans. James Graham-Luján and Richard L. O'Connell [New York: New Directions, 1963] 194). One of the characters in a much later work, *The Public* (see chapter 4 of the present study), alludes directly to *A Midsummer Night's Dream:* "If love is pure chance and Titania, Queen of the Fairies, fell in love with an ass, then, by the same reasoning, there wouldn't be anything extraordinary about Gonzalo drinking in the 'music hall' with a boy dressed in white sitting on his lap" (*The Public and Play Without a Title: Two Posthumous Plays,* trans. Carlos Bauer [New York: New Directions, 1983] 43–44). I want to thank Christopher Maurer for pointing out to me the importance of the forest as one of Lorca's central images of poetic fantasy and imagination. Some examples are in Lorca's lecture "The Poetic Image of Don Luis de Góngora": "The poet who is about to make a poem (and I know this from experience) has the vague feeling he is going on a nocturnal hunting trip in an incredibly distant forest" (*DS* 72), and in the

suite "In the Forest of the Lunar Grapefruits (A Static Poem)" (*CP* 353–55).

18. See Carlos Feal, "El Lorca póstumo: *El Público* y *Comedia sin título*" (The Posthumous Lorca: *The Public* and *Play Without a Title*), *ALEC* 6 (1981): 48.

19. For an elaboration on the hermaphrodite, see Allen, *Psyche and Symbol* 195–203.

20. The Spanish reads: "mi cintura y tus caderas" (my waist and your thighs). A much closer English rendition is found in *The Rural Trilogy: Blood Wedding, Yerma, and The House of Bernarda Alba,* trans. Michael Dewell and Carmen Zapata (New York: Bantam, 1987) 61: "The moon nails us together. / My loins are fused to your thighs."

21. See Gibson, *A Life* 398, 401.

22. Allen (*Psyche and Symbol* 144–47) also points out the obvious connection between singing and fertility and between biological and artistic creativity in *Yerma.* While Allen finds Yerma responsible—not Juan—for her incapacity to "sing," this reading sees in both of them the effect of religious and societal norms that inhibit any fruitful exchange between man and woman.

23. See Luis Fernandez-Cifuentes 171.

24. See Francisco García Lorca, *In The Green Morning: Memories of Federico,* trans. Christopher Maurer (New York: New Directions, 1986) 217–18.

25. The theme of the bath of love appears frequently in the collections of traditional and popular poetry that Lorca knew well, even from childhood. (See Mario Hernández, "La muchacha dorada por la luna" (The Girl Turned Golden by the Moon), *Trece de nieve,* 2d series, 1–2 [1976]: 212.)

26. For Christopher Maurer ("The Black Pain," rev. of *Federico García Lorca: A Life,* by Ian Gibson, *New Republic* 1 Jan. 1990: 33), Lorca's work is alien to the carpe diem spirit because the object of his desire is never specified: "His subject is longing that has no object, no hope of satisfaction, no center."

27. For an elaboration on Juan's kiss and its implications, see C. B. Morris, "Lorca's *Yerma* and the 'beso sabroso,' " *Mester* 10.1–2 (1981): 68–81.

28. For the image of the withering childhood, see Allen, *Psyche and Symbol* 150.

29. Bettina L. Knapp, in a different reading, offers an archetypal reading of the play and views Victor as Lorca's mythical Abel, Juan as Cain, and the child whom Victor leads by the hand as suggesting the arrival of the Son of Man ("Federico García Lorca's *Yerma*: A Woman's Mystery," *Women in Twentieth-Century Literature: A Jungian View* [University Park and London: Pennsylvania State UP, 1987] 12–13).

30. See Gibson, *A Life* 436.

31. For symbolical and structural elements in the play, see Vicente Cabrera, "Poetic Structure in Lorca's *La casa de Bernarda Alba,*" *Hispania* 61.3 (1978): 466–70.

32. Cabrera 466–67.

33. J. Rubia Barcia ("El realismo 'magico' de *La Casa de Bernarda Alba*" [Magic Realism in *The House of Bernarda Alba*], *Federico García Lorca,* ed. Ildefonso Manuel Gil [Madrid: Taurus, 1973], 312) points out Bernarda's denial of reality and compares it with don Quijote's, with the difference that Bernarda is blinded by her totalitarian pride.

34. See Bettina L. Knapp, "Federico García Lorca's *The House of Bernarda Alba*: A Hermaphroditic Matriarchate," *Modern Drama* 27.3 (1984): 384. Knapp points out the usual association of houses with the feminine principle "because they are containers and protectors." Various critics have seen the house and its sterility as an image of the womb (see Cabrera 469).

35. "Phalogocentrism" is a neologism coined by French philosopher Jacques Derrida to describe Western culture's belief in the Phallus and Logos as absolute truth. For an explanation of Derrida's basic terms and philosophical tenets, see the "Translator's Preface" to Jacques Derrida, *Of Grammatology,* trans. Gayatri Chakravortry Spivak (Baltimore and London: Johns Hopkins UP, 1976), especially pp. lxii–lxxxvii. For the meaning of Maria Josefa's name, see Herbert Ramsden's introduction to his edition of *La casa de Bernarda Alba* (Manchester and New York: Manchester UP, 1983) xliii.

36. For an analysis of Maria Josefa's craziness, see Ricardo Domenech, "Simbolo, mito y rito en *La casa de Bernarda Alba*" (Symbol, Myth, and Ritual in *The House of Bernarda Alba*).*La casa de Bernarda Alba y teatro de García Lorca,* ed. Ricardo Domenech (Madrid: Cátedra, 1985) 207.

37. For an analysis of these associations, see Domenech 206.

38. Domenech 207.

39. For a reading of the symbolism of Poncia's name, see Herbert Ramsden's introduction to his edition of *La casa de Bernarda Alba* xliii.

40. Domenech points to the Christological and ritual aura of the sheep carried by the grandmother, María Josefa, and identifies the sheep with Adela, since she is sacrificed, and with the child she carries, who will never be born, perpetuating the fruitlessness (200–201).

41. Carolyn Heilbrun and Catharine Stimpson, "Theories of Feminist Criticism: A Dialogue," *Feminist Literary Criticism: Explorations in Theory,* ed. Josephine Donovan (Lexington: UP of Kentucky, 1975) 72.

42. Heilbrun and Stimpson 68.

43. C. Michael Wells ("The Natural Norm in the Plays of F. Garcia Lorca," *Hispanic Review* 38.3 [1970]: 3110 points out the absurd and conflictive situation of Lorca's characters—placed between natural instincts and societal rules—which anticipates playwrights like Beckett and Ionesco.

CHAPTER 3

Lesser-Known Poetry

This chapter will discuss Lorca's lesser-known poetry collections, the familiarity of which is gradually increasing as all aspects of Lorca's work continue to attract critical attention. Lorca's youthful *Book of Poems* (1921), which was overshadowed for decades by the author's more mature works, is available in Ian Gibson's 1982 critical edition. In this work can be seen the origin of some of Lorca's major themes and images. *Songs* (1927) and *Suites* (written between 1921 and 1923), thematically related, though less structurally fixed than *Poem of the Deep Song* (1931), appear as a distinct cycle of Lorca's production, particularly after more precise boundaries between these two collections were established by a 1983 publication of a compilation of the suites. A number of odes, also dating from the 1920s, reflect Lorca's experimentation with artistic form and poetic images in the Gongorine and avant-garde styles. Lorca's poetry of the 1930s—in particular, *Diván del Tamarit* (*The Divan at Tamarit*, 1940), which has already been the subject of a number of critical works, and *Sonetos [del Amor oscuro]* (*Sonnets [of Dark Love]*), first published in authorized form in 1984 to a great deal of interest even outside of academic circles—is very much open to further readings, as are his plays from that same period.

Early Works

Lorca's contact with avant-garde groups in Madrid in the early 1920s and the admiration he and his generation shared for Góngora are reflected in his collections from the 1920s in a greater concern for artistic form and emphasis on the image. The aesthetics of the imagination, as the metaphoric transformation of reality, prevail in these works. Their innovative character culminates in *The Gypsy Ballads,* a collection situated at a crossroads in Lorca's aesthetic development (see chapter 1 of the present study). The mythic character of *The Gypsy Ballads* allows the exploration into realms outside logical representation. This exploration is fully pursued in Lorca's later works through the aesthetics of the inspiration.

Book of Poems

The somewhat autobiographical *Book of Poems* in many ways serves as a mirror of Lorca's childhood and adolescence in the Granadine vega.[1] These poems express Lorca's nostalgia for the union with nature and the religious faith he enjoyed in his childhood, the crisis brought about by temporal awareness and sexual awakening, and the subsequent alienation and loss of faith. "Encrucijada (Julio de 1920)" ("Crossroads [July 1920]," *CP* 58–61) illustrates the young author's critical stance toward his life and poetry:

> Oh, what sorrow to have
> poems off in the distance
> of passion, and a brain
> all stained with ink!
>
> Oh, what sorrow not to have
> the happy man's fantastical
> shirt—a tanned skin,
> the sun's carpet.
>
> (Flocks of letters
> wheel round my eyes.)
> Oh, what sorrow the ancient
> sorrow of poetry,
> this sticky sorrow
> so far from clean water!
>
> Oh, sorrow of sorrowing
> to sip at the vein of lyric!
> Oh, sorrow of blind fountains
> and mills without flour!
>
> Oh, what sorrow to have
> no sorrow, to spend life
> on the colorless grass
> of the hesitant lane!
>
> Oh, the deepest sorrow:
> the sorrow of joy, a plow

cutting furrows for us
where weeping bears fruit!

(The cold moon rises
on a paper mountain.)
Oh, sorrow of truth!
Oh, sorrow of the lie!

The repeated apostrophe (the addressing of a person or a personified thing rhetorically) calls attention to the subjectivity of the poetic speaker articulating his sorrow, a typically Romantic stance. However, the speaker's sorrow and feelings of alienation from nature are expressed through the confrontation with poetic language. The apostrophes point to the speaker's presence in the poem as an artist struggling with language, caught in the crossroads of different artistic traditions. "Passion" (as opposed to reason), "the happy man's fantastical shirt," a "tanned skin" (images of his fusion with the sun and nature), and "clean water" nostalgically allude to a direct contact with the world and to a lost language that was able to transparently reflect it. Instead, the speaker now confronts a language in which the ink (representing the materiality of the words) impedes linking directly with the referent, and in which words can no longer be made to reproduce mimetically the plenitude of nature. The alphabet is no longer the instrument used to create worlds by naming them, but rather its flocks of letters obscure the direct perception of the world through the eyes. The recognition of the autonomy of poetic language parallels the speaker's awareness of his estrangement from nature.

Poetic self-consciousness increases with the references to the "ancient sorrow of poetry" and "the vein of lyric" which characterize poetry as a discourse traditionally associated with the expression of feelings. The emotional content of poetry becomes "sticky" because the repetition of sentimental formulas and clichés clouds the sincerity of the emotion. The speaker realizes that experience cannot be transparently expressed in disregard of language as the means of representation. Unlike the childhood state, to which this early book is a nostalgic farewell, the speaker is forced to accept the existence of external things as different from himself. The distance from nature's language of vitality provokes the images of dryness and lack of productivity ("Oh, sorrow of blind fountains / and mills without flour"). No matter how artificial sorrow may become in the poetic text, its complete absence would mean the "colorless grass" and "hesitant lane" of a life without passion. Sorrow is ingrained in joy and therefore is the root of all feelings ("The sorrow of joy, a plow / cutting furrows for us / where weeping bears fruit"). Later in Lorca's poetry, this sorrow will become the Gypsy *pena* (pain) of Deep Song (see chapter 1 of the present study). The "paper mountain" at the end of the poem reverses the image of the rising sun. It suggests premonition and fatality, which are associated with the moon in Lorca's writings. The "paper mountain" the poet is accumulating in his attempts to write refers also to the act of writing itself. The aesthetic crossroads is an ethical one as well: "Oh, sorrow of truth! / Oh, sorrow of the lie!" Confronting the truth or falsity of language necessitates wrestling with the truth or falsity of personal beliefs, a question found at the core of this early collection of poetry.

Beginning with this early collection, the moon imbues Lorca's writings with the foreboding, premonition, and fatalism that is traditionally associated with that symbol. As evident in "Crossroads," poetic writing is marked by a nostalgia for an original fusion with nature that time has dispersed. This accounts for the recurring themes of pain and sorrow in many compositions and for the reiterated tone of loss, frustration, and unfulfillment in Lorca's poetry.[2]

Suites

The title of *Suites* may refer to an instrumental-music form (dating from the seventeenth and eighteenth centuries) that consists of a series of dances. It could also allude to a modern instrumental composition with several different movements. Lorca worked on these poems for three years (1921–1923), but they were not published as a collection during his lifetime. The book we have today was compiled by the French Hispanist André Belamich (published in 1983), who recovered poems dispersed in archives, magazines, or among friends to whom Lorca gave autographed copies. Belamich also incorporated the *Primeras Canciones* (*First Songs*), published in 1936, into this book.[3]

Suites and the book *Songs,* which will be discussed later, were written simultaneously and express similar formal and thematic concerns. They reflect the period when Lorca lived at the Resi in Madrid.[4] During this time he came in contact with the avant-garde movements of the time, Spanish ultraism in particular. As the name indicates (*ultra* means "beyond"), the *ultraísta* poets sought to create a language that would go beyond its boundaries as a verbal medium. Images were not supposed to represent reality but to reinvent it. Rather than constructing a discursive and narrative elaboration, the poet adopted a carefree tone to create effects of immediacy. Sentimentality was discarded unless used ironically or humorously.

The suites are brief and schematic poems in which Lorca experiments with words and rhythms as ways of approaching a particular subject from different angles. Themes often have a cosmic projection that are represented by sun/ moon, sky/earth, day/night polarities. Each pole reflects the other in a game that forces the speaker to conclude: "Nature: eternal / Narcissus" ("Sesame," *CP* 203). The different elements in nature cannot be perceived as complete entities, for their meaning, or identity, is paradoxically both present and absent. As in a reflection ("The reflected is / the real," affirms Lorca in the same poem "Sesame," *CP* 203), the real is always somewhere else. The self-reflexivity of nature is emphasized in the poems through images of mirrors and other objects that connote different planes of representation—fans, roulettes, wheels of fortune—and by refrains and parentheses used in parallel structures. In the center of this meditation is the speaker's subjectivity, where all reflections meet. The presence of the speaker points to two essential features in Lorca's writings: the intensity of emotions to which Lorca always aspires regardless of the demands of poetic form, and the solitude of the human heart in the midst of a world of reflections, where no fusion with the other is ever totally possible.

In *La suite de los espejos* (*Mirror Suite, CP* 168–78), the reflecting mirror is the textual space where the author attempts to articulate reality, only to see it diffuse in the ever-slippery nature of words. One of the poems in this suite, "Initium" (*CP* 174–75), reads as follows:

> Adam & Eve.
> The serpent cracked
> the mirror
> in a thousand pieces,
> & the apple
> was his rock.

In Lorca's Eden the mirror represents the original transparency, the immediacy, of the world. The serpent smashes the transparency of the world with a fitting weapon, an apple that embodies the power of knowledge. By assigning the image of a rock to the serpent's destruction of innocence, Lorca brings a concreteness, a tangibility that, introducing the distance time places between subject and object, word and world, serves to magnify the tragedy of the fall. Hence, the sign of the serpent is often synonymous with the moon as a symbol. As a celestial body associated with phases and changes, the moon represents the shadow of time that fogged the transparency of the paradisiacal mirror.

The meditation about knowledge provoked by the apple is picked up again in the suite *Newton* (*CP* 306–13). The first poem in the suite, also entitled "Newton," refers to Isaac Newton's law of gravity as the last apple to fall off the tree of knowledge (*CP* 306–7). However, that does not mean the mystery has been elucidated. Thus, Newton is described scratching his Anglo-Saxon nose while the white moon shines its inscrutable light over the trees. The speaker continues to wonder: "But who joins waves / with sighs? / And stars / with crickets?" ("Armonía/Harmony," *CP* 308–9). Clues are all around but remain unexplained. Adam's and Newton's apples are the two cut breasts of the child named Innocence, but the apple's mystery still continues. The speaker wonders about the nature of the apple as a powerful symbol of knowledge, a spherical shape encompassing the secret of existence. Why was this fruit endowed with such a meaning of revelation? Why not the orange or the pomegranate? This question makes the speaker a successor to Adam, Paris (in Greek mythology, he awarded the apple of discord to the goddess Aphrodite), and Newton, who all caressed the apple but had no idea what it meant ("Pregunta/Question," *CP* 310–13).

En el bosque de las toronjas de luna (Poema extático) (*In the Forest of the Lunar Grapefruits [A Static Poem]*) and a second draft, *En el jardín de las toronjas de luna* (*In the Garden of the Lunar Grapefruits, CP* 352–97), contain an ambitious suite dealing with a personal and poetic journey to a world—a forest or garden of possibilities—that never was but should have been. This suite encompasses the concerns that occupy the other much briefer compositions, especially the fragmentation of the mirror in the original vision, as expressed through the recurring mirror image and its variety of reflections and perspectives. The traveler/poet seeks that marvelous garden in every mirror of his house (again a symbol of the text itself) by attempting various "geometries with words & rhythms" (*CP* 353). He confesses that "a pure & intact soul" (*CP* 355) would not experience his curiosity. This implies that the poet's search is not an innocent one, because it is self-conscious and aware of the distance that separates the seeker from the sought.

"A sharp & elegiac feeling for things that haven't been—good & evil, large & small" (*CP* 369) is what inspires the poet's journey in this suite and explains a major part of Lorca's writings. It is the desire or longing for something that remains undefined and unreachable.

> From behind my eyes
> hermetic song breaks open—
> song of the seedling that
> did not ever flower.
>
> (*CP* 371)

These lines, from "Perspectiva" ("Perspective," *In the Garden of the Lunar Grapefruit, CP* 370–73), place the garden of possibilities behind the speaker's eyes, at an angle or perspective hidden from the accepted one. The possibilities that never were but should have been are suggested in that "hermetic song" whose mystery can be approached only from the other side of convention.

The end of this suite is a return to the morning, indicating that the journey has been a nocturnal voyage. It has also been a journey into the inner world. Hence the poet/traveler cries: "My soul, boy and girl, / be silent, *silent!*" ("Amanecer y repique/Wake Up/Ring Out," *CP* 396–97). That call to his soul, where sexual boundaries do not apply, is an attempt to silence his inner world, or garden, and to adjust to daily life. The garden of the grapefruits of the moon is that space where things never were, the context of continuing desire that never comes to fruition.

Suites is a youthful book mixing a musical and seemingly free tone with profound existential and artistic concerns. In contrast to the often discursive tone of *Book of Poems,* the conciseness of the suites shows an artist with greater control over his craft. The suites are variations that illustrate mental states concentrating on time, death, and the nature of poetry. Like the traveler to the garden of the grapefruits of the moon, Lorca frees himself from common sense, the great enemy of poetry, and sets out to uncover what remains unexpressed from the accepted perspective. Although Lorca appears playful and carefree, the seriousness of his quest is evident. The impossibility of mimetically capturing reality leads to new experiments with words and structures. The result is a series of constructions and dismantlings, the goal of which is to resist the natural tendency to construct fixed perspectives.

Songs

Although not published until 1927, *Songs* comprises Lorca's poetic work between 1921 and 1926.[5] The book consists of eleven titled sections of generally brief poems filled with striking images reflecting the avant-garde movements of the time. A good illustration of these aesthetic principles is "Nocturno esquemático" ("Nocturne in Outline," *CP* 414–15), a poem whose title implies a graphic perspective that favors greater attention to form and rejects all traces of sentimentality:

Fennel, serpent, and rushes.
Aroma, trail, and half-shadow.
Air, earth, and apartness

(The ladder stretches to the moon.)

This poem attempts to approach the same subject from many different angles and is thus similar to cubism, an artistic style that emphasizes abstract structure by displaying simultaneously several different perspectives on the same object and fragmenting its form. The nocturnal atmosphere is sketched through three images that refer by metonymy (a figure of speech in which the name of an attribute or a thing is substituted for the thing itself) to three different levels of reality: the fennel refers to the sense of smell and to the air; the serpent to the trail, or sense of touch and to the earth; and the reeds to gloom or shadows, and finally to solitude. The careful structuring of this brief poem, and the seeming simplicity of its concise images, attempt to capture the essence of reality. The elements in the first three lines correspond to one another; they can thus be read in their horizontal relation to each other (in the linear development of the poem), as well as in their vertical relation to their corresponding elements in the other two lines. The intention seems to be to juxtapose the various elements in order to create the simultaneity that will subvert the normal temporal sequence of conventional language. If read sequentially, with each line following the other, the meaning falls heavily on the word *apartness* (or solitude in the original). The moon, an expected presence in a nocturne, is the repository of the movement of desire depicted in these three elements: the fennel reaching upward, the serpent downwards, and the rushes toward the half-shadow, or "penumbra," associated with marshes, rivers, and other wet areas where rushes grow.

A triptych of great interest is "Tres retratos con sombra ("Three Portraits With Shading," *CP* 452–59), about French poet Paul Verlaine (1844–1896), Spanish poet and Nobel laureate Juan Ramón Jiménez (1881–1958), and French composer Claude Debussy (1862–1918), accompanied respectively by Bacchus (Roman god of wine), Venus (Roman Aphrodite, goddess of love), and Narcissus (mythological figure who fell in love with his own image reflected in water). Each portrait consists of a main poem on the historical figure, and a minor one, printed in smaller type, about the mythological figure presented as his shadow. The triptych structure reappears in other poetry collections (see chapter 1 of the present study) and reflects the author's attempt to deal with a topic from various angles, thus avoiding the static nature of a single viewpoint. History and myth are brought together as two sides of the same reality.[6] The historical portrait offers the "official" side of the subject, while his mythological shadow articulates the repressed side.

The official portrait of Verlaine presents the aristocratic poet of melancholic and abandoned gardens as evoking a song of plenitude, of fullness that he will never utter:

> The song
> I'll never speak,
> on the tip of my tongue fell asleep.
> The song
> I'll never speak.

(*CP* 453)

Lorca has Verlaine sing the song of fulfillment he sought in his writings but never attained, the song "filled with lips," "with hours," "Song of stars alive / in perpetual daytime skies" (*CP* 453). Verlaine's shadow is Bacchus, who, like a panther (an image of desire and instinct), tries to seize Verlaine's laurel wreath. Symbol of immortality and glory, the laurel marks Verlaine as the sublime artist striving for pure poetry, but it also freezes him into a prototypical image that takes away the tension of his art. By bringing forth his shadow in Bacchus, Lorca is unmasking the underside of desire in Verlaine's art.

Juan Ramón Jiménez's poetry is also traditionally associated with purity: "In the infinity of white, / snow, spikenard, and salt flat, / his fantasy went astray" (*CP* 455). As the epitome of the sublime poet, Jiménez has transcended beyond the here and now into a level of "whiteness" where thought is almost totally absent. His shadow is Venus:

> The dead maiden
> in the shell of the bed,
> stripped of blossom and breeze,
> ascended in unending light.

Both portrait and shadow emphasize the inertness and stasis of these prototypes of poetic purity and beauty. They also call attention to the wound that pierces the apparent harmony of these figures. For Jiménez, it is "In the infinity of white / what a clean, long gash / his fantasy left!"; for Venus it is "The dead maiden / plied love from within" (*CP* 455, 457). By piercing through the surface appearance of harmony, Lorca addresses the hidden wound that keeps these figures alive.

Lorca conveys Debussy's music as a play of reflections:

> My shadow glides in silence
> over the watercourse
> . . . .
> A glow arises in my breast,
> the one mirrored in the water.

(CP 457)

These lines allude to Debussy's music as a self-reflexive, artistic expression that foregrounds its own formal structure. Hence his shadow is Narcissus, the representation of artistic consciousness. The self-conscious exploration in Debussy's art (like Narcissus's) runs the risk of losing itself in its own activity. The speaker warns Narcissus about falling into the water, but when it happens he simply states: "When he vanished into the water, / I understood. But I shan't explain" *(CP* 459). The poet's refusal to explain art's self-reflectivity alludes to the tautological nature of an explanation that will only return upon itself.

This triptych illustrates several concerns about artistic ideals. A chief concern is the quest for pure poetry, which, attempting to emulate music, strives to achieve a level of verbal expression devoid of the burden of representation and other dross. Lorca recognizes the value of such an ideal and the undeniable self-reflexive nature of art, which explains why Narcissus is central in quite a few poems as well as why formal elements mirror one another. Nevertheless, Lorca also points to the danger of falling into an excessive abstraction that would deny the reality of human pain and desire. This meditation reiterates what Lorca had already formulated in *Book of Poems,* that is, the need to fuse aesthetic with emotional concerns, for in their tension resides the truth of the work of art.

"Academic" Poetic Exercises in the Gongorine Style

In letters to friends in 1928 (the same year *The Gypsy Ballads* was published), Lorca refers to a book of odes he plans to publish that is written in a style entirely different from the ballads. He mentions *Oda al Santísimo Sacramento del Altar (Ode to the Most Holy Sacrament of the Altar)* and *Oda a Sesostris (Ode to Sesostris)* as "precise *academic* things" that he is writing for the sake of discipline. To one of his epistolary friends, the Colombian poet Jorge Zalamea, who seems to be experiencing conflicts between his emotions and his art, Lorca suggests: "See to it that your state of mind does not filter into your poetry, because it will play you a bad trick by exposing the purest in you to the eyes of those who should *never* see it" (*SL* 143). He further advises his friend to "sketch out a plan of your desire and live within it, always within a norm of beauty" (*SL* 143). The "purest in you" is, for Lorca, the inner truth that should only be expressed out in the open after having been transformed through art. Writing the odes is thus for Lorca an exercise in developing a formal structure within which to frame or hide personal feelings.

In 1927, in commemoration of the tercentenary of Don Luis de Góngora's death, Lorca wrote *Soledad insegura (Fragmentos)* (*Uncertain Solitude [Fragments]*, *CP* 760–63) in the style of the *Soledades* (*Solitudes*) by the baroque master. This poem was never finished nor published in any of the special issues of magazines and journals dedicated to the tercentenary. This fact may reflect Lorca's discomfort with a poetic technique that he deeply admired for its high sense of artistry but which he felt constrained the expression of emotions within too rigid a structure. This fragment, along with *La sirena y el carabinero* (*The Siren and the Carabineer*, *CP* 758–61), published in 1927, echoes concerns about form similar to those expressed in the letter of 1928.

The adjective *uncertain* before *solitude* suggests Lorca felt insecure vis-à-vis the great baroque master, or perhaps that he wanted to inject a note of humor about the enterprise he has undertaken. Written in hendecasyllabic verses, Lorca's solitude reflects the Gongorine spirit in both its mythological references and the well-crafted images. However, unlike Góngora's language, which can ultimately be understood after one becomes familiar with its most common metaphors and allusions, Lorca's images cannot always be deciphered and made to adjust to the norms of the outside world. Also, contrary to the luminous reality of Góngora's poetry, Lorca portrays a night-filled scene with unsettling songs: "Words of glass and dark breeze, / round ones, yes, are spoken by mute fish," while the centaur sings on the shore "with a limitless pain of spikenards" (*CP* 761, 763). These voices speak a language of desire bound by the highly formal and classical tone of the fragment. Other foreboding signs threaten the apparent harmony of the increasingly uncertain solitude: "Wolves' eyes slumber in the shadow" (*CP* 763) and the voice of Philomela is filled with the sorrow of the passionate south, of desire. (Philomela is a mythological figure who was raped by Tereus, king of Thrace, who then cut out her tongue and hid her in a lonely tower. Later she was changed into a swallow, and her sister Procne into a nightingale, although in some versions their roles are reversed.) The voice of someone shipwrecked, who corresponds to the young man (*joven*) in Góngora's *Solitudes,* is heard "in the dark horror," singing about the unhappiness of a nation of people "who look in vain for the sea" (*CP* 763). His song echoes similar frustration of other Lorcan compositions, yet here Lorca has made it fit within the formal boundaries of Gongorine aesthetics.

Oda a Salvador Dalí (*Ode to Salvador Dali, CP* 588–95) also follows the Gongorine aesthetic as delineated by Lorca in his lecture on the baroque author (see chapter 5 of the present study). It was finished in 1926, after Lorca's stay in Cadaqués at Dalí's house on the Mediterranean coast, where he had spent Holy Week of 1925. This visit to Catalonia and his contacts with the avant-garde intellectuals of the region had an important effect in Lorca's aesthetic reflections. The ode comments on a phase then just beginning in Dalí's career, when he was busily developing cubist principles under the inspiration of Spanish painters Juan Gris (1887–1927) and Pablo Picasso (1881–1973). The poem has five parts in alexandrine verses. The first, about the objectives of the new aesthetic theory, presents Dalí as the paradigm of the search for purity and asepsis (in the sense of "detached," "objective") in the new art, far from the shadows, reflections, and vagueness of the "Impressionist fog" (*CP* 589). The new artist now "treads firmly on the cobbled streets"(*CP* 589), returning to objective reality all its presence. All things can be measured because the real, with its volumes, profiles and shapes, is the main focus.

Lorca joins in this new adventure when he writes: "A desire for forms and limits overwhelms us" (*CP* 589); he advocates doing away with the impressionists' lack of definition. Cadaqués's landscape of sharp lines offers a model for the new aesthetics. Its horizon is free of "wounded handkerchiefs" (*CP* 589)—an image of anguish, painful anxiety, or farewell—because no mystery is hidden there. To that landscape belongs Dalí, whose art is addressed in section 3:

> Oh Salvador Dalí, of the olive-colored voice!
> I do not praise your halting adolescent brush
> or your pigments that flirt with the pigment of your times,
> but I laud your longing for eternity with limits.
>
> (*CP* 591)

While Lorca criticizes young Dalí's technique (for a "halting adolescent brush"), he does admire the quest of his friend, and that of the new art, for the "eternal" that can be found in the present, with all its limitations and boundaries. Dalí is a "sanitary soul"—referring to the "aseptic" or detached elements of the painter's art—fleeing from "the dark jungle" of impressionism (*CP* 591). His imagination has discovered that the world, even in its most mysterious or impenetrable forms, possesses an order that the artist has the responsibility to decipher. Even the stars (as images for the mystery all quests seek to penetrate) "reveal the perfect schema of their courses" to the eye willing to look closely (*CP* 591). Dalí's inspiration remains a matter of reason, "up in the head," never going down closer to the heart. Such motivation is the opposite of the inspiration provided by the passion and ecstasy of the god of wine, Bacchus, and all his disorderly forces, as suggested in the references to "loving vines" and to the "chaotic force of curving water." Dalí's art is based on a direct approach to the world and finds beauty in the world's concrete presence. Dalí loves "a matter definite and exact," and his art is a song of praise for the straight line and pure geometric form (*CP* 593).

Lorca is deeply touched by his friend's quest for what has possible explanation, but he also recognizes Dalí's fear "of the feelings" that await him in the streets, which could threaten the "objectivity" of the art the Catalan painter was creating. It is possible to find here the same concerns as in the triptych on Verlaine, Juan Ramón Jiménez, and Debussy, discussed above. In Lorca's repeated praises of the new aesthetics (as exemplified in Dalí's art), one recognizes his own efforts to discipline his art through constantly working with form in order to objectify his emotions. However, the ode is above all an homage to the friendship between these two artists: "The light that blinds our eyes is not art. / Rather it is love, friendship, crossed swords" (*CP* 595). Lorca offers his ode as an artistic exercise that he has consciously performed, resorting to the use of formal elements he has admired in his friend's art. However, he indicates the impossibility of disregarding the emotion whose shadow so threatens the claims to objectivity of the new art.

In his lecture "Sketch de la nueva pintura," 1928 ("Thoughts on Modern Painting"), Lorca discusses some of the ideas he elaborates poetically in "Ode to Salvador Dalí," such as the diffusion of form in impressionist paintings due to the invasion of light. Cubism, by returning to volume and form, allowed painting to become an autonomous art, freed from servitude to reality. However, "Ode to Salvador Dalí" subtly points to the reaction after 1926 against excessive objectivity, which brought the return to instinct, to inspiration, to the subconscious, suggested already by Lorca when referring to Dalí's fear of the emotion he could encounter in the streets, away from the asepsis of his studio. The coming of surrealism would mark a different artistic route for each of the two friends. The ode attests to Lorca's joining in his friend's enthusiasm for pure art devoid of servile dependence on reality, while remaining aware of the limitations implicit in such a search. Surrealism invited the artist to delve into the dark regions of the self away from rational control. Dalí would follow that invitation and try to make his friend join in. Yet Lorca maintained there was a poetic logic in his writings (*SL* 135). His refusal to lose himself in the dark realm of the subconscious signals the personal and artistic split that occurred between the two friends.

The other great work of this period is *Oda al Santísimo Sacramento del altar* (*Ode to the Most Holy Sacrament of the Altar*, *CP* 598–609), dedicated to Lorca's fervently Catholic friend, the musician Manuel de Falla, who was shocked by its images. Only the first two parts, "Exposición" ("Exposition") and "Mundo" ("World"), were published in 1928.[7] Lorca wrote the last two sections, "Demonio" ("Devil") and "Carne" ("Flesh") in 1929 in New York. This ode was considered by Lorca a poem of great intensity, perhaps the greatest one he ever wrote (*SL* 144). "Exposition" deals with Christ's real presence in the Host, as prescribed by Catholic dogma, not simply his symbol or image. The Host stands as a paradigm of the harmony the speaker is struggling to reach in the midst of a divided world. The Host offers to him a God in diminutive, anchored in a perfect and harmonious form, a specific illustration of "the eternity with limits" for which Lorca and Dalí longed:

> Oh, Form whose limits express the concrete
> multitude of lights and cries that I hear!
> Oh, snow surrounded by icebergs of music!
> Oh, flame crackling over all our veins!
>
> (*CP* 601)

The apostrophe concentrates the reader's attention on the form of the Host. Limits are opposed and preferred to the multiplicity of voices dispersing the original unity that the Host encapsulates. However, as such a symbol, the Host remains detached from the suffering below, high up in its monstrance, something to be looked at and admired but not to be shared.

In "World," the setting is night in the urban context. Anonymous employees in skyscrapers have fallen asleep exhausted by inhuman work, while on other floors, prostitutes show their wounded breasts. In this sad night of the world, the nightingale of love is continuously assassinated. The Host is depicted again as the place "where the card and wound are entwined in song," the "Junction where the age and the moment call," and the "Changeless Sacrament of love and discipline!"(*CP* 603) The Host is the meeting point of history and the present, of concrete, naked shapes corresponding to the ideal of objectivity without distracting reflections (the flat playing "card") and the "wound" of desire that those forms attempt to articulate.

In "Devil," the devil arrives on Sunday, God's day, imposing his blinding presence. The devil does not entice his victims by his seeming to be a beautiful woman or a young adolescent; he attracts people with the charm of a momentary pleasure. The simple unity of Jesus' presence in the visible form of the Host offers the perfect challenge to the beautiful enemy with his myriad manifestations, colorful but all false; Host and devil represent the opposition between unity and dispersion. The Host offers the perfect fusion of form and spirit, while the devil, "prodigious magician of fires and colors" (*CP* 605), entices victims with the variety and gaudiness of his signifiers and multiplicity of options, but is devoid of an anchor or substance.

The second stanza of the last section, "Flesh," presents a scene of primordial innocence tainted by the blood of passion: "Eve, gray and streaked with torn purple" (*CP* 607). The following stanzas describe desire ("The fig trees arrived with burning flowers") destroying "the white walls of discipline." Above it all is Jesus' flesh, the Corpus Christi, or Body of Christ, "of absolute silence," where harmony is found. The dispersion creating the darkest night of the world, the multifaceted appeal of the devil, and the attempts of the flesh to persist can be redeemed only by Christ's vanquished flesh in the Host.

Plagued by personal and artistic conflicts, Lorca writes this ode as a call to Jesus for help. Each section of the ode ends with apostrophic appeals to the harmonious fusion of the Host, calling attention to the living presence of this symbol of harmony. However, the ode articulates the tension between the living quality of the Host emphasized by the direct address, and its inertness as a fixed symbol. The harmony of the Host is shaped and willed by the apostrophic act of the text that insists on appealing to it, and thus remains framed within the formal, fictive boundaries of the poem itself. The ode succeeds as an artistic project but fails as a program for personal faith. Even though Lorca always remained faithful to Christ as the supreme paradigm of love, he was unable to accept Catholic orthodoxy because of its distance from, and disregard for, the fragmenting of the human spirit.

The unfinished *Oda y burla de Sesostris y Sardanápalo* (Ode and Jest of Sesostris and Sardanapalus) was described by Lorca as "full of humor, weeping and Dionysian rhythm" (*SL* 134). Humor, along with exotic setting and characters, masks very personal concerns. The setting is Egypt, where Lorca placed the origins of Deep Song in his lecture about this musical art (see chapters 1 and 5 of the present study), alluding also to the link between Gypsies and Egyptians. As in Deep Song, the Dionysian elements here are mixed with lament or suffering in addition to the humor and irony that Lorca always found to be essential in carrying life's burdens. Sardanapalus is a fictitious figure, a pederast identified as the last Assyrian king. The name *Sesostris* perhaps alludes to Sesostris III the Great, an Egyptian conqueror.[8]

This ode consists of twelve quartets in alexandrines, seven about Sardanapalus, two about the Greeks, and the last three about Sesostris. The historical frame serves to objectify an intense sexual conflict, distancing it from the present and from personal feelings. Also, Egyptians and Greeks mark the origin of Eastern and Western civilizations. But, unlike the traditional ode praising the deeds and glory of the subject at hand, Lorca's ode provides the intimate side of the official history. Sardanapalus embodies an obscure and ambivalent sexuality associated with the color green, as opposed to the red of vital passion. Lorca insists on the painful nature of this sexuality, comparing sex with a *zarzamora,* or blackberry surrounded with thorns, the fruit of sterility itself. Sesostris embodies desire: "Inside his nakedness / nightingales of blood and bumblebees sang" (*Oda y burla de Sesostris y Sardanápalo,* 13); these are images of sexuality. Both figures illustrate a desire depicted as unnatural; hence their association with images of corruption and pain. The Egyptian and Assyrian settings are places of decadence. In contrast, the Greeks are depicted as tough sailors very unlike the corrupted and effeminate Sardanapalus. The sailor occupies an important role in Lorca's writings and drawings as an image of sexual freedom, and Greeks represent a culture where homosexuality was openly practiced. Lorca's ode offers both understandings of homosexuality while also implying the different developments emerging from each: the Eastern one identified with decadence, the Greek classical one with the purer way. "Ode to Walt Whitman," from *Poet in New York* (see chapter 1 of the present study), presents a similar confrontation between a pure and corrupt homosexuality, with a preference for the first that is not so clearly expressed in this ode. The insistence on the hidden nature of the desire embodied by Sardanapalus and Sesostris, and on the pain that it entails, are aspects that Lorca remarks on frequently and that account for the contradictory views he had about his own sexuality.

Later Works

By the end of 1928, the important lesson of Góngora is superceded, as Lorca writes to his friend Jorge Zalamea (*SL* 139); Lorca now seeks a return to inspiration, to instinct, to "a sort of VEIN-OPENING poetry." After Lorca turned away from the ideals of objectivity, and from Góngora's aesthetics of the imagination dominant in his early works, his poetry begins to explore the side of human experience that the order of reality represses, liminal areas where artistic control faces the unknown and where life confronts death.

The Divan at Tamarit

The word *divan* refers to, among other things, a collection of poems in Persian or Arabic, usually by one author. *Tamarit* was the name of a *huerta,* or small farm, owned by one of Lorca's uncles. As Ian Gibson explains, "The word Tamarit means 'abundant in dates' in Arabic." Lorca loved this *huerta,* "with its wonderful views of the Sierra Nevada and the poplar groves of the vega," even more than his own, the Huerta de San Vicente.[9] Lorca's divan dates from 1931–1934, and it comprises eleven gacelas and nine casidas, two types of Arabic stanzas. Lorca adopted the Arabic names not so much because of the direct influence of Arabic metric patterns as the evocation of a world with which he felt deeply identified. Already, in his *Book of Poems,* the Arabic and the Gypsy, along with the ancients, are viewed as open to the expression of desire. They are thus opposed to the restrictions imposed by the official religion and social mores of contemporary Western culture.

This book is a meditation about the I-you relationship in the Tamarit garden, a poetic projection of the speaker's subjectivity. This space has Granada, the poet's native city and the source of so much of his inspiration, as background. The dichotomies of Granada, a city divided between its Arabic past and its Christian present, between its Gypsy anguish and its external restraint, echo that of the author himself, fragmented between desire and social restrictions, love and its undoing in time. *The Divan at Tamarit* captures the aesthetics of that agony made word on the page. "Gacela primera. Del amor imprevisto" ("I. Ghazal of Love Unforeseen," *CP* 654–55) provides the key to understanding the rest of the collection.

> No one understood the perfume, ever:
> the dark magnolia of your belly.
> No one ever knew you martyred
> love's hummingbird between your teeth.
> . . . .
> Between plaster and jasmine
> your glance, pale branch of seed.
> I searched my breast to give you
> the ivory letters saying: Ever.
>
> Ever, ever, my agony's garden,
> your elusive form forever:
> blood of your veins in my mouth,
> your mouth now lightless for my death.

The speaker addresses a beloved whose type of passion (intimated with *perfume*) is misunderstood and unknown, perhaps because of an unnatural sexuality the beloved represents: the belly is a "dark magnolia," a flower normally white but here alluding to a kind of dark, obscure sexuality. The beloved's passion is also destructive, for it martyrs the bird of love ("hummingbird") in its embrace (the bites and violent kisses in the passionate exchange.[10] The verb *martyrs* has a Christly connotation; again Lorca refers to Christ as the paradigm of suffering love. The speaker perceives his love as similar to Christ's, since it is not only condemned by all the rules of convention, but is also consuming.

The boundaries of "plaster and jasmine" (or deadly dryness and fertility) frame the lover's glance within opposite tendencies, which explains the sterility of this desire ("pale branch of seed"). Therefore, the speaker confesses to having tried to inscribe his love in the activity of writing in the hope that it will thus survive ("the ivory letters saying: Ever"). However, words are elusive markers in which meaning cannot be retained. The speaker's mouth, or his poetry, is filled with the blood of the beloved's vitality, thus becoming the marking of love's demise. Instead of securing love for eternity, writing is the inscription of its dissolution. The last lines also reverse the meaning of the Christian communion, for the lovers' communion does not bring forth life, but rather consumes it.

This hidden passion, identified with homosexuality in particular and with desire in general, becomes a paradigm of the artistic conflict facing Lorca. If homosexual desire confronts extinction with its own expression, the attempts to articulate it in language succeed only in capturing the trace or agony of that desire. Thus the Tamarit garden, scenario for the I-you relationship, becomes the double of the garden of agony in Gethsemane, paradigm of Christ's abandonment and suffering. The speaker feels alienated from the other half of humanity, those who live under the protective cover of religion and societal norms. For them, the promise of love in the paradisiacal garden is still possible, while the speaker is painfully aware of the betrayal it masks. The poetic image of the garden of Tamarit/garden of agony (suggesting the actual space where the erotic relationship takes place, as well as the poem as the space where it is articulated), is elaborated in several poems (ghazals 1, 4, and 7, and qasidas 2 and 5) as a place blocked off by the walls of frustration.

The garden of agony is not only spatially but also temporally marked. Necessarily part of a cyclical rhythm (day/night, sun/moon), desire is constantly confronted by its annulment in death. Several poems (ghazal 9 and qasidas 8 and 9) depict the continuous pattern of morning ending in night, night in morning, as a cycle of anguish without relief or resolution: "I can see the struggle of wounded night / wrestling in coils with midday" (ghazal 2, *CP* 657). Night is wounded by the inevitable coming of its opposite, noon. Both extremes struggle, forming the image of a serpent that in many other poems is identified with the moon. Thus, in ghazal 8 (*CP* 662–65), the moon is endowed with the mouth of a serpent because she drinks the blood spilled in the night of love that she herself first inspired with her game of seduction but later only betrayed. Equally, love is betrayed in an embrace in which the lovers (ghazal 1) are trapped in a knot/communion that consumes rather than nurtures. "Casida IX. De las palomas oscuras" ("IX. Qasida of the Dark Doves," *CP* 678–79) illustrates this conflict:

> Through the laurel's branches
> I saw two dark doves.
> One was the sun,
> the other the moon.
> Little neighbors, I called,
> where is my tomb?
> In my tail, said the sun.
> In my throat, said the moon.
> And I who was walking
> with the earth at my waist,
> saw two snowy eagles
> and a naked girl.
> The one was the other
> and the girl was neither.
> Little eagles, I called,
> where is my tomb?
> In my tail, said the sun.
> In my throat, said the moon.
> Through the laurel's branches
> I saw two naked doves.
> The one was the other
> and both of them were neither.

The laurel brings to mind the myth of the nymph Daphne, who escaped Apollo's advances by being changed into a laurel tree. It thus suggests the sublimation of reality and desire implied in art, as well as connoting the wreath of glory and immortality for a poet (or "laureate"). The laurel has a second set of implications as the setting for a question of existential and cosmic proportions, the location of the speaker's tomb. Through artistic transformation, objects, people, and animals are made to signify other realities. Hence the two dark doves are the objectifications of sun and moon as images of the passage of time; the sun's tail ends in the moon's throat, when at dusk, daylight is engulfed by the night. This cosmic image illustrates the onanism the speaker perceives in the cycle of day/night, life/death, fertility/frustration, for it is a cycle devoid of outlet or result. Tail and throat are two sides of the same reality of failed desire, the site of the tomb. This bipolarity frames life, which the poem portrays as a naked girl (line 12). Life is thus naked and defenseless, since it is trapped in the cycle of sun and moon, although it (the girl) is neither of them. Life is not only the sun nor only the moon, neither day or night, neither the appearances of reality and passion nor their hidden or repressed side, but a constant shifting of reflections in which fulfillment remains elusive. This game of differences leads to no resolution, and those opposite poles seem to cancel each other out: life is neither day nor night; it is defined by what is not, by what is "other," thus it leaves humankind with no definite truth for comfort.

Various poems (qasidas 4, 6, 7, and ghazals 2, 8, and 10) express the desire to escape from that cycle by submerging oneself in the unconsciousness of the sea (ghazals 8 and 10) or in a wounded hand (qasida 6), representations of the speaker's suffering love offered as support in the journey to death that life ultimately is. Another attempt to escape is expressed in the rose (qasida 7), an image of the speaker's desire to transcend the passage of time and achieve fulfillment. In Lorca's poem, the rose seeks to go beyond its own nature, beyond beauty and death, in an attempt to supersede the existential cycle, striving toward something that remains unknown and undefined.

These poems seem to conclude that there is no escape from the life-death cycle. Finding that transcendence is impossible, the speaker expresses the desire to flee from the vision of death and emptiness to which the quest inevitably leads. There lies his tragic situation, placed between his desire and the death and emptiness its realization would reveal. That critical point is developed in several poems about the sunset, an image for the impossibility of maintaining the moment of fulfillment. Ghazals 3, 5, and 11, and qasidas 1 and 3 depict that moment of confrontation with death, that point where opposites fuse. The fatal effects of such a union attest to the failure of human desire and the frustration of a sense of completion. *The Divan at Tamarit* seems to conclude that even in its earlier forms life is tainted by death, that in fulfillment absence is already inscribed, and that the harmony in the center is unreachable.

Love's fulfillment is thwarted by time, as depicted in the succession of contrasting images of day/night, sun/moon, erotic climax/frustration, a cosmic cycle in which the speaker is imprisoned. The moon-serpent is in this book (as elsewhere) the poetic depiction of time as a movement ceaselessly turning upon itself. It is also the image depicting the self-reflexive nature of language, with a double edge for the poet. Language is the poet's only instrument for self-expression, but it is also a tool that keeps enclosing him in the same cycle of fulfillment and frustration from which he first tried to escape by writing. Words express desire, while they keep fulfillment at a distance with their own material presence. Lorca's writings are marked by a desire to articulate what is absent or unreachable. *The Divan at Tamarit* is the artistic elaboration of an experience in the interstices between presence and its dissolution, between being and nothingness. This collection expresses the impossibility of actualizing a passion that from the outset is trapped in time.

Six Galician Poems

On several occasions, as a university student, lecturer, and director of the theater group La Barraca, Lorca visited Galicia, a region in northwestern Spain. Most of his Galician poems were written in the period 1932–1934 and first published in 1935. It is likely that they were first written in Castilian, or in Lorca's own deficient Galician, and later corrected by some of his Galician friends.[11] In them, Lorca sings of a mythical Galicia with similarities to his native Granada, a vision perhaps attributable, as Lorca indicated in his lecture "On Lullabies" (*DS* 19), to the Galician songs that, filtering through Castile, arrived in Andalusia and contributed to the development of the typical Granadine mountain song.

Each of these six poems touches upon a distinctive feature of Galicia and its inhabitants: the perennial Galician rain in its most representative city, Santiago; Galician religious celebrations; emigration; the Galician melancholy and frustration as articulated by the image of a drowned boy; the Galician Romantic poet Rosalía de Castro (1837–1885); and the supernatural occurrences so frequent in the region's folklore. "Madrigal â cibdá de Santiago" ("Madrigal for the City of Santiago," *CP* 684–85) is addressed to "my sweet love." This reference could be to the city itself or to the poet's love, not necessarily a person but his passion or desire. Hence, the poem does indeed fit the definition of a madrigal as a short lyric usually about love. The poem identifies Santiago's persistent rain and distance from the sun as tears that the city (and region) shed for a sunny and happy past, the "ancient morning," or pristine origin, when no shadows existed between the *I* and the world. That distance causes fear and trembling of the heart (the speaker's sense of self) at the end of the poem. The madrigal is thus a sad song about the absence of love that the frequent Galician rain laments.

"Romaxe de Nosa Señora da Barca" ("Ballad of Our Lady of the Boat," *CP* 684–87) refers to a popular celebration in honor of the Virgin patroness of sailors. The poem begins and ends with a chorus about the *ruada*, or night celebration, in honor of the festival of the Virgin. Her image, which is transported through the streets in a religious procession, arrives at the church at dawn, when the poem ends. The celebration presents the Virgin with all who perished at sea, "the misty dead," as they are called in the ballad. A popular legend also describes the Virgin as going in her boat to the rocks to rescue the victims of shipwrecks.[12] The Virgin is thus the mother who presides over this maritime region where so many die at sea. The poem depicts the Virgin and Galicia as pietà images offering their motherly nurturing to their dead children. This image seems to encapsulate the sense of nostalgia, of life's transience, inspired in Lorca by the rainy and misty Galician landscape. The sea, which gives much life to Galicia, also takes it away.

In "Noiturnio do adoescente morto" ("Nocturne of the Drowned Youth," *CP* 688–89), the body of a youth is found in the river. The speaker urges people from all parts of the Galician region to go silently to the ford to see the body before the river takes him to the sea, where it will dissolve. The fact that the whole region is called to witness suggests the symbolic meaning of that dead boy. Drowning, like wounding in the throat, is a recurring image in Lorca's work signifying the ultimate frustration of vital impulses. The adolescent represents life cut down in its prime. Since his death encompasses all of Galicia, he embodies that region's desire for life that continues to be thwarted.

"Canzón de cuna pra Rosalía Castro, morta" ("Lullaby in Death for Rosalía de Castro," *CP* 688–91) is dedicated to the poet Rosalía de Castro, whose grave Lorca visited during one of his trips to Galicia in 1932. The poem begins with an urgent call to wake up: "Arise, my friend, / for the roosters are crowing." This call contradicts the poem's designation as a lullaby, as does the association in the title of the lullaby, or cradle song, with death. The lullaby's rhythm is evoked in the following lines:

> The plows come and go
> from Santiago to Bethlehem.
> From Bethlehem to Santiago
> comes an angel in a boat.

> (*CP* 691)

Santiago and Bethlehem are pilgrimage centers: Bethlehem as the site of the birth of Jesus; Santiago as the burial place of apostle Santiago (James) and final destiny for many pilgrims in the Middle Ages. According to legend, Santiago brought Christ's gospel to the Iberian peninsula and then returned to Jerusalem, where he was killed by Herod. His body was returned to Galicia in a boat sailed by an angel. Lorca's poem recalls the history of the region, juxtaposing the pilgrimages to Santiago's tomb with the speaker's own pilgrimage to Rosalía's grave site. The refrain, urging Rosalía to wake up from her grave, attempts to counteract the sleepy, dreamy atmosphere into which the region has fallen. It calls on Rosalía, the poetic voice of Galicia, to rise and give renewed spiritual guidance. Covered by the green grass so typical of the Galician landscape, Rosalía's "bed" is her grave, where her body is one and the same with her land:

> Galicia stretched out and silent,
> harrowed with unhappy grasses.
> Grasses that cover your bed
> and the black fountain of your hair.

> (*CP* 691)

The Galician landscape is thus a cradle and a grave, a mother whose caring mingles life-giving with death or frustration. In this poem, however, the speaker calls for new life to emerge from death. The combination of lullaby and rousing call is echoed in Lorca's lecture on lullabies (see chapter 5 of the present study). Unlike inert stone monuments, lullabies are living elements that speak for their region of origin. Spanish lullabies are very different from their counterparts in other parts of Europe. They are sad and melancholy, intended not only to put the child to sleep but also to wound its sensitivity. Spanish lullabies usually evoke a land—the poetic realm—to which the child is taken. Rosalía's lullaby takes the poetess back into the history of pilgrimage of her region. Rosalía becomes an active participant in her own lullaby, and her tomb/cradle (like Bethlehem/Santiago) becomes a place where death can be the source of new life.

In "Danza da lúa en Santiago" ("Dance of the Moon in Santiago," *CP* 690–93), a mother becomes gradually mesmerized by the moon's dance until she is totally lost in its fatal white light. The moon's dance of death and eroticism illustrates the contradictory fusion of life and death Lorca perceives in the Galician landscape. The image of the mother/moon is also the Virgin in "Ballad of Our Lady of the Boat" (who is often identified with the moon) and Galicia itself, a mother who nurtures her children with life's ultimate message, death.

Lament for Ignacio Sanchez Mejías

Lament for Ignacio Sanchez Mejías is a four-part elegy dedicated to a close friend of Lorca. Ignacio Sánchez Mejías (1891–1934) was a bullfighter and also a highly educated man. His *finca,* or country house, in Seville was a gathering place for poets and artists. After retiring from the bullring he decided to return in 1934, at the age of forty-three. He was gored on August 11 of that year and died two days later in Madrid. Lorca probably wrote his elegy in 1934; it was published in 1935. The elegy befits the tone of loss and absence that pervades Lorca's poetry, while allusions to the theme of bullfighting can be found in some of his other works.[13] This particular elegy is an extended reflection on death as well as a meditation on the power or failure of poetry to counteract the gradual fading of one's powers before it. In his lecture on *duende* (*DS* 51) Lorca described bullfighting as the context where *duende* expresses its force most fully. In bullfighting, two opposing forces confront each other: "The bull has his orbit and the bullfighter has his, and between these orbits is a point of danger, the vertex of the terrible play." That point of danger is where the *duende* struggles to maintain the agonistic tension between the bull's instinctual force and the bullfighter's sense of precise form and measurement. Bullfighting thus becomes an image for the creative process. Writing with *duende* entails a constant struggle to balance formal control with emotional force. If Ignacio's goring attests to the fatal loss of that equilibrium, in writing that loss would entail artistic failure.

The first section of the work, "La cogida y la muerte" ("The Goring and the Death," *CP* 696–99), repeats obsessively the verse "a las cinco de la tarde" (*at five in the afternoon*). The death did not have to occur at that time, but the exactness of the hour is used as a poetic device to fix the attention on that hour and counteract the dissolution brought about by the tragic death. Inscription and fading, stasis and temporality, are thus contrasted and fused here, as throughout the elegy. They reflect the purpose of the elegiac genre to mark the absence of something or someone. This first section moves from poetic symbols connoting the whiteness of death as the fading of all traces ("the white sheet" and "basketful of lime" brought for the body), to images of metals, glass, oxide, arsenic, and iodine referring to the medical treatment of gored Ignacio and to his impending death. Reason and measure have been defeated by the instinctual power of the bull. The order of things has been turned upside down: sequential time is fixed in the delirious repetition of "At five in the afternoon," the bullfighter's wounded body becomes a place where death lays eggs, and his bed becomes his coffin. The central presence is the bull who, although killed, has vanquished the bullfighter.

Section 2 of the work, "La sangre derramada" ("The Spilled Blood," *CP* 698–703), repeats the verse "No, I refuse to see it!," referring to the bullfighter's blood on the sand. Just as the bullfighter attempts to vanquish death with reason, the writer's craft is a constant attempt to fill the void between words and life. Ignacio's spilled blood attests to the crossing of boundaries, the smudging of life's normal profile. The poem then moves to the mythic level of the moon, an image related to the cow, the bull, or the oxen, from the similarity between the horns and the crescent. The moon, like an old mother who swallows up the sun at sunset to give birth to it again at dawn, licks the blood that will warm her paleness and coldness. The blood of life is thus integrated into the moon, the destiny of all the dead. Ignacio is thus the son sacrificed and incorporated into the realm of the mother who first gave him birth. Consequently, Ignacio is described going up the stairs leading to the realm of the moon:

> Ignacio mounts the steps,
> shouldering his full death.
> He looked for daybreak
> and daybreak there was none.
> He seeks the clean line of his profile
> and sleep leads him astray.
> He looked for his shapely body
> and found his gaping blood. (*CP* 701)

Ignacio's ascent seems to lead him toward some type of transcendence where he could be immortalized. Just as the line or the word on paper seeks to leave an imprint, Ignacio wants to make the line that will delineate his profile, thus leaving the imprint of his existence. However, all the elements that might effect such a transformation are ineffectual. Daybreak, or the order of light, never comes, so the space is filled with the whiteness of the moon; "the clean line of his profile," or the imprint of his being, is dissolving in dreams, the realm of the subconscious and the night, and the shape of his body dissolves in the spilled blood. The game of bullfighting/writing has lost the necessary equilibrium between opposing tendencies.

Section 3 of the work, "Cuerpo presente" ("Presence of the Body," *CP* 704–7), begins with an address to a stone, possibly the stone at Ignacio's grave. The stone is a symbol of the opacity and muteness of death, of the impossibility of linking up with existence after death. It is as if the elegy's attempt to paint a portrait of Ignacio were faced with the unsurmountable obstacle of death. On that stone where Ignacio lays, his decomposing body is covered by "pale sulphur" (*CP* 705). He is the victim, the son sacrificed on the altar of the great mother, the deadly moon. His body is present, but as a sign doomed to dissolution, since it is decomposing. Once a luminous form, Ignacio's body is now "punctured through and through" (*CP* 705).That punctured body signals the void invading the writing of the elegy and threatening to disclose the futility of its project of inscription. The body now present is becoming absent, its outline being irremediably effaced. The result is silence: "No one is singing here" (*CP* 705). The deictic *here* refers to death from which there is no escape. To that *here* of death the speaker convokes "men with harsh voices" (*CP* 705), a type of natural being whose close contact with nature would counteract death. At the end, the speaker indicates that Ignacio's body will get lost in "the round bullring of the crescent / moon" (*CP* 707), the place where it is believed all the dead end.

In the fourth and last section of the work, "Alma ausente" ("Absence of the Soul," *CP* 706–9), death is effacing Ignacio's profile, making him unrecognizable even to those to whom he was most familiar: "The bull does not know you, nor the fig tree, / nor horses, nor the ants on your floors" (*CP* 707). The repetition of the phrase "does not know you" emphatically proclaims the effacement of Ignacio, which is reiterated in the refrain "because your death is forever." Nevertheless, the speaker sings for him, for poetry will preserve Ignacio's memory forever: "No one knows you. No one. But I sing you— / sing your profile and your grace, for later on" (*CP* 709). Knowing Ignacio means maintaining his memory in a movement that looks toward the past, while in poetic singing, memory is projected into the future. Hence the elegy will preserve the memory of this man for generations to come. However, this writing is marked with "words that moan" (*CP* 709). Just as a flamenco dancer's movements and a guitar strumming articulate the existential frustration of desire, the words of the elegy are circles, for they can express Ignacio's identity only by turning back on, by referring to, themselves. The elegy cannot bring back Ignacio. It can only maintain his memory in the self-reflective movement of the text

Sonnets of Dark Love

In 1984 the Madrid newspaper *ABC* published eleven sonnets dating from 1935 that were based on manuscripts found in the García Lorca family archives. Lorca referred to these pieces simply as sonnets, but poet friends seem to have heard him call them "sonetos del amor oscuro" (sonnets of dark love, *CP* 849). The connotations of "dark love" as homosexual, secret, and forbidden passion, the taboo surrounding Lorca's writings after his death and during Franco's regime, and a pirated edition of these poems in 1983 (known as the "Granadine edition in red"), contributed to an aura of mystery and expectancy around these sonnets, as well as to a complicated editorial and publishing history.[14]

There are other Lorcan sonnets, published at various times and compiled in the different editions of the *Obras completas* (Complete Works). Most were written to honor admired artist friends, such as Spanish composers Manuel de Falla or Isaac Albéniz (1860–1909) (*CP* 728–29, 732–33), or on the death of a friend ("En la muerte de José de Ciria y Escalante" ["On the Death of José de Ciria y Escalante"], *CP* 726–27), or, in the case of "A Mercedes en su vuelo" ("For Mercedes in Her Flight," *CP* 734–35), for a daughter of the Counts of Yebes, who died as a child. Others closely follow the baroque tradition of writing a sonnet to thank someone for a gift while praising the gift giver ("Soneto a Carmela Condón, agradeciéndole unas muñecas" ["Sonnet to Carmela Condón, Thanking Her for Some Dolls"], *CP* 728–31).

Ten of the eleven sonnets published in *ABC* were written on stationery from the Hotel Victoria in Valencia, where Lorca stayed in November 1935. They are addressed to an absent beloved, expressing Lorca's personal experience as well as offering an artistic creation that surpasses concrete personal boundaries. These eleven sonnets thus form a cycle around the theme of love. They are written against the background of a great tradition of such authors as the baroque Spanish poets Quevedo (1580–1645) and Góngora and the mystic Saint John of the Cross (1542–1591), echoes of whom are found in the Lorcan sonnets. Another antecedent is Shakespeare, whose influence is evident in other works by Lorca, from *The Butterfly's Evil Spell* to *The Public*. Both Shakespeare and Lorca express a tragic feeling of time, but Shakespeare believes in the strength of love to confront time, and he defends marriage, procreation, and art as means to overcome temporal destruction. Lorca, on the other hand, does not find an escape, and his love is fatally marked by time.

The "dark," clandestine nature of homosexuality results from society's repression; Lorca feels urged to articulate it, especially in his later work (*The Public*, for instance). Hence these sonnets are filled with rhetorical devices (apostrophes, command forms, and deictics) that point to the urgency of the passion—a passion always threatened with dissolution on being expressed. In "Soneto de la guirnalda de rosas" ("Sonnet of the Garland of Roses," *CP* 712–13) there is an urgent call to enjoy love before it is too late—a carpe diem or carpe florem—to weave the garland of roses even though time will destroy the lovers in their own embrace. The sonnet alludes to the tragic love of Venus and Adonis, and to love's intertwinement in the skein of time (referring to Adonis as a god who dies in the winter to be resurrected in the spring). The speaker insists on the need to go on weaving in order to impede death. As elsewhere in Lorca's writings, weaving love is associated with the act of writing. Nevertheless, time's triumph is inevitable and the weaving/writing may be a futile activity, but necessary to live.

In other sonnets, the *tejer*, or weaving of the garland of love, becomes the *alacrán* (scorpion) of suffering that gnaws in the speaker's chest and gradually turns his poetry into "a pulseless lyre" ("Llagas de amor" ["Wounds of Love"], *CP* 714–15). The speaker in these sonnets is in a trance-like state of *viva muerte* ("living death"; "El poeta pide a su amor que le escriba" ["The Poet Asks His Love to Write Him"], *CP* 714–15), a state commonly alluded to in mystic writings. "El poeta habla por teléfono con el amor" ("The Poet Speaks with His Beloved on the Telephone," *CP* 716–19) is one of the few examples in which speaker and beloved unite, though within limitations:

> Your voice watered the dune of my breast
> in the sweet wooden booth.
> South of my feet, it was Spring,
> and north of my brow, a fern blossomed.
>
> Within that narrow space a pine of light
> sang out, but with no dawn, no seed to sow;
> and my lament for the first time
> hung coronets of hope upon the roof.
>
> Sweet and distant voice, spilling for me.
> Sweet and distant voice, tasted by me.
> Distant and sweet voice, muffled softly.
>
> Distant like a dark and wounded doe.
> Sweet like sobbing during the fall of snow.
> Distant and sweet, and caught in the marrow!

This poem fuses the highly conventional sonnet structure with the reference to the modern invention of the telephone and the telephone booth, in which the speaker is conversing with his beloved. The most salient aspect in the tradition of the sonnet is the high status of this type of poem for the expression of sublime love. In the modern era, the experience of love is twice removed, not only by the formal structure of the sonnet, but by the telephone as well. Both sonnet and telephone are substitutes for the absent beloved, proxies for the missing object of desire. In Lorca's sonnet this distance from the actual experience is contrasted by a love discourse highly charged with sexual connotations.

The beloved's voice has a fertilizing effect of water on the dry heart of the speaker ("dune"), and since this process is facilitated by the telephone booth, this space is qualified as "sweet." The booth and the telephone itself come to occupy the same position as language in facilitating love's discourse. The blossoming south and north the speaker refers to the fulfilling nature of the experience that can be easily read at both the erotic and poetic levels. Upon hearing the beloved's voice, there is an erotic and poetic blossoming/orgasm that materializes in the sonnet: "South of my feet, it was spring, / and north of my brow, a fern blossomed." *South* could refer to the lower parts of the body (loins and genitalia) while *north* could point to reason and logic. The fact that the north makes the fern blossom (an impossibility, for ferns do not blossom) indicates the extent to which the speaker has discarded the censorship normally imposed by the head. The depiction of the experience through images of nature contradicts the artificiality of the medium by which it is facilitated (booth/telephone and sonnet). This contrast creates a tension between direct experience and mediation, reality and substitute, that is at the core of the sonnet.

The "narrow space" (line 5) is the telephone booth, which symbolizes what narrow limitations words place on emotions. It also refers to the physical containment of the speaker as contrasted with the intensity of the emotional experience. The "pine of light" is not only the booth itself transformed now into a luminous tree because it resonates with the conversation), but also a reference to an erection. The orgasmic experience accounts for the coronets of hope, although the speaker knows this song lacks dawn or seed. The erotic and artistic blossoming is onanistic, with no outcome beyond its own articulation.

The game of reflections played by the adjectives *sweet* and *distant* refers to the game of presence and absence in the poem as well as in language itself. The voice is sweet because of the blossoming it provokes, but emotionally distant because of the physical distance between the lovers that the telephone so pointedly reflects. The muffled voice through the telephone represents how reality is also "muffled" in the word and its distance from the object. The voice is distant like a dark and wounded doe, a mystical image of the beloved that here refers to the secrecy and pain of homosexual love. The beloved's voice is like sobbing during a snowfall, for it won't be heard. The snowfall image suggests the sexual discharge, after which passion dissolves. Similarly, language's inscription is threatened by its distance from the world. The voice of dark love is in the marrow because it is one and the same with the speaker's being. It is the voice of the existential and artistic struggle between presence and absence, desire and frustration.

Lorca's sonnets depict love as an experience always struggling against time and societal repression. The speaker insists on articulating love's voice, even if it proves to be a futile attempt. Lorcan writing means leaving a mark on life and love through the writing of words on the page, as the spilling of the blood/ink of human suffering, with all its Christly connotations. Societal and temporal restrictions may repress love's voice or threaten to turn its embrace into the web of death, but the process of weaving it must continue.

This commitment to writing explains the great variety of poetic forms with which Lorca experimented. In *Suites* and *Songs,* long, discursive lines are discarded in favor of formal devices that are intended to capture a world in motion. In the Gongorine phase, form is a solidly built structure, aimed at counteracting the passage of time. The trance-like quality of Lorca's later writing stems from his awareness of the artificiality of poetic form and his knowledge that this form is the only means available for expression.

Notes

1. The period 1917–1918 was for Lorca, according to his brother Francisco's account, one of *exaltación literaria* (literary intensity) ("Primeros escritos de Federico" [First Writings by Federico], *Federico García Lorca y su mundo.* Translated by Christopher Mauer as *In the Green Morning* [New York: New Directions, 1986] 161). During that time, the young author wrote poems in which sentimentality is mixed with sexual feelings. Ian Gibson (*Federico García Lorca: A Life* [New York: Pantheon, 1989] 62–77) points to the rebelliousness against Catholic dogma in Lorca's early writings and to the malaise and uneasiness about a God that allows his children, including his son Jesus, to suffer. Gibson finds an evangelical root in these compositions, in which the young author identifies with Christ (67). These early compositions, most of which are still unpublished, are permeated with the conflict between religion and sexual demands, Christ and Satan, as exemplified in Lorca's first published collection, *Book of Poems.*

2. For a detailed commentary on the *Book of Poems,* see Candelas Newton, *Lorca: "Libro de poemas" o las aventuras de una búsqueda* (Lorca: *Book of Poems* or The Adventures of a Quest) (Salamanca: Universidad de Salamanca, 1986) and *Lorca, una escritura en trance: Libro de poemas y Diván del Tamarit* (Lorca, Writing in a Trance: *Book of Poems* and *The Divan at the Tamarit*)(Amsterdam and Philadelphia: John Benjamins, 1992).

3. Christopher Maurer, in *Collected Poems* (New York: Farrar, Straus & Giroux, 1991), reedited the poems published by Belamich with changes in the chronology and in

the texts based on biographical information not available when Belamich published his edition. Quotations from *Suites* are here taken from *Collected Poems,* and cited parenthetically.

4. See Gibson, *A Life* 141.

5. Originally published as *Canciones,* Philip Cummings translated the collection, with Lorca's assistance, during Lorca's stay at Cummings's house in Eden Mills, Vermont, in August 1929. The translation was published in 1976 as *Songs,* ed. Daniel Eisenberg (Pittsburgh: Duquesne UP).

6. For Paul Ilie ("Three Shadows on the Early Aesthetic of Lorca," *"Cuando yo me muera . . ." Essays in Memory of Federico Garcia Lorca,* ed. C. Brian Morris [Lanham, New York and London: UP of America, 1988]) this triptych polarizes myth and "poeticized biography" (26). In my reading the triptych presents the tension between history and myth as two aspects of the same reality.

7. In *Revista de Occidente* 22.66 (1928): 294–98.

8. First published as *Oda y Burla de Sesostris y Sardanápalo* (Ode and Joke of Sesostris and Sardanapalus), ed. Miguel García-Posada (Ferrol: Esquío, 1985), with a very useful textual analysis. Translations are my own.

9. Gibson, *A Life* 386.

10. Close readings of the poems in *The Divan at Tamarit* are offered in Newton, *Lorca, una escritura en trance,* and Andrew A. Anderson, *Lorca's Late Poetry: A Critical Study* (Leeds, Eng.: Francis Cairns, 1990). Anderson, among other critics, points out the Christly connotations in this Ghazal.

11. See Anderson, "Who Wrote *Seis Poemas Galegos* and in What Language?," *"Cuando yo me muera . . .": Essays in Memory of Federico García Lorca,* ed. C. Brian Morris (Lanham, New York and London: UP of America, 1988) 139. Anderson identifies 1932 as the year when Lorca visited Rosalía de Castro's grave (129).

12. My thanks to Lolita Gómez Posada for conveying to me some of her personal knowledge of Galician folkloric traditions.

13. For a perceptive reading of the role of elegy in Lorca's writings, see Christopher Maurer's introduction to *Collected Poems,* esp. xxiii–xxxvii.

14. For a close reading of Lorca's sonnets, see Candelas Newton, "Los paisajes del amor: Iconos centrales en los *Sonetos* de Lorca" (Love's Landscapes: Important Icons in Lorca's *Sonnets*"), *Anales de la literatura española contemporánea* 11.1–2 (1986): 143–59, and Anderson, *Lorca's Late Poetry* 275–399.

CHAPTER 4

Lesser-Known Plays

Early Dramas and Puppet Plays

Between 1917 and 1923 Lorca wrote several plays now considered juvenilia: *Del amor. Teatro de animales* (Of Love: Theater of Animals), the unfinished *Cristo (Tragedia religiosa)* (Christ [A Religious Tragedy]), the dramatic dialogue *Jehová y el ángel* (Yahweh and the Angel), and *Sombras* (Shadows).[1] A typical feature of these early dramatic writings is the unorthodox depiction of religious figures. God the Father is an unloving and decrepit presence in whose kingdom Christ, and other subversives like him, are kept in chains for preaching love. This rejection of conventional religious doctrine is indicative of the young author's crisis, caught as he was between his incipient sexual urges and his Catholic upbringing. While the church and God the Father imposed restrictions upon human desire and insisted on the separation between the body and the spirit, Christ's sacrifice exemplified the difficult fusion of opposites (the divine and the human, the spirit and flesh). Christ epitomizes the tension at the core of Lorca's view of art and life between desires and the outside order of reality, between pathos and form. As the character of the pig says in *Del amor,* liberation and art will be possible only when Christ's message of love operates in the world.

The polarity between reality and desire, idealism (or imagination) and the outside world, is apparent in Lorca's first theatrical production, *El maleficio de la mariposa. Comedia en dos actos y un prólogo* (The Butterfly's Evil Spell: Comedy in Two Acts and A Prologue), performed in March 1920.[2] The scene is a colony of beetles where everything is going well until one of the members, the Boybeetle, falls in love with a butterfly who fell into the colony after one of its wings broke. While he despairs at an impossible love, since the butterfly's impulse is to fly high and away from the colony, he is unable to enjoy or value the love that Sylvia, another beetle, offers him. As a poet, Boybeetle is committed to seeking the ideal star in his imagination, which the butterfly fully embodies. But when he attempts to reach that ideal, the butterfly flies away. Boybeetle's dreams, and the affected kind of poetry he represents, are gently mocked by the author, and contrasted with the gluttony and grotesqueness of Scorpy, a scorpion who thinks only of drinking and eating. Lofty ideals are thus confronted with the exigencies of the body, pointing to a dichotomy that recurs repeatedly in Lorca's writings and that he is able to treat with some humor in the character of Scorpy.

The prologue to the play presents an idea that will be central in Lorca's theater: that of love being "born with the same exaltation in all planes of life" (*FP* 194). For Lorca, love is not a sentiment shared only by humans, much less only by heterosexual beings, but a desire found in all forms of life. It is not difficult to see the beetle colony, a minute setting somewhere under tall grass, as a microcosmic representation of the existential condition of human beings subjected to events over which they have no control. As Lima remarks, the insects' absorption in their own lives, their pettiness, and their concern for riches reflect human blindness that does not usually see beyond itself.[3] When it does (as in the case of Boybeetle), the dreamer is punished for it. The beautiful butterfly is a cruel joke on poor Boybeetle, who will never reach her heights, but will nevertheless be fatally marked by the desire for her. The speaker of the prologue (the director or the author, although his identity remains ambivalent) points to the fatal wound that beauty can and does inflict when he says how Death can disguise itself as Love. This remark implies that love, as an impulse leading beyond the boundaries of reality, inflicts suffering and ultimately death. The impossibility of winning the Butterfly's love results in Boybeetle's death, implied at the end, though the final act of the play remains a fragment in the only surviving original manuscript.

With these animal characters and a decor of huge daisies, as seen from the beetles' viewpoint, Lorca was trying to present a different perspective and stir the audience out of its passivity and usual expectations.[4] This does not seem to have worked, however, as the play was a complete failure. The public was unable to accept the sight of insects voicing such lyrical feelings, and booed the play loudly. In a fairy-tale atmosphere, this play dramatizes the conflict found at the core of Lorca's theater; that is, the struggle to enact a fusion of ideal and reality, desire and its object, word and referent, no matter how difficult or impossible. In this early play, as in later ones such as *The Public,* Lorca uses animal characters to defy the traditional irrational/rational polarity and the accepted placement of humans at the center of meaning.

Lorca's interest in puppet theater was constant, as is attested by the various works he wrote in that genre starting in the 1920s. He was very much concerned with resurrecting the old tradition of *cristobitas,* or puppets, since they represented for him the popular soul of Andalusia and the origin of theater. Puppets do not have to imitate real types, as human actors do, for they are just what they are, unabashedly fictional, the antithesis of mimetic acting. Hence, for Lorca, they offered the possibility of overcoming the mannerisms and "acting" that plagued the stage at the time.[5] The puppet convention could do away with the "realistic" pretensions then common in conventional plays, thus allowing Lorca to indulge in the unabashed artificiality of theater.

Cristobical (FPP 11–16) is an undated fragment, possibly the first puppet play Lorca intended to write. He later abandoned it to work on *Los títeres de Cachiporra. Tragicomedia de Don Cristóbal y la señá Rosita. Farsa guiñolesca en seis cuadros y una advertencia (The Billy-Club Puppets: Tragicomedy of Don Cristóbal and Miss Rosita: A Guignolesque Farce in Six Scenes and An Announcement)*. An *advertencia,* or announcement, precedes this play, just as the prologue did *The Butterfly's Evil Spell.* This technique, which Lorca also used in other plays, is intended to establish a direct contact with the audience, which the author considered essential for theater. Here it is Mosquito, "a mysterious personage, part ghost, part leprechaun, part insect" (*FP* 15), who addresses the audience, requesting silence so that the performance about to begin may be heard. Mosquito offers a commentary in which two types of theater are contrasted: the theater of the bourgeoisie, in which the audience falls asleep, and a more popular type of theater for "plain people." The former is described as a place of "gold and crystal" where Mosquito and his company, representing "the wit and poetry of the Andalusian people," felt imprisoned. The latter is associated with open fields and with nature in general. This polarity—of art as a conventional form or as the expression of true human emotions—foregrounds the question of form and content, of the autonomy of art and communication, that all of Lorca's works tackle from different angles. Later plays, such as *The Public,* delve into the nature of a theater that, aware of its own artificiality, integrates self-reflexivity with the expression of pathos or passions.

In this tragicomedy, Rosita loves Cocoliche, who has no money, while her father wants her to marry the rich Cristóbal. As in other plays, desire is thwarted by an external force-here, the father's authority and his code of materialism. Cristóbal is always the bully, just as Rosita represents the archetypical sentimental theatrical female. Currito is Rosita's previous lover, who has gone all over the world in search of a love that remains elusive. He is the typical mysterious romantic lover who is sad because his love is somehow inherently an impossibility. By resorting to these cliché characters, Lorca is calling attention to the degree of acculturation implicit in the "normal" association of those characters with bullying, coquetry, or parental intransigence, thus making it all the more evident that we are seeing a theatrical performance.

In 1923, in celebration of the Epiphany (6 January), the day Spanish children receive their Christmas gifts, Lorca prepared, in collaboration with Manuel de Falla and others, a party at his Granada house that included a presentation of a puppet theater and music. For the occasion he wrote *La niña que riega la albahaca y el príncipe preguntón* (*The Girl Who Waters the Basil and the Inquisitive Prince, FPP* 3–9), based on an old Andalusian folk tale.[6] Some elements in this early play will reappear in later works: the play's division into "engravings" instead of acts; the motif of "singing" with erotic connotations; the "wound of love"; and the motif of the mask or disguise.

The social element is present from the outset with the contrast between the Shoemaker—the "terribly terribly poor" father of the Girl—and the Prince. The nobleman, who from his palace has seen the Girl watering the basil plant, a symbol of love, disguises himself as a peddler of grapes in order to be able to speak with her. She will later disguise herself as a Magician, with a hat full of stars, in order to go into the palace and cure the Prince of his melancholy. On stage was Lorca's drawing "Garden of the Tree of the Sun and the Tree of the Moon," which projects the scene onto a cosmic scale. Moreover, the Prince and the Girl always meet at a very early hour of the morning, enacting the moment when night and day merge. In this children's play the young author resolves the polarity of sun/moon—a frequent one in his writings—in the union of the Prince and the Girl in marriage, while it is impossible to tell "if the sun or the moon shines more brightly" (*FPP* 9). The result of this harmony of opposites is an "imp of joy" that dwells only "under the pillow of the child who is pure" (*FPP* 9). Only the purity implicit in childhood and in the "wild things" of nature can effect the fusion of opposites. While other Lorcan plays dramatize the impossibility of such a union, Lorca makes full use of the childlike and theatrical nature of puppet theater for this happy resolution to work. Author and audience are fully aware of the artificiality of the puppet performance. It is only within that realm of artistic awareness that the "happy ending" is possible.

Puppet theater appealed to Lorca because its theatricality allowed an artistic freedom that realism in conventional plays did not permit. In *Retablillo de Don Cristóbal. Farsa para guiñol*, 1931 (produced 1935) (*In the Frame of Don Cristóbal: A Puppet Farce, FPP* 17–31), the Poet, addressing the audience in a prologue, defends the puppet's simple language as evidence of the innocence and honesty absent from the refined speech of conventional plays. The play's exchange between Poet and Director turns on a question of aesthetics: whether to maintain stereotypes and thus give the audience what it wants, or change them and break away from customary expectations. While the Poet would like to experiment with creating free and imaginative characters, the Director, aware of the demands placed upon theater by its links with society, insists on respecting the conventions the audience is accustomed to seeing. Thus the Poet accuses the Director of shutting the players up "in a tiny iron cage." The dilemma between artistic freedom and the demands of the audience will be explored in depth in *The Public.*

The puppet genre was important to Lorca as a medium for experimenting with artistic questions that would be developed in later plays. Even as late as 1934, after working on his more experimental plays, Lorca proclaimed the importance of puppet theater by proclaiming Don Cristóbal as the "mainstay of the theater" in *Diálogo del poeta y Don Cristóbal* (*Dialogue of the Poet and Don Cristóbal, FPP* 33–36), which preceded the performance of *The Billy-Club Puppets* in Argentina that year.

Reality and Artistic Transformation

Mariana Pineda

Lorca started work on the play *Mariana Pineda. Romance popular en tres estampas* (*Mariana Pineda: A Popular Ballad in Three Engravings*) in 1923, although it did not premiere until 1927. The work is based on a historical liberal uprising in the nineteenth century against the absolute rule of King Ferdinand VII. Mariana Pineda, twenty-seven years old, was executed in Granada in 1831 for her role in the uprising.[7]

In the play she is a widow around thirty years old, mother of two children, and in love with the insurgent Don Pedro de Sotomayor. Because of her love for him, she has agreed to embroider the flag of his liberal cause. When the conspiracy is discovered and Don Pedro flees to England, leaving Mariana behind, she refuses to reveal the names of the conspirators, even though Pedrosa, the king's agent, has promised her freedom in exchange. She feels cornered by Pedrosa, who pressures her excessively, until she is sentenced to die. At that point, she explodes in a cry for freedom: "Now I am Liberty itself. Love made me so!" (*MP* 175).

Lorca does not follow history to the letter, preferring to incorporate into the plot the popular ballads and legends about the local heroine, which he had known since childhood (*OC* 1:1139; *OC* 2: 945). Since those early years in Granada, Lorca, as he confessed, felt a special attraction to the figure of Mariana. From his window he could see the statue that the city had dedicated to her in one of its plazas. Mariana embodies, for him, the spirit of Granada (*MP* 3), a city that represses its passion behind the white walls of its enclosed *cármenes* (villas with walled gardens), behind the mask of social propriety. As Granada is a city turned upon itself, Mariana's passion is proclaimed by her silence—by not naming the conspirators—and ultimately by accepting death.

The play opens and closes with a popular ballad about Mariana sung by children in the streets of Granada (*MP* 12). Thus framed, the play is offered as a poeticized, literary form referring to its own theatrical nature. This self-reflexivity permeates the various aspects of the play: stage directions, characters' attitudes, dialogues, and costumes. Lorca's intention was to create a play with a Romantic flavor, hence the use of "engravings," or curtains, painted by Dalí, that framed the scene as though it were an old photograph (*OC* 1:1139–40). Stage directions call for stereotyped poses so as to re-create the atmosphere of the period more accurately. Thus, in the first "engraving," Mariana is sitting on a chair with "her profile to the audience," while Fernando, a young officer in love with her, faces her, the couple thus looking like "an engraving typical of the period" (*MP* 7, 65). The play is offered as an exquisite artistic construct in which the "historical realism" of Mariana's tragic story of love, freedom, and abandonment is framed within its well-defined formal structure.

On the flag of freedom Mariana sewed "the one real love" of her life (*MP* 157). Like writing, embroidering is a way to express one's dreams and desires. It may be a punishable action, however, for it dares to articulate a passion that society represses. Hence, Mariana's red thread (like the red thread of the women weaving like the Parcae in *Blood Wedding*) is described as a knife-wound in the air, suggesting that the act of embroidering her love/dreams on the cloth will bring her death. While Mariana appears like a modern version of the Parcae, shaping with every stitch the destiny of her relationship with Don Pedro, her embroidering represents subversion to the repressive forces of the king, a threat to official authority. With every stitch Mariana shapes her love, while she is simultaneously unweaving her own self, since her embroidering ultimately brings her destruction. The embroidering is thus the ironic image with which Lorca articulates the dilemma of desire being repressed or censored as it is being expressed.

People are the captives of their dreams, Mariana realizes: if they let the dreams go, the dreamers then become entrapped by their own limitations, but if they choose to stand by their aspirations, fulfilling them exacts a high price. Imagination and desire, as depicted in the act of embroidering, are opposed by reality. A network of images depicts Mariana in relation to the sacrificed bull in a bullfight, with her neck pierced by arrows of repression. The blood coming from the wound is symbolically equivalent to the thread with which she embroiders the flag of freedom and which she offers in the name of love. Lorca frequently associates the neck and throat with the voice of poetry, which, like Mariana's embroidering, is silenced for daring to express its desire. When she is to be executed, Mariana declares she is dead already. She has become aware that, for her dream of love to be allowed to exist, she has to become the embodiment of love sacrificed for demanding its freedom. The thread of blood with which she embroidered her passion finally flows freely.

Mariana's death acquires different levels of meaning. While she is publicly accused of endorsing a subversive type of freedom, her sacrifice becomes a cry for the existential freedom to feel and express one's love. This is a right that the tragic end of most of Lorca's characters negates. Besides, Mariana has been abandoned by Don Pedro, a situation repeated in other plays. Her stubborn refusal to reveal the names of the conspirators and her willingness to die in spite of Don Pedro's abandonment point to a proud and uncompromising attitude tinged by a desire for vengeance. To reveal the names of the conspirators would force Mariana to admit Don Pedro's deceit and the futility of her dreams. Hence, by remaining silent and paying the price of her own life, Mariana proclaims in public the truth and value of the dreams for which society punishes her.

The similarity between Mariana's death and Yerma's (for killing her husband Juan) lies in the fact that both heroines choose death (either a physical death or a living death) rather than compromise their desire. Similarly, Adela, in *The House of Bernarda Alba,* strangles herself when, after she has openly expressed her desire for Pepe, she believes he is killed. Desire admits of no compromise. The tragedy of the character is thus to be reduced to aspiring to something whose very nature requires that it remain out of reach.

The Shoemaker's Prodigious Wife

A first version of *La Zapatera prodigiosa (Farsa violenta en dos actos y un prólogo) (The Shoemaker's Prodigious Wife [A Violent Farce in Two Acts and A Prologue])* dates from 1930; another was presented in 1933 in Buenos Aires, to which Lorca added music and dancing (*OC* 1:1142). In the prologue, written in 1929–1930, the author indicates that he is no longer intimidated by the audience. Therefore, he is not there to ask for the audience's forgiveness or good will, but rather to tell the audience to be more artistically open to new and unconventional perspectives. While he talks, the Shoemaker's wife interrupts him, for as an embodiment of the poetic impulse, she wants to come out from behind the stage and express herself. Boundaries between reality and fiction are thus crossed directly, confronting conventions of theatrical realism; the audience is to understand that theater is the place of artifice, not a servile replica of reality.

The theme is the commonplace one of the young woman married to an older man. The Shoemaker is fifty-three years old and his wife is eighteen. He married her to have company in his old age; she married him because she was an orphan without means of support. Meanwhile, she is constantly dreaming of all the suitors she gave up, admirers existing more in her imagination than in real life. The whole village gossips about the couple's unequal relationship, and they themselves argue constantly. She accuses him of being the cause of her unhappiness, while the Shoemaker, a quiet man who never liked gossip, accuses her of being too outgoing and talkative, a behavior that the village misconstrues as deliberately flirtatious. There is a direct reference here to the inside-outside dichotomy that appears frequently in Lorca's work and is a central concern in this play. The wife is extroverted and, like other Lorcan characters, has been chastised for daring to express her desire. She likes to go out and to fantasize about things in disregard of the rules of propriety. The Shoemaker, on the other hand, guards his privacy and is very concerned about other people's opinion. As a consequence, he feels very repressed.

At the end of act 1 the wife finds out that her husband, incapable of tolerating the turbulent marriage, has left her. In act 2 she has opened up a tavern to support herself. When the Shoemaker has been gone for four months and Don Mirlo and various youths are courting her, the wife has decided to remain faithful to her marriage vows. Her fantasizing is now focused on the figure of her husband, to whom she has transferred all the dreams she first concentrated on her other suitors. The Shoemaker returns disguised as a puppeteer, who, he claims, shows in the works he performs how life is from the inside. The Shoemaker/puppeteer recites a ballad in two parts about a tanner and his wife. The first part parallels his own life with his wife, with the addition of some "creative" touches of his own. The tanner is described as poor, weak, and clearly abused by his stubborn, disagreeable young wife. By exaggerating how helpless the tanner is in the face of his wife's uncaring behavior, the Shoemaker's seems to intend initially to make his wife—whose impressionable and childlike personality has been clearly stated—feel guilty and vulnerable. As if trying to compensate for those innuendos, he then continues with a section praising the tanner's wife's physical beauty. The Shoemaker is thus also preparing his wife for what comes next. The tanner's wife's beauty attracts many suitors, who are described in ways reminiscent of the suitors in the fantasies of the Shoemaker's wife. The husband is portrayed as a decent man who has to suffer humiliation because of what his wife did. The trick works, because the Shoemaker's wife, "who has been sighing, bursts into tears" (*FP* 93).

The second part narrates what could happen if the tanner's wife followed her desire: the death of her husband at the hands of one of the suitors. The recitation is stopped when shouts are heard offstage. As though replicating fiction, the youths, who have been courting the Shoemaker's wife, are having a knife fight over her. The Shoemaker's wife is visibly upset and declares her innocence. In the conversation that ensues between her and the disguised Shoemaker, she confesses her love for her husband. He does not reveal his identity until he is totally certain of her fidelity and commitment. Through the artistic disguises of puppeteer and ballad recitation, the Shoemaker has revealed himself, expressing feelings that he would never dare to reveal without the artifice of art. Artistic creation is thus shown to be the medium for articulating the true feelings of the character, while society's strict, repressive rules reject that truth. The boundaries between reality and fiction, truth and fantasy, are not as clearly defined as society would claim, for art reaches truth in more ways than "reality" ever could. The ballad artifice has a direct impact on the Shoemaker's wife as well, who all along has violently rejected reality in favor of fantasy. She now declares her love for her husband, perhaps not so much for the passion he will bring her as for the warmth and safety he represents. Convinced that his wife has passed the test, the Shoemaker reveals his identity. They decide to resume their lives together and to forget about what other people say. In the end, they are arguing just as they were at the beginning. However, they have come to a better understanding of who they are, instead of wishing for things that cannot be. The wife will put her dreams in perspective and the Shoemaker will free himself of the constraints of public standards.

Only when the wife recognizes the value of what she has *in reality,* and only when the Shoemaker learns to view her fantasizing as her way of expressing herself, and resorts to fantasy himself (his disguise), can they both live together. Fantasy and reality, or desire and an "acceptable" way of fulfilling it, thus find a harmonious compromise, or at least an accommodation, in this play. Imagination, or artistic transformation, enlightens both characters and their situation in society, while their more or less successful accommodation depends on how far they are willing to accept reality and the compromises that it imposes on personal aspirations and dreams.[8]

The Love of Don Perlimplín and Belisa in the Garden

Amor de Don Perlimplín con Belisa en su jardín. Aleluya erótica en cuatro cuadros y un prólogo. Versión de cámara (The Love of Don Perlimplín and Belisa in the Garden: An Erotic Lace-Paper Valentine in Four Scenes: Chamber Version) dates from 1925.[9] Perlimplín, a fifty-year-old bachelor, has always lived with his books. His servant, Marcolfa, convinces him to marry because he will need someone to care for him when she is gone. He confesses that he fears women, but Marcolfa takes him to a window from where he sees Belisa, a neighbor's daughter, barely dressed and singing a song full of childish eroticism. Finally, Marcolfa—with the help of Belisa's avaricious mother, who tells her daughter that happiness is based on money, which Perlimplín has—convinces him to marry. Perlimplín is awakened to desire and love when he watches Belisa through the keyhole while she is getting dressed for the wedding ceremony. That night he confesses to her how love, by the sight of her body, had wounded him.

At this point, two Sprites appear on stage. They draw a curtain over the scene in the couple's bedroom, sit on the prompter's box, face the audience, and begin an exchange filled with double meanings and contradictions. Their conversation centers on the covering/dis-covering of the scene; it is thus reminiscent of the inside/outside dichotomy of *The Shoemaker's Prodigious Wife.* They cover the scene so that the audience will be motivated to uncover its truth. This game of covering and uncovering announces the two concepts of theater that will be confronted in a later play, *The Public:* "theater beneath the sand" (searching beyond appearances), and "theater in the open air" (with the symbolical meaning of remaining at the level of outside conventions). The Sprites are intent on covering up Perlimplín and Belisa so that all is not totally evident and mystery remains. They are magic spirits whose function is to protect the artifice of theater from the invasion of crass realism.

Although conventional wisdom would doom Perlimplín's and Belisa's relationship because of the difference in age and sexual experience of the two, the Sprites suggest other possibilities that might upset such expectations. Their function is to undermine the self-evident, to obscure all-too-easy interpretations, to produce ambivalence and ambiguity. By drawing a gray curtain over the scene, the Sprites also bring to the attention of the audience the artificiality of theater as a spectacle. As they themselves point out, evidence is one thing, "I have seen," and hearsay is another, "It is said" (*FP* 116). The Sprites leave through the darkness, or hidden reality, from which they came, after having injected the scene with uncertainty. As embodiments of the underside of reality, the Sprites question the certainty of the order of reason and objective reality.

When Perlimplín appears in bed the next day crowned with two huge golden horns—showing he is a cuckold—conventional wisdom concludes that the Sprites covered up Perlimplín's humiliation. However, the Sprites' warning about the deception of appearances should alert us to other possibilities, which the play fulfills. While Perlimplín was sleeping, the five balconies in the room were opened. Through them, five men, representatives of the five races of the world, came and "enjoyed" Belisa. This hyperbole connotes the unlimited nature of desire. Rather than feeling resentful, Perlimplín adopts the attitude of a father ready to protect Belisa and to be her confidant. As he says, now that he has experienced love, he understands Belisa's tragedy, a young woman filled with passion but married to an older man who could never satisfy her. He asserts he is above the world's ridiculous morals and conventions. As suggested by the Sprites, Perlimplín has undergone a transformation that is going to subvert the audience's expectations about his character.

Artifice, or disguise, intervenes in this transformation. Since Perlimplín knows that he will never be the lover Belisa desires, he creates an imaginary lover who sends Belisa passionate letters. In them, he confesses his desire for her, but not for her soul, as those afraid of desire would want (and as the audience would expect old Perlimplín to wish for)—but rather for her body. When, at the end, Perlimplín, through his creation of the mysterious lover, meets Belisa in the garden, he is planning to kill himself. His intention is to free himself from his obsession with Belisa's body, the representation of the enigma of desire that he cannot decipher.

Belisa goes to the garden, hoping to find there the fulfillment of her passion, the garden of delights. Instead, she is confronted with a lover who dies in her arms. By dying, her secret lover can never leave her, yet remains forever unreachable. Marcolfa tells her she is now another woman because she is dressed "in the most glorious blood of my master" (*FP* 130). The Christly connotations are pervasive. In scene 2 "all the objects on the table are painted as in a primitive Last Supper" (*FP* 120); the garden reminds us of the "garden of agony," or Gethsemane, and Perlimplín appears clothed in a red cape. Because his blood has been spilled, that is, because desire has again been sacrificed rather than compromised by reality and its limitations, Belisa changes from a woman who knows only how to enjoy sexual love to one who can feel love in all its intensity and scope.[10] With Perlimplín's "sacrifice" however, the ambivalence is preserved, for it appears tainted with the revenge of the old man who is afraid of failing the woman who demands only action. As the critic John Lyon indicates, Lorca leaves us with contradictory interpretations: is Perlimplín's act self-sacrifice "to 'save' Belisa and 'give her a soul,'" or is it "an act of revenge?"[11] As the Sprites suggested, conventional views have been jolted. At the end, Belisa is left alone asking where the young lover is, feeling a passion that will never find its aim, with a longing that will never be fulfilled.

Both Mariana and Perlimplín choose to die rather than compromise their love. The element of pride and vengeance in their death is directed not only against the beloved who does not reciprocate their feelings but also against an existential condition that inherently limits their aspirations. Replicating Lorca's own view of artistic creation, Mariana's and Perlimplín's artistic act is self-immolation and the denunciation of an existential condition that denies their right to fulfillment. Like the act of writing words on the page, Mariana's and Perlimplín's presence (in the embroidering as in the imaginary lover) is maintained only by the absence of the desired object that they purport to represent. Their self-affirmation through artistic transformation entails their dissolution in death.

Similarly, both the Shoemaker and Perlimplín, at first afraid to act, resort to creating a fantasy to give their wives insight into the nature of love. As Lyon indicates, both of these plays deal with the role of imagination in love, or art in the articulation of love. However, they also deal with the tension between art and reality at the heart of Lorca's production. They reveal that art, while surpassing reality, is inherently bound by it. Imagination, or artistic creation, makes Belisa aware of a much deeper dimension of love. Yet it also makes her aware of the tragic impossibility of attaining that new realm of desire. Because she has now been exposed to imagination, her reality seems to her diminished and will never be fully satisfying. In Perlimplín's case, seeing Belisa's real and concrete body framed in the keyhole awakens his awareness of and capacity for feelings.[12] As he becomes aware of the body in all its presence, he realizes that the body, as the site of desire, can never be possessed.

In both plays, the men grow more mature when they realize they have to overcome society's conventions and morals. Through imagination, that is, through their exposure to the realm of art, they learn more about themselves, their loves, their lives. As Lyon remarks, Lorca recognized the human need to fantasize, to go beyond common expectations and limitations. But he also recognized the tension between social pressures and personal desire. His characters' artistic creation is an attempt to articulate a balance between these two poles.[13] Both Perlimplín and the Shoemaker create their own fantasy play. The difference is the denouement: happy for the Shoemaker, tragic for Perlimplín. Lorca is showing not a formula but different outcomes of different personal quests. These characters' creation of a play-within-the-play reveals the autonomy of art, as well as its unavoidable link with reality and social convention.

Dialogues

During 1925 and 1926, Lorca wrote several dramatic dialogues that are called his *teatro breve* (short plays). He referred to them as pure and naked poetry (*SL* 62), thus emphasizing the importance of their artistically constructed structure over any pretensions of realism. These dialogues reflect the influence of Dalí, of surrealism in general, and of Sigmund Freud. The importance of the dream as a language system of meaning in these dialogues (as in Lorca's later plays *The Public* and *Once Five Years Pass*), recalls Freud's *The Interpretation of Dreams,* published in Spanish in the 1920s. Although it is not certain that Lorca read Freud, it is certain that he moved in intellectual circles where discussions about psychoanalysis and its tenets —repression, dreams, the unconscious—played a central role as they related to artistic endeavors such as surrealism. Dalí, whose admiration for Freud is well known, was a likely conversation partner for Lorca on these matters. The Lorca-Dalí friendship was at its peak in the period between 1926 and 1928, and the topic of modernity was a constant in their discussions.[14] An expression of these aesthetic concerns was *gallo,* an avant-garde journal Lorca cofounded with a group of Granadine writers in 1928. This publication recognized the influence of Dalí and other painters, including Giorgio de Chirico and Pablo Picasso.

Freud indicates that the dream has both a manifest and a latent content. It is possible to read Lorca's dialogues and experimental plays as the manifest content of a latent content that we, as readers, are called to interpret. Plots do not correspond to realistic or conventional models or develop logically, nor do they conform to the automatic association of ideas that surrealism advocated. These texts combine seemingly unrelated elements that do not reach a conclusive end, leaving them open to a variety of association of ideas. This lack of coherence is only apparent, for these dialogues possess their own internal logic. Although there are no clear temporal or spatial references, the characters, designated by generic or symbolic names, are paradigmatic of basic human situations. These plays dramatize the situation of the character faced with the welter of information impinging in his/her decisions. They also exemplify the artist's confrontation with the multiplicity of systems that play upon his/her articulation of the word.

El paseo de Buster Keaton, 1928 (*Buster Keaton's Outing*), reflects the passion Lorca and his friends at the Resi felt for films. Keaton is presented on his bicycle, a simple fellow whose lack of self-awareness allows him to enjoy the urban landscape of Philadelphia in spite of its ugliness. Lorca may have been attracted to Keaton for the physical nature of his comedy, devoid of tricks, which probably reminded him of the puppets. This play evolves around two levels of verbal interaction: the purity and simplicity of the exchanges among the characters and the highly literary stage directions. Keaton's encounters with two girls (an American and one with a nightingale's head) fail because of conventional sexual, religious, and literary codes that determine his actions even before he comes into the picture. By juxtaposing the innocent unawareness of the character with a highly codified world, Lorca foregrounds the constructedness of reality and of art. Buster Keaton's final mumbling suggests just how hard a time this innocent character will have in the midst of a self-conscious world.[15]

Failure is also the ending for *La doncella, el marinero y el estudiante,* 1928 (*The Maiden, the Sailor, and the Student*). The maiden embroiders on pillow-cases all the letters of the alphabet so that her male companion can call her whatever name he chooses. She seems to represent a type of verbal system whose letters can be chosen to articulate the desired identity or object. By choosing the letter *M,* a *marinero* (sailor) appears, and with him, the possibility of expressing freedom and adventure. However, the authoritative figure of the ship's captain prevents even the attempt at this. When she picks the letter *E,* an *estudiante* (student) invites her to express herself more intellectually, which leads to inaction. Afraid of the passage of time, the student resists movement (just as the character of the Young Man will do in *Once Five Years Pass*). The maiden, however, rejects both idleness and adventure as unviable for the artistic or verbal expression she represents. So she thinks of possibly jumping from letter *Z* out of the alphabet and thus into the abyss of nonarticulation. However, she is held back by Emilio Prados (1899–1962) and Manuel Altolaguirre (1905–1959), two friends of Lorca and members of the same poetic generation who played a vital role in the editing and printing of many books by various poets of the group. This brief dialogue expresses a central concern in Lorca's life and aesthetics. If the personal and aesthetic freedom of the sailor was what surrealism proclaimed, a liberation from the immobilizing effects of excessive intellectualism, Lorca was also concerned about the risk of nonarticulation if reason were totally disregarded.

In *Quimera* (*Chimera,* scheduled for publication in 1928, in the failed third issue of *gallo*), a quest is undertaken by Enrique, whose name is the Spanish equivalent of *Heinrich,* the name of the protagonist in *Faust.* The title of Lorca's dialogue points to the dreaminess of the work itself. An old man, perhaps a representation of Enrique's fears and doubts about his expedition, tries to hold him back by reminding him of his fear of horses (often symbols of unchained passions in Lorca), and of possible natural dangers (a cyclone, or the sea, also connoting uncontrolled passion). When Enrique leaves, his wife stays behind, consumed with desire for him. His six children ask him to bring them back different animals (a squirrel, a lizard, a mole) or minerals. The child is a frequent symbol in Lorca's works of the protagonist's desire for personal and artistic fulfillment. The six children could represent Enrique's desires within the limits of a conventional family. Their various requests point to Enrique's confusion about his identity. It is possible to suggest symbolic meanings for those requests on the basis of popular belief. The word *squirrel* can be used in Spanish to refer to someone who is restless, sharp, and very lively. The word for lizard (*lagarto*) is used as a safeguard against bad luck, and also connotes an inferior status of life. Finally, the mole is invoked to describe someone who is clumsy and unable to surpass the subterranean level of existence.

Enrique's children want him to bring back to them animal symbols that point to Enrique's repressed sexuality. However, they later seem to prefer minerals, which would connote just the opposite. Instead of bringing forth what is repressed, the request for minerals could represent the intention to petrify, or silence, desire. The children's fight about their requests indicates Enrique's own confusion about his own self and desire. It is possible that Enrique is escaping a life of falsity within a conventional heterosexual relationship; or perhaps his escape is just a chimera in which, again, frustration prevails. His wife is left in the house while he gradually disappears and a cold wind blows up outside. By leaving the safety of conventional family life, Enrique is exposing himself to all sorts of risks, as the old man suspected. In the end, Enrique's daughter is left behind crying for the squirrel she truly prefers over the minerals. She is the next one to feel the longing—the restless squirrel—that will send her on her own search, thus continuing the endless line of unfulfillment.

The "Unperformable" Plays

Lorca characterized the following plays as unperformable because they were so experimental and avant-garde: *El público. Escenas de un drama en cinco actos* (*The Public: Scenes from A Drama in Five Acts,* finished in 1930), *Así que pasen cinco años. Leyenda del tiempo en tres actos y cinco cuadros* (*Once Five Years Pass. A Legend of Time in Three Acts and Five,* finished in 1931), *Comedia sin título* (*Play Without a Title,* also called *El sueño de la vida* [*The Dream of Life*], of which there is only the manuscript of the first act), and *La destrucción de Sodoma* (*The Destruction of Sodom,* composed about 1933 of 1934), which has been lost. It has been said that these plays were Lorca's temporary flirtation with surrealism until he rediscovered his true roots in the rural tragedies. However, the analysis of these works proves that they were no mere experiments; these works show how far ahead of his time Lorca was. As he remarked, the rural trilogy, on which he worked alongside these plays, was written in order to establish his personality and to win respect (*OC* 2:1016), but his true purpose in theater was exemplified by these "unperformable" pieces. More recent critical evaluations convincingly discard the classification of these plays as surrealistic and connect them closely with the early twentieth-century German cultural movement called expressionism. Emphasis on the visual, a major element in expressionism, characterizes Lorca's theater in general, and much of his poetry as well. Lorca himself denied the surrealistic affiliation of his work by insisting on the internal, poetic logic of their structure. Expressionism was a powerful presence in the theater of the 1920s. Its tenets coincide with Lorca's views on theater, in particular its rejection of realism; instead, theatricality, or the visual articulation of subjective realities, was emphasized, as in August Strindberg's and Frank Wedekind's plays, and characters became the visual shape of a particular type or idea.[16] These principles are illustrated in Lorca's experimental pieces.

The Public

The first version of *The Public* was finished in 1930. Lorca very likely wrote it simultaneously with *Poet in New York,* since both works, as André Belamich indicates, are written in the same state of exasperation and fury, of loneliness and alienation.[17] Lorca openly declared that this play could not be premiered because no one would want to stage it and because the public would not tolerate seeing itself mirrored by it (*OC* 2:929). It does offer a challenge to the expectations and conventional attitudes of a typical audience, for it exposes the hypocrisy of society in general as well as of the bourgeois theater in particular. Lorca's intent in this play is to invert a well-known drama, such as Shakespeare's *Romeo and Juliet,* in order to show the hidden side that tradition has silenced. His objective is thus to deconstruct the edifice of conventional literary and cultural evaluation by which meanings are fixed and offered as the only correct view. In this process, other repressed aspects are exposed, such as the homosexual tendencies of many characters, and the artificiality of theater is contrasted with the naive realistic expectations of bourgeois plays and audiences.

Scene 1 shows the office of the play's Director with a blue decor, X-ray photographs in the windows, and a huge image of a hand on the wall. These elements point to a search delving into levels beyond surface reality. The X-rays suggest a penetration into the innermost part of the theater as spectacle and, simultaneously, into the self. The hand, a frequent image in Lorca's work as well as in that of Dalí, is a symbol of creativity (writing/painting) and loving support, as well as the instrument of onanism. The hand sign thus fuses art and passion with solipsism and sterility, which are some of Lorca's recurring concerns. Three men in tuxedos come in and congratulate the Director for the success of his production of *Romeo and Juliet.* This is the level of objective reality, with Shakespeare's play as the subtext for *The Public*'s text. Man 1 voices Lorca's unconventional project for this play. He speculates on the possibility that Romeo and Juliet could be more than merely human, thus suggesting that love could occur under any guise and not just between human beings. The Director, who at this point is a faithful mouthpiece for conventional views, insists that Romeo and Juliet could never stop being a representation of ideal love, since tradition has so decreed. While Man 1 would like theater to go beyond the surface meaning, Man 2 views theater as an artificial medium concerned only with the external and conventional view.

Man 1, also identified as Gonzalo, is willing to kill himself in order to inaugurate the theater "beneath the sand," where that inner reality will be disclosed, and thus end the open-air, or conventional, theater. The Director perceives that such a theatrical change would be terribly received by the public. It means getting rid of the railings on the bridge, a metaphor referring to the barriers that prevent theater from delving into the truth. The public would be outraged, because theater is a pastime and not a place to face uncomfortable truths. Man 1 is determined to expose the Director, who, in a pathetic gesture, tries to find refuge in the convention of heterosexual love by calling Helen (the prototype of female beauty) for help. At this point, the Horses' trumpets are heard. Man 1 goes to the back of the stage to open the door and let them in, because there is ample room for everything and everyone in the theater he wants to inaugurate. Associated with the audience earlier in the play, the Horses expose the level of reality and subjectivity that a conventional audience keeps hidden or repressed. The borders between the two, clearly stated in traditional plays, are here overstepped, as when Man 3 brings out a folding screen that, like a fan, covers and reveals at the same time. When the Director is forced to go behind the screen, he comes out as a young boy dressed in white satin with a small black guitar. This could mean that another identity of the Director's has been revealed: that of a young boy with homosexual tendencies. Both Man 2 and Man 3 also go behind the screen, coming out in outfits that reveal their hidden desires. In this process of disclosing, categories defended by social standards, such as gender, lose their fixedness, thus putting into question the "natural" truth of accepted norms and codes. The discovering process becomes a succession of costumes that fail to reveal a true identity or essence while foregrounding the form as an empty sign.

Scene 2 is entitled "Roman Ruin" and presents two figures, one wearing vine leaves, the other bells. They are transpositions of the Director and Man 1, also with the names of Enrique and Gonzalo. Their dialogue-dance is charged with sadomasochism, each alternately adopting the role of master or slave. Though at first the figure with vine leaves is stronger, the roles are later reversed and s/he is subjugated to the figure with bells. The constant change in their identities recalls the folding screen in the previous scene and the interplay between the inner and outer realms. When the figure with vine leaves blows a silver whistle, a child dressed in a red net falls from above, calling the Emperor. The Emperor enters with the Centurion and four horses and trumpets, offering a scene of sexual potency. In accordance with the power implied in his title, the Emperor takes the child into the ruins. In spite of his apparent control, the Emperor is not fulfilled, because he is searching for the fusion and unity in perfect love. This character embodies the kind of authoritarianism that denies all ambivalence, ambiguity, or difference in order to preserve the illusion of coherence and unity. When he returns, it is indicated that he has killed forty boys who refused to tell him whether they were the "one." He then orders the figure with vine leaves to undress, revealing underneath a white, plaster, naked body, a symbol of the empty or uninhabited body. The Emperor embraces him because "one is one" (*PP* 15). If the "one" is associated with a white and naked plaster body, ideal unity comes to be synonymous with nothingness, emptiness. Man 1, the figure with bells, and the Director cry treason, while the figure with vine leaves and the Emperor embrace.

Scene 3 presents a wall of sand, a gelatinous moon, and a huge green leaf, possibly referring to the theater beneath the sand, the hidden reality over which the moon always presides, and to nature or the forest, in which the characters are searching. The wall opens, and Juliet's crypt in Verona appears. This figure, the paradigm of ideal love, speaks from the other side of life, from the grave. She rejects the promises of everlasting love made by White Horse 1, because she knows love is but one fleeting moment. White Horse 1, plus the three other white horses and Black Horse that appear with Juliet, are possibly the same horses which, in scene 1, represent on stage the hidden side that the Director wants to repress. In their obvious color symbolism, the white and black horses represent the polarity between life and death. The Black Horse, however, knows that love needs to pass its light (or idealism) through dark heat, through the "obscure fevers" (*PP* 25) of sexual desire. So Juliet accepts the Black Horse's vision and refuses to be deceived again by the blandishments of the three white horses. Juliet makes a stand against the tradition that depicts her as the symbol of idealistic love. From the side of death, Juliet knows that the word *love* is a deceit, a broken mirror, an empty sign.

Man 1 accuses the white horses of still searching for the idealized Juliet because they have not looked into their true inner selves. He himself claims to have struggled to get to see the naked form of the Director, the truth of theater and of the self. However, he admits that his attempts may prove unsuccessful because forms keep refracting themselves endlessly. He calls out for Enrique-Director, who enters dressed in a very delicate ballerina outfit with a pale yellow mask; then s/he takes off her dress and appears in a bathing suit covered with bells. The constant change of forms affecting all characters suggests the lack of unity or cohesiveness of their personas and the impossibility of reaching the truth or essence of anything or anyone.

Scene 5 takes place near some back arches and stairs leading to a theater, and on the right is the façade of a university. Center stage is occupied by a vertical bed with a Red Nude crowned with blue thorns, obviously a Christ figure. This is the hidden side—or theater beneath the sand—of *Romeo and Juliet,* as though the audience were seeing X-ray photographs of the performance. This interplay between the various levels of theater reinforces the self-reflexivity of this play, a central feature of the artistic project this work represents. Just as a Male Nurse offers the Nude a glass of gall to drink and prepares to pierce his side —with clear Christly connotations—some students come in speaking of a revolution: the audience that has been seeing the performance of *Romeo and Juliet* is asking for the death of the Director. The revolution broke out when the Director, in the middle of the experimental production of the play *Romeo and Juliet,* opened up the trap doors and allowed the public to see the inner workings of the theater under the sand, thus disclosing its game of masks. Convinced by Man 1, the Director tried to prove that Romeo and Juliet did not need to be man and woman for the scene to work; the character of Juliet was performed as if she were a boy of fifteen. The audience, an example of the bourgeois public that Lorca considered to be the true enemy of authentic theater, could not take it, and it revolted and killed the actors. The greatest victim of this revolution seems to be the Nude, who repeats Christ's words: "Father, forgive these people for they don't know what they are doing" (Luke 23:34). This figure of the Red Nude, a transposition of Man 1/Gonzalo, represents the solitude of the search for authenticity in art and love.

The concluding scene, between the Director and the Prestidigitator, or Magician, is a dialogue about theater. The Magician indicates the need for some kind of curtain or sleight of hand to alert the audience that a metamorphosis is going to occur. In turn, the Director claims to have resorted to a play as well-known as *Romeo and Juliet* because he wanted to show the unexpected, the hidden through the accepted. The inner/outer dynamic, as established by the polarity "theater in the open air/ beneath the sand," is the focus of this play. It is also the mechanism allowing the audience to become aware of the interplay in artistic signs between truth and artifice, identification and aesthetic distance. For this purpose, the Director tried to destroy false theater by exposing its artificiality, but the public could not stomach it. His project led to the death of the actors, for by his attempting to show the hidden side, the void behind the sign was revealed.

A woman dressed in black comes in, looking for her son Gonzalo, but she is only given a moonfish with a thin thread of blood coming out of its mouth. This image is related to the death of the Red Nude, a Christly representation pointing to the failure of Christ's redemption and to the impossibility of giving life to the son as a symbol of generative life, love, and creativity.[18] This figure of Gonzalo/Man 1/Red Nude, the moonfish, is an image of solipsism, of loneliness that cannot overcome itself, of the raw solitude defining human nature. Like the reenactment of Christ's sacrifice in the Mass, Man 1-Gonzalo-Romeo-Red Nude is martyred in this play for attempting to go to the innermost truth of things, for trying to reach the roots of love and identity. The Director and Servant complain of cold, since they have exposed themselves and are therefore condemned by society and the public. The Magician is the only one who feels comfortably warm because he still believes in covering up his true identity with masks.

With the resources and possibilities of the theater beneath the sand Lorca searches into the sphere where life and death fuse, that obscure area from which the *duende*-inspired work emerges, a scary environment into which the true poet has to delve no matter how afraid of it he may be. Yet this play deals also with technical concerns that Lorca had about theater as a multileveled spectacle; about the relationship between author and audience; about the elusiveness of essence in the constant struggle against the mask and endless metamorphoses; about the right of love to occur in all forms, especially the right of homosexual love; about the defeat of expectations in order to stir the audience and its bourgeois beliefs. In the complicated action of this play, it is as though Lorca were consciously and revolutionarily dismantling the four walls inside which so many of his characters were forced to live in fear of society's attacks. Yet in peeling off the first masks, others appear, forever masking the truth. Each character is, in Roland Barthes's words, "a construction of layers . . . whose body contains, finally no heart, no kernel, no irreducible principle, nothing except the infinity of its own envelopes."[19]

The title of *The Public* is a direct reference to the audience within the play. The interaction of theater and audience concerned Lorca starting with his early plays, as expressed through prologues, warnings, and interviews, and the issue took on even more importance after his return from America in 1930. Lorca's objective was to educate the artistic taste of the audience, but he understood that, in order to achieve that intellectual goal, the play had to affect the audience with the pathos of its characters and scenes. The play had to interact both intellectually and emotionally with the audience. This is the interaction that the Director attempted in *The Public,* referring to it as "un dificilísimo juego poético" ("an extremely difficult poetic trick," *PP* 45). At the intellectual level, the audience in *The Public* is made aware of the artificiality of theater: masks, costumes, and folding screens are displayed on stage. Theater is turned inside out, manifesting the impossibility of escaping from the mask and its artifice. But the project of *The Public* was to penetrate through the mask and reveal "el perfil de una fuerza oculta" ("the profile of a hidden force," *PP* 44), the dark force of love, which, like a dagger, pierces the heart with the pathos of its unfulfilled desire. And this "poetic trick" can be achieved only in the audience to which the title appeals. The spectator/reader is confronted with an unending succession of masks, disguises, and forms. The fact that it does not end shows that the search for unity fails, but this failure instills in the audience pathos that refuses to succumb to artistic and existential frustration.

Once Five Years Pass

Once Five Years Pass was finished in August 1931. It was performed in English in 1945 in the Provincetown Playhouse of New York, and it premiered in Spanish in 1954 in Puerto Rico. It has been adapted to ballet as well as a radio play and in a television version (*OFYP* xv).

In act 1 the setting is the Young Man's (Joven's) library, a representation of his mental world, where he wants to remain because he is afraid of the outside.[20] As in other plays, characters confront an outside world that offers possibilities of personal fulfillment as well as a set of rules and restrictions on desire. These people can either conform to the outside demands or oppose them; in either case, the consequences are tragic, for there is no easy way to harmonize these two opposing realms. In *Once Five Years Pass,* the Young Man insists on having the windows shut, because outside, all things are constantly moving, disrupting his inner atemporal world, his solipsism. Since his mental images do not coincide with reality, reality is to be deleted from his consciousness. The conflict between the subjective and objective realms facing the Young Man parallels that between the autonomy of art as a system and its link with reality. At the outset, the Young Man is a representation of the artist who has chosen to alienate himself from reality. He wants to remain within his mental world, his inner language and its own set of rules. The outside world is rejected because its constant changing subverts the stability of the inner world.

This play becomes the Young Man's mental quest for his own identity through the experience of love, which in Lorca is often identified with that of art.[21] The effect time has on love—this play is subtitled *Legend of Time*—applies to art as well.

The five years refers to the period of time the Young Man agreed to wait for his Bride. This period has passed, and now it is time to claim her. She has been on a world tour with her father to have time to think about marriage. The Bride is the prize awaiting the Young Man's search, a search he has willingly delayed because he has relished the anticipation more than the actual fulfillment. As in other plays, to delay pleasure, or go against it because of honor or denial, has fatal consequences.[22] The other extreme is the Typist, who is in love with the Young Man. She represents the prize at hand that the Young Man rejects because he would rather delay his pleasure in favor of the idealized image of the Bride. In the context of the play as a quest for sexual and artistic identity, the Typist represents a kind of love demanding direct fulfillment. The Typist profession suggests a form of writing/behavior directed to capture reality within a fixed and concrete set of signs. There is no room for vagueness or indeterminacy in the Typist's approach; each of the signs in her code corresponds to a referent or concept. The Young Man, because of his sexual indeterminacy and his detachment from the outside world, rejects this option. He would like to desire and love her, but he cannot.

The Old Man (Viejo) and Friend 1 (Amigo 1) seem to be representations of the Young Man.[23] The Old Man agrees with the Young Man's denial of time's passing and keeps telling him how his Bride will stay youthful and beautiful if he keeps her as a dream within himself. If she is seen in her reality, she will age, affected by the air, that is, by time passing. Friend 1 is the image of the present, of acting and doing. If the Old Man anticipates what the Young Man will become if he continues his fruitless, procrastinating life, Friend 1 offers the opposite alternative. He is fully identified with the outside world and its continuous change, and thus he dissolves in a succession of forms, submerged, as he is, in a constant process of making numerous sexual conquests and then losing them. Friend 1's alternative is also unviable, since he, like the Typist, is too superficial for the Young Man and his search for true identity, no matter how falteringly he pursues it. When the three characters (the Young Man, the Old Man, and Friend 1) go behind a folding screen, a dead child with a cat appears. Dressed for burial in his first communion outfit, the child could be an image of the Young Man's childhood. If the Old Man represents the rejection of the present and Friend 1 is the embodiment of the ever-changing present, the child is a past forever lost. All three characters portray the impossible link with an outside world, where temporal change makes fulfilling fusion impossible. The cat is identified as female, rather than male, and described as blue with red spots, possibly wounds inflicted by children. The cat may be the projection of the Young Man's homosexual tendencies as a child and the attacks other children inflicted upon him. That blue cat, the color of idealism, is marked with the red of pain and suffering. The child is said to be the son of the Concierge (who also appears as First Mask) at the Young Man's building. She had that son with Count Arturo, a man from a very different social class. Their union is fruitless and conflicts with societal standards, as can be seen in the fact that the child is dead. This character offers another example of the failure of the son, the fruit of the personal and artistic search. When both child and cat are grabbed by a large hand, the other three characters come out again from behind the folding screen. They are going to bury the Concierge's dead child. Also, the Young Man's servant, Juan, informs him that he needs to remove from his bedroom a cat the children have killed. Thus, the previous scene, which seemed a projection of the Young Man's mental world, now becomes part of reality. The outside and the inside are overlapping, thus foregrounding the question of the boundaries between reality and art.

Friend 2, another representation of the Young Man, looks fragile, which associates him with the Dead Child as a representation of the Young Man's homosexual tendency. The stage directions indicate that this role could be played by a girl. If the Old Man is what the Young Man can expect to become in time and Friend 1 is a present caught up in superficiality, Friend 2 is the desire to return to childhood unconsciousness before time and reason confronted the Young Man with his conflicting tendencies. Friend 2's desire is voiced as follows: "I'll go back for my wings, / . . . I want to die at / the break of day! / I want to die just / yesterday!" (*OFYP* 58–59). At the end of act 1, the Young Man is faced with four options. The Old Man points to the impossibility that either the sign or desire could link with the outside world, since the world is in chaotic flux. Word and object remain distant because of the time separating the expression of the word from the object it represents. The Old Man uses language that implies waiting forever for a fusion that will never be. Friend 1 claims to represent that fusion between word/desire and object, but it would come at the expense of dissipating one's desire in the world. Friend 2 wants to return to the word its pristine original congruence with the object, when time did not exist, while the Typist offers a system of signs with which to encapsulate reality—if one is willing to pay the price of freezing it into a fixed form.

In act 2 the Bride has returned from her trip. At this point the Young Man is to receive the prize for which he has been waiting. The Bride represents the

Young Man's fruitful link with reality, but their meeting proves to be a failure. She is confused about her plans for marriage because of her relationship with the Rugby Player, the embodiment of physical force, of conventional existence, and of sexual libido. By comparison, the Young Man comes across as frail and devoid of vitality. She notices that his kisses are cold and that his hand is like wax. Each is trying to find in the other the mental image they had formed of each other, but their meeting proves the falsity of both preconceptions. The Young Man does not know what to do now with a love he has maintained for five years but which has no recipient. His love is rapidly becoming empty, as represented by the Mannequin dressed in a wedding gown. This character points to the total dissociation of the Young Man's dream from any reality outside, and also shows the emptiness of all the dreams of wedding, procreation, hope, and artistic creation implied in the character of the Bride. The Mannequin protests, demanding her fulfillment. The failure of the wedding implies that the son whom the Young Man and the Bride will never beget would also fail. However, the Young Man, filled with unexpected enthusiasm, finally runs outside in search of the woman who loves him—very likely the Typist.

In act 3 the Harlequin and the Clown explain their presence with a circus in town. However, these figures move in a type of dream world, perhaps the Young Man's unconscious. They sing: "Oh Dream travels on over Time. / It floats like a ship on the sea. / And no one can make a seed burst / in the heart of the sailing Dream" (*OFYP* 122–23). If time destroys everything, so does dreaming, since nothing comes of it. In view of the fruitlessness of his waiting and his quest, the Young Man wanders back home through the forest, which becomes an image of his mental state of confusion and loss.

The Typist appears with First Mask (the Concierge), who is dressed in loud yellow. Roles have been exchanged, because the Typist is now the one who wants to hold back, although she is certain that the Young Man loves her now because he has waited five years for her. The Typist's association with First Mask may imply her loss of a direct link with reality. She no longer speaks in the present tense, but rather in the past or future tenses. The Young Man is the one who emphatically insists in enjoying the present time. He wants the Typist—but only after having failed with the Bride, the true object of his desire. However, his decision to act upon his desire is doomed to failure, because it implies resignation to a lesser good, thus frustration. There is perhaps an element of vengeance in the Typist, who, once spurned by the Young Man, now has the chance to inflict pain on him. As the Young Man's dreams decay, the child, or potential he has inside, feels locked up.

Through the servant, Juan, we find out that the Mask/Typist was probably the Concierge whose son, the child she had with a count who later abandoned her, died. As a character placed at the level of objective reality, the Concierge/ Typist is identified with the Mask, since they deny inner truth. They are both rejected by the more idealistic quester, the Young Man/Count, who in turn fails because his quest denies reality. "Real" characters adopt imaginary appearances, showing the convergence of both planes but also their ultimate incompatibility. As Allen indicates, Juan the servant is perhaps the only real character.[24] He always moves so as not to awaken his master, he opens and closes windows, and informs the audience of the identity of the Concierge and of the death of her child. He thus organizes and structures the Young Man's dream, endowing Lorca's so-called surrealistic plays with poetic logic.

At the end of the play, the scene moves back in the library, where the air is filled with the smell of flowers from the garden. The Young Man has returned from his trip/quest. He is back in the enclosed realm of his mind, and he feels weak and empty. Three card players, who resemble the Parcae, have come to play for his Ace of Hearts, which represents the human heart of the Young Man filled with blood, with obvious Christly connotations.[25] The three card players talk about other people, who, when confronted with death, were able to escape by relying on their vitality. In this game the Young Man is presented with one last chance to come up with the vitality he needs to be a fruitful human being, sexually and artistically. The Young Man's card is an Ace of Hearts, which Player 1 shoots by the bookshelf. This action suggests a denunciation of the Young Man for having led a life devoted to intellectualism at the expense of vitality. The Young Man has lost everything. Death is the result of having committed the crime of endlessly delaying love and pleasure.

As evident in the Young Man's case, it is impossible to lock oneself up in an inner world, avoiding contact with the outside. Lorca himself declared that artists have to laugh and cry with their people. Lorca might be implying that a solipsistic exploration into one's own dreams, as the surrealists were proposing, could lead nowhere. The Young Man idealized the object of his love/art to the point of emptying it of reality, making it sterile. He lost his own child, the one of flesh and blood that he might have had, as well as the one of his artistic creation. However, the Young Man's attempts to come out of himself and live at the level of objective reality, accepting the rules prescribed by society, also prove a failure. This failure is evidence of the impossibility to harmonize inner desires with the outside world. The Young Man's search has taken him on a journey with no successful outcome. The play ends where it began, in the Young Man's library/mind (*OFYP* xvi).

Contrary to the typical values of conventional bourgeois plays of the time (which emphasized unity, realism, and concealment of all traces of the work as an artificially constructed structure), Lorca's dramatic dialogues and "unperformable" plays foreground the cultural and literary conventions involved in their own construction. Roland Barthes's critical designations of the readerly and the writerly text are useful in establishing the difference and modernity of Lorca's dialogues and "unperformable" plays with respect to the theater that was popular at the time. While the readerly text calls for a reader who passively receives the text and accepts its emphasis on coherence, unity, and "the *mastery of meaning,*" the writerly text engages the reader in the production of meaning. Rather than unity, Lorca's writerly plays emphasize heterogeneity and contradiction.[26] These texts do not fulfill the reader's expectation for a closure, or dénouement, where all contradictions are solved. Instead, these plays reject all final closure and emphasize reading as a process. By presenting characters in a state of psychological fragmentation, Lorca questions the dominant subject position in traditional texts. He reveals, instead, the cultural conventions that are an intrinsic part in the formation of the subject. By referring to these plays as "unperformable," Lorca showed that he was aware of the defiance they presented to the "horizon of expectations" of the period. As defined by Hans Robert Jauss and Hans-Georg Gadamer, theoreticians of the aesthetics of reception, the "horizon of expectation" that these Lorcan texts so directly question is the frame of reference constituted by the prevailing ethical, cultural, and literary elements at the time, including the spectator's or reader's knowledge of artistic/theatrical conventions.

Doña Rosita, the Spinster

Doña Rosita, the Spinster or *The Language of the Flowers: A poem of 1900 Granada, Divided into Various Gardens, with Scenes of Song and Dance* premiered in Barcelona in December 1935. Lorca described it as a bourgeois comedy, filled with sweet ironies and evocations of past times: 1890, 1900, and 1910, in particular (*OC* 2:969–70). The three acts correspond to these three different periods and to the three stages in Rosita's life: youth, maturity, and old age, also represented by the colors of the dresses she wears. In this play Lorca portrayed the tragic aspect of Spanish provincial society, and particularly the tragedy of the middle class spinster in a country where such a status is perceived as pitiable, humiliating, and shameful (*OC* 2:975).

The subtitle, *The Language of the Flowers,* refers to Rosita's uncle, who was able to produce a rare species of rose, the *rosa mutabile,* or changeable rose, a flower red in the morning, even redder at noon, white in the evening, and faded at night. Lorca first heard of the *rosa mutabile* in a passage from an eighteenth-century botany book that a friend read to him (*OC* 2:1016). The language of flowers, like that of fans or handkerchiefs, is a code whose signs stand for certain feelings. In lieu of a direct manifestation of passion, the lover may send red roses to his beloved, or a bouquet of white lilies may be placed at the altar of the Virgin to symbolize her purity. Lorca chose the *rosa mutabile* as the poetic sign of passion as subject to the passage of time (*OC* 2:1010). This idea is embodied by the main character, Rosita, whose name is the diminutive of *rosa* (rose). "Through the sky, immobile" the rose always "looked for some-thing else," writes Lorca in "VII. Qasida of the Rose," from *The Divan at Tamarit* (*CP* 677). That "something else" is the forever delayed fulfillment of the rose as a symbol of perfection and fulfillment.[27] As her name indicates, Rosita em-bodies a desire that never coincides with its object, while her passion withers away with time.

A twenty-year-old girl when the play starts, Rosita lives with her aunt and uncle, because her parents died when she was a child. With them lives the housekeeper, the *ama*. The uncle spends his days taking care of the many rare varieties of flowers in his greenhouse, while the housekeeper complains because she prefers fruits—quinces or oranges—filled with vital juices, over the indoor flowers, which remind her of death and other sad things (*FP* 133–34). This initial contrast between nature in the open air and nature enclosed—the inside/outside polarity—is central to the play. The uncle's greenhouse is the enclosed garden that Lorca identifies with his native city of Granada. Growing flowers there represents a type of artistry distant from the outside, open nature. It is an activity that favors preciosity, refinement, and attention to detail, quali-ties of the "Granadine aesthetics" that are the subject of this play and that Lorca elaborated in his 1926 lecture on Soto de Rojas (see chapter 5 of the present study). The character of the housekeeper represents the direct apprehension of the outside world, which Lorca associates with simple country folk, not city people. Hence the housekeeper wants to eat fruits rather than smell sophisti-cated flowers.

When the play starts, Rosita appears on stage wearing a rose-color dress in the style of 1900, and she is all movement and energy. She does not like to sit down and embroider, and her only wish is to go out and do things. The nephew, who is Rosita's boyfriend, comes in to tell his aunt that he has to leave for Tucumán, in South America, to take care of his father's estate. The aunt soon realizes that his departure will be extremely painful for Rosita: "You are going to shoot an arrow with purple ribbons in her heart. Now she'll find out that linen isn't merely to embroider flowers on, but also to dry tears" (*FP* 139). The arrow and purple ribbons are a clear reference to the pain Rosita will suffer. The aunt and housekeeper foresee the painful future that awaits Rosita after her boyfriend's departure. While he will go across the ocean to a life in open nature, Rosita is left behind enclosed within the four walls of her house. The cloth, as the surface on which to embroider pretty flowers and Rosita's trousseau, will fade without ever being used.

The nephew would like to marry his cousin, but the aunt dissuades him until his future is assured. Besides, he might take up with a Tucumán girl, the aunt says. The Spanish expression she uses is *pegar la hebra,* or "thread the needle," another reference to the activity of embroidering or sewing—which doubles as writing—used in relation to sexuality and love. Act 1 ends with a romantic conversation between the two cousins against the background of a musical étude by Czérny. The scene has all the overtones of romantic dramas. In this exchange, and in spite of the cousin's promises to return, Rosita foresees the loneliness that awaits her. Love spills poison on the lonely soul and "will weave with land and wave / the garments of my death" (*FP* 147), Rosita remarks. In her fiancé's absence, Rosita will embroider the white sheets for their nuptial bed that will in time become her cloth of tears and finally her shroud.

This closing scene of act 1 dwells on the artificial. Rosita and her boyfriend express their passion for one another in highly sophisticated terms set in verse. The direct enjoyment of their love is displaced by the flow of verbal images, by a language that calls attention to itself. The character of Rosita, from this point on, becomes fully identified with the symbol that her name represents. Rosita embodies the rose symbol as she strives to reach a fulfillment that can never be identical to the desire she, as a rose, represents.

When act 2 opens, fifteen years have passed since the cousin left. The uncle conducts a conversation with a Mr. X—a possible suitor for Rosita—in which two opposing attitudes are evident. While the uncle rejects new technological advances, Mr. X is a fervent defender of them. Lorca is mocking this character's pretensions of modernity, much as he is ridiculing the rancid conventionalism of Granadine society. The housekeeper complains that she keeps putting unused table cloths away, just like the unused sheets Rosita is still embroidering. Rosita seems unaware of time passing, living in a world all of her own, one which is as she would like it to be, not as it really is. She is still dressed in pink, but the style has changed noticeably. Unlike in the first act, when she liked only to go out, now she prefers to stay inside, for going out forces her to acknowledge the passage of time, as evidenced in all the changes in her surroundings. When the Ayolas—ladies of the Granadine society—come to visit Rosita, they sing a song in which the women's desire is masked behind the language of flowers: "The flowers have a language / for maids who are in love" (*FP* 168). Unable to fulfill their passion in real life, these women are reduced to enjoying the vicarious pleasure that language gives them. This game comes to a head when a letter arrives from Rosita's cousin proposing marriage by proxy. Rosita is very happy, but the housekeeper has difficulties reconciling a proxy with what marriage is for her, the union of two people in the full sense. "Let him come in person and get married" (*FP* 171) cries the housekeeper.

In act 3, ten more years have gone by, and the uncle has died. The proxy never arrived, and it is known that the cousin married eight years earlier. Rosita appears in a pale pink dress in the style of 1910, and she has aged visibly. Both the housekeeper and the aunt suffer for her because she is buried alive. As the housekeeper puts it, hers is an open wound from which a thin thread of blood pours out continuously, and there is no one to come with cotton, bandages, or cooling snow to soothe it (*FP* 176). While other Lorcan characters undergo a violent and quick death, Rosita's is a slow process of withering, a distilling of suffering that, like the thread of blood or the words inscribing her pain, dry up as they leave their mark. The arrival of Don Martín, an old teacher of rhetoric, brings Rosita's quiet tragedy into focus. When Don Martín recites some lines from a drama he has written, the fossilized language echoes the world to which Rosita has remained anchored, and her profound tragedy becomes a cliché, as petrified as the words expressing it. Lorca was highly critical of the excessive conventionalism of the Granadine society of the turn of the century, but he was saddened by the quiet tragedy of its demise as embodied in the character of Rosita. While accepting the inevitable arrival of the new world of technology, Lorca illustrates the plight of people like Don Martín and Rosita. Still enslaved by the demands of their disappearing social class, these characters are forced to face the coming of a society in which their pretensions to elegance and propriety are confronted by a heedless, crass materialism.

Since the house was mortgaged by the uncle to pay for Rosita's dowry, Rosita, the aunt, and the housekeeper are forced to move out. Rosita knows her cousin has married, and each year she has felt more as though people were pointing fingers at her, the increasingly ridiculous spinster still waiting for love. Her dreams of marriage have proved to be a lie. Now she is reduced to going "around and around in a cold place, looking for a way out that I shall never find" (*FP* 184). Rosita is the rose, the sign of a desire that can never go beyond itself. Although she is convinced she will never marry, her torment continues, for her hope, her desire, is still alive. At the end, she is dressed all in white, the clear representation of her fading as a flower of love. The wind is blowing hard, and it is announced that it will not leave any roses alive.

Lorca described this play as calm life on the outside but scorched inside (*OC* 2:1010). For Ian Gibson, Rosita's quiet tragedy echoes that of Granada, a city yearning for the sea, but enclosed within mountains.[28] The narrow views of the Granadine bourgeoisie, patterned after a strict moral and religious code, repressed all spontaneous expression of desire. This repression was, for Lorca, the gravest crime one can commit against oneself. The poetic equivalent would be a word that becomes stultified in preciosity, for fear of the risk it would entail to delve into realms beyond the boundaries of reason and propriety.

Unfinished Plays

Lorca's unfinished plays consist of fragments, notes, and dramatic works-in-progress dating from 1926 until the end of Lorca's life that remained in his family archives after the war started in 1936. Perhaps the most relevant is *Comedia sin título* (*Play Without a Title,* or *The Dream of Life*) possibly started in 1935, which was found in the 1960s by Francisco García Lorca among his brother's papers and first published in 1976. There is only a draft of the first act, dated August 1935 (*PP* xvii–xviii). It is another one of Lorca's "impossible" plays about seeing and saying the truth without fear, about loving and acting according to that truth rather than continuing to repress it. This fragment is related to *The Public,* since both present a play within the play and are influenced by Shakespeare, here by *A Midsummer Night's Dream.* It is as though Lorca had decided to let all the theater's trap doors open, as the Director tells the public in another one of Lorca's unfinished plays, *Dragon,* of which we know only the prologue, dating from around 1928.

In *Play Without a Title,* the Author needs to liberate himself from the pressure the public has placed upon him and go to unexplored territories. The public pays to come to the theater to be entertained. However, the Author is ready to expose truths even if the audience is not willing to face them. Lorca continues his project of making the theater a medium to change people's views, of stirring the audience's comfortable bourgeois beliefs and lives. The Author wants to overstep the boundaries of the theater and have men and women of flesh and blood, not just actors. Conventional boundaries between theater and reality are tested by the exchange between the Author and various spectators, and by the juxtaposition of the fantastic atmosphere of Shakespeare's play with the reality of workers and social upheaval that this fragment represents. As in *The Public,* the "truth" of the characters remains elusive in the constant change of outfits, while "real" emotions are confronted with their theatrical counterparts. The interplay of imagination and reality in Lorca's earlier plays continues in these later works in the question of art—of theater and theatrical conventions, of the poetic sign—and its link with reality.

The French critic Marie Laffranque lists other recovered fragments, including *Posada,* 1927 or early 1928 (Inn), scenes from *Rosa mudable,* 1928 (Changeable Rose, or *Rosa mutabile*), *La destrucción de Sodoma,* 1936 (The Destruction of Sodom; initially referred to as *Las hijas de Lot* [Lot's Daughters]); *La bola negra,* 1936 (The Black Ball), and others.[29] The first act of *Los sueños de mi prima Aurelia,* possible from 1936 (The Dreams of My Cousin Aurelia), has been preserved. It is based on one of Lorca's favorite cousins, Aurelia, for whom Lorca probably entertained feelings of puppy love as a child. It takes place in 1910, the same year Doña Rosita's world falls apart, and the year that symbolically meant for Lorca the end of his childhood, when the family moved to the city away from Asquerosa (today, Valderrubio). These fragments attest to continuous theatrical activity on the part of Lorca from 1926 until his death in 1936. For Laffranque, these unfinished plays not only clarify the trajectory of Lorca's complete theatrical works but also let us see more clearly some of Lorca's major concerns.

Lorca's theater constantly experimented with new approaches so as to articulate the playwright's existential and artistic concerns, and ultimately to communicate them to the audience in the hope of contesting its conventional beliefs. Lorca's plays include human as well as animal and puppet characters. They are classified within a great variety of genres—comedy, tragicomedy, farce, romance, dramatic dialogue, alleluia, legend, drama, tragic poem—while their divisions range from acts to scenes, engravings, and *cuadros* (frames). This wide range of genres and structures reflects Lorca's continuous experimentation with different ways of expression. The author's attention to the theater as an artistic construct goes hand in hand with his denunciation of the hypocritical claims to realism in bourgeois theater. Most of Lorca's plays deal with the inside/outside polarity, also articulated as covering/uncovering, or the mask versus true identity. Bourgeois theatrical realism is but a mask to disguise the uncertainty and ambiguity at the heart of human nature. By uncovering theater's false realism, Lorca reveals the false naturalness of social constructions and the instability of what is perceived as real.

Notes

1. Eutimio Martín discusses *Del amor. Teatro de Animales* in "Federico García Lorca, ¿un precursor de la 'teología de la liberación'? (Su primera obra dramática inédita)" (Federico García Lorca, A Forerunner of the "Theology of Liberation"? His First Play Still Unpublished), *Lecciones sobre Federico García Lorca* (Lessons on Federico García Lorca), ed. Andrés Soria Olmedo (Granada: Ediciones del cincuentenario, 1986) 27–33. In *Federico García Lorca, heterodoxo y mártir* (Federico García Lorca, Heterodox and Martyr) (Madrid: Siglo XXI, 1986) Martín discusses Lorca's other dramatic juvenilia (see especially part 2, section 4, 200–60). For the theme of God the Father and Jesus, see Javier Herrero, "The Father Against the Son: Lorca's Christian Vision," *Essays on Hispanic Themes in Honour of Edward Riley,* ed. Jennifer Lowe and Phillip Swanson (Edinburgh, Scotland: Department of Hispanic Studies, U of Edinburgh, 1989) 170–99.

2. The standard translation of *The Butterfly's Evil Spell* is collected in *Five Plays: Comedies and Tragicomedies,* trans. James Graham-Luján and Richard L. O'Connell (New York: New Directions, 1963) 191–236. This volume also includes *The Billy-Club Puppets, The Shoemaker's Prodigious Wife, The Love of Don Perlimplín and Belisa in the Garden, Doña Rosita, the Spinster,* and music for the plays. References to the plays collected in this volume, abbreviated as *FP,* will be cited parenthetically. For translations of *The Girl Who Waters the Basil and the Inquisitive Prince, Cristobical, In the Frame of Don Cristóbal: A Farce,* and *Dialogue of the Poet and Don Cristóbal,* see *Four Puppet Plays, Play Without a Title, The Divan Poems and Other Poems, Prose Poems and Dramatic Pieces,* trans. Edwin Honig (Riverdale-on-Hudson, N.Y.: Sheep Meadow Press, 1990). References to the plays collected in this volume, abbreviated as *FPP,* will be cited parenthetically.

3. *The Theatre of García Lorca* (New York: Las Américas, 1963) 66.

4. See Francisco García Lorca, *In the Green Morning: Memories of Federico,* trans. Christopher Maurer (New York: New Directions, 1986) 137. Luis Fernández Cifuentes, in *García Lorca en el teatro: La norma y la diferencia* (García Lorca in His Theater: The Norm and the Difference) (Zaragoza: Prensas Universitarias, 1986) 29–44, draws attention to the "transgressive" nature of *The Butterfly's Evil Spell* when viewed in relation to the bourgeois and conventional plays that were popular at the time. Lorca's play threatens the audience's expectations about the characters' and actors' bodies, about space and time, action and dialogue.

5. In chapter 2 of *García Lorca en el teatro,* Fernández Cifuentes presents a thorough study of Lorca's puppet theater as a paradigm of freedom (63–94).

6. See Francisco García Lorca, *In the Green Morning* 144.

7. See p. 1 of *Mariana Pineda,* trans. Robert G. Havard (Warminster, Wiltshire, Eng.: Aris & Phillips, 1987). References to this play and introduction, abbreviated as *MP,* will be cited parenthetically.

8. My thanks to Andrew A. Anderson for his comments on a draft of this chapter.

My reading of this play is indebted to his study on the play, *La Zapatera Prodigiosa,* Critical Guides to Spanish Texts (London: Grant and Cutler, 1991). John Lyon, in "Love, Imagination and Society in *Amor de don Perlimplín* and *La zapatera prodigiosa," Bulletin of Hispanic Studies* 63.3 (1986): 235–45, analyzes the role of imagination in love as the element linking *La Zapatera* and *Don Perlimplín.* For this critic "La Zapatera is not aware of what she has" until she awakens to love through imagination (237).

    9. *Don Perlimplín* is subtitled *aleluya,* which in Lorca's childhood, as his brother Francisco explains *(In the Green Morning,* 182*),* were large sheets of "colored paper, each with a series of drawings . . . making up a story. Each engraving was explained by two lines of verse." See also Margarita Ucelay,"De las aleluyas de Don Perlimplín a la obra de Federico García Lorca" (From the "Aleluyas" of Don Perlimplín to the Work of Federico García Lorca), *Federico García Lorca: Saggi critici nel cinquantenario della morte,* ed. Gabriele Morelli (Fasano, Italy: Schena Editore, 1988) 96.

    10. For Lyon, Perlimplín's death gives Belisa "a spiritual dimension which, from lack of imagination, had previously been denied to her" (238).

    11. Lyon 241.

    12. For Perlimplín and Belisa imagination needs to be understood "as an expansion of consciousness, a fruitful contact with the mystery of the world, not as escape into fantasy or opting out of 'reality'" (Lyon 238, 241).

    13. Lyon 244.

    14. See Rafael Santos Torroella, *La miel es más dulce que la sangre. Las épocas lorquiana y freudiana de Salvador Dalí* (Honey Is Sweeter Than Blood: The Lorcan and Freudian Periods of Salvador Dalí) (Barcelona: Seix Barral, 1984) 93.

    15. See Gwynne Edwards, *Lorca: The Theatre Beneath the Sand* (London, Boston: Marion Boyars, 1980) 48–50. The standard translation of *Buster Keaton's Outing* is included in *Once Five Years Pass and Other Dramatic Works,* trans. William Bryant Logan and Angel Gil Orrios (New York: Station Hill Press, 1989). This collection also includes *Once Five Years Pass, The Maiden, the Sailor and the Student, Chimera,* the film script *Trip to the Moon,* and other works. Page references to the translations included in this volume, abbreviated as *OFYP,* will be cited parenthetically.

    16. For the study of Lorca's "unperformable" plays in connection with expressionism, see Carlos Jerez-Farrán, "La estética expresionista en *El público* de García Lorca" (The Aesthethics of Expressionism in *The Public* by García Lorca),*Anales de la literatura española contemporánea* 11.1–2 (1986): 111–27, and Andrew A. Anderson, "*El público, Así que pasen cinco años* y *El sueño de la vida*: Tres dramas expresionistas de García Lorca" *(The Public. Once Five Years Pass,* and *The Dream of Life*: Three Expressionist Dramas by García Lorca), *El teatro en España. Entre la tradición y la vanguardia 1918–1939,* ed. Dru Dougherty and Francisca Vilches de Frutos (Madrid: CSIC, Fundación García Lorca, Tabapress, 1992) 215–26.

    17. André Belamich, "Claves para *El público," Federico García Lorca: Saggi Critici nel cinquantenario della morte,* ed. Gabriele Morelli (Fasano, Italy: Schena Editore, 1988) 109. For Belamich this play denounces existential deceit in all its forms;

a series of masks or costumes never reaches the core of true being, which remains elusive. Love is also a lie, a game of mirrors and an endless spiral (111–13). In 1976 Rafael Martínez Nadal, a friend of Lorca's, published a facsimile edition in London of an incomplete manuscript of this play given to him by Lorca, who had requested that the manuscript be destroyed if anything happened to him. During the Civil War, Martínez Nadal entrusted the manuscript to a friend and did not recover it until 1958. It was not published until 1976 because Lorca's family was still hoping that one of the later complete manuscripts could be located. Martínez Nadal believes there must have been at least two other manuscripts of this play. See also Rafael Martínez Nadal, *Lorca's 'The Public': A Study of His Unfinished Play and of Love and Death in the Work of Federico García Lorca* (London: Calder and Boyars, 1974); and María Clementa Millán's introductory study in her edition of this play (*El público* [Madrid: Cátedra, 1987] 13–112). For the translation of this play and of *Play Without a Title*, see *Federico García Lorca:* The Public *and* Play Without a Title. *Two Posthumous Plays,* trans. Carlos Bauer (New York: New Directions, 1983). Page references to the translation included in this volume, abbreviated *PP,* will be cited parenthetically.

18.   For the moon/fish image, see José Angel Valente, "Pez luna" (Moon Fish), *Trece de nieve,* 2d series 1–2 (1976): 191–201.

19.   Roland Barthes, "Style and Its Image," *The Rustle of Language,* trans. Richard Howard (New York: Hill and Wang, 1986) 10.

20.   See Lima 158.

21.   For a reading of *Once Five Years Pass* as a search for sexual identity, see Dennis A. Klein, "'Así que pasen cinco años': A Search for Sexual Identity," *Journal of Spanish Studies XXth C.* 3.2 (1975): 115–23. For a detailed psychological reading, see Rupert C. Allen, *The Symbolic World of Federico García Lorca* (Albuquerque: U of New Mexico P, 1972) 61–157.

22.   See Gibson, *A Life* 315.

23.   See Lima 158.

24.   Allen, *The Symbolic World* 153–54.

25.   For an elaboration on the three players, see Allen, *The Symbolic World* 144–53.

26.   Roland Barthes, *S/Z* (Paris: Seuil, 1970) 174, 5–6.

27.   Marie Laffranque establishes the correlation and contemporaneity of Lorca's "qasida" and *Doña Rosita* in "Federico García Lorca, de *Rosa mudable* a la 'Casida de la rosa,' " *Lecciones sobre Federico García Lorca,* ed. Andrés Soria Olmedo (Granada: Comisión Nacional del Cincuentenario, 1986) 279–300.

28.   Gibson, *A Life* 404–5.

29.   See *Teatro inconcluso: Fragmentos y proyectos inacabados,* ed. Marie Laffranque (Granada: Universidad de Granada, 1987), especially the study-prologue, 7–99.

CHAPTER 5

Prose Works, Visual Arts, and Music

This chapter will address some areas of Lorca's artistic production that have received much less critical attention than his theater and poetry, but whose variety attests to the scope of the author's talent: his prose works, drawings, his foray into the field of cinema, and his musical activity.

Prose Works

The prose works discussed here include Lorca's first published book, *Impresiones y paisajes,* 1918 (*Impressions and Landscapes*), his lectures, and a series of prose poems, or narrations.[1]

Impressions and Landscapes

Impressions and Landscapes was subsidized by Lorca's father and published in a limited edition. Censorship during the Franco regime did not permit the complete version of this book to appear until the eighteenth Aguilar edition of the *Obras completas* (Complete Works) in 1973.[2] The book is a series of articles from four educational trips, under the direction of Don Martín Domínguez Berrueta, professor of theory of literature and the arts, in which Lorca participated while enrolled at the University of Granada between June 1916 and September 1917. The group of students visited places of cultural and artistic interest in Andalusia, Castile, León, and Galicia.

As the title indicates, this is a series of impressions or reflections upon the landscapes of the various places the group visited. The inner and outer realities are thus fused in the text, corresponding to Lorca's aesthetic theory at this time. In the prologue the young author states how the artist should be open to all emotions from the outside world, which should then be internalized and transformed in order to be offered to the reader as the artist's own spiritual reaction to sensorial reality (*IL* 3). The various elements in the landscape are apprehended as signifiers or visual images of a signified, or content, that is no other than the "soul" of that landscape. These articles are not intended to be faithful depictions of the physical reality of the landscape, but transformations; they are filtered through the artist's self in an interpretative process.

This filtering of outside reality in the transformation that is the creative process entails uniting pathos and form at the point where the expressive character of the work of art resides. Starting early in his career, Lorca was aware of the social resonance of art, and he was concerned about the impact religious art, and art in general, could have on the public. Common people modeled their visions of the afterlife on vulgar images of saints like those of holy martyrs St. Cosmas and St. Damian, whose statues Lorca saw at the collegiate church in Covarrubias: "two stupid-faced manikins garbed in faded damask, with heads of hair stiff and pressed down, and with very big, very dusty hats" (*IL* 40). These artless representations were thwarting the imagination and artistic sense of the people. In his *Impressions and Landscapes,* Lorca repeatedly condemns the gaudiness of the paintings and sculptures in most of the churches, convents, and monasteries he visited, mainly in Old and New Castile. He recognizes that some works display excellent artistry but lack true pathos, while in others, the emotions of horror and fear, directed to impress the ignorant faithful, are overdone at the expense of artistic balance and good execution (*IL* 23). Lorca's *Impressions and Landscapes* offers a commentary not only on art, and on art's central role in shaping the aesthetic and ethical sense of the audience, but also on the role of religion. The young author expresses his belief in the interconnection between religious and aesthetic elements in the work of art. The religious aspect should be "subordinated to the aesthetics," as Martínez Nadal indicates, while aesthetics is required for the transmission of a richer and more faithful religious message.[3]

The group's visits to several convents and monasteries allow the young author to express his unorthodox views about religion. The insistence of the official church on separating spirit and form, soul and flesh, and its rejection of human desire as sinful, were for Lorca the source of much human suffering. He was therefore quick to condemn the cloistered life of monks and nuns as un-Christian, since it favors seclusion over a life of sharing love with others. Love is the search for a harmonious fusion between body and soul, flesh and spirit, emotion and form, the individual self and the outside world. At this early age, Lorca clearly perceived the distance separating official religion from the heart's tragedy and desires, and from the world surrounding it.

In his critical commentary of this book, Lawrence H. Klibbe remarks on the lack of references to the great world events taking place at the time, such as the World War I and the Russian Revolution.[4] However, such direct references would not fit within the aesthetics of this book, which shows that

Lorca is not interested in reporting, but in offering his personal impressions of the landscapes and places he visited. While openly involved in public causes— as attested in interviews and declarations—and committed to creating an art (especially theater) that communicated with the audience, his works (his later plays in particular) seek to achieve communication without bypassing the work as an artistic construct. Social awareness is found, however, in several sections of *Impressions and Landscapes,* about the people's destitution, especially peasants, and about the anguish, barrenness, and poverty of the land, especially in Castile, where the fields are "all kneaded with blood inherited from Cain and Abel" (*IL* 7). Castilian men are enslaved by nature, while the women are sacrificial victims of their own procreating nature, forced to repeat the same cycle of poverty (*IL* 17), as Lorca himself witnessed at the old Castilian inn. In "An Orphanage in Galicia" (*IL* 126–27), he directly addresses social injustice to children. These concerns continue to be expressed, especially after the author's return from America, in different declarations on the need for social equality and justice. Time and its eventual erasure of all vitality is another essential concern in this first book, as seen in the comments on the sepulchers of Burgos and in the section on gardens. The heavily decorated sepulchers in many churches attested to the human desire for immortality, but the young author saw them covered with dust and their names almost erased. In "A Romantic Garden" (*IL* 99–102), the world of the madrigal, of laces, silks, vases, of the eternal romantic *she,* of the fair hands upon the keyboard, has given way to the railroad. The garden is now the cemetery for all those relics from the past. Yet, if at first the young writer rejected the loss of the romantic garden, at the end he accepts it in view of more urgent demands, such as hunger: the flower garden has to give way to the vegetable patch.[5]

The emphasis placed on the subjective transformation of reality is further developed in the essay "Granada (Paraíso cerrado para muchos)" (Granada [Paradise Closed for Many], *OC* 1:936–40), in which the author elaborates on the Granadine aesthetics of the diminutive. Granada's taste for reduced dimensions is determined in great part by its location. The city is surrounded and limited by hills. Unlike Seville or Malaga, both open to the sea, Granada is closed within itself. Lacking space, it keeps its imagination within the boundaries of very detailed and elaborate works. Thus the typical structures in Granadine aesthetics are the small garden and chambers. In "Semana Santa en Granada" (Holy Week in Granada, *OC* 1:941–44), Lorca elaborates on the personality of his native city, fragmented between its Arabic nature, as represented by the Alhambra (Arabic palace), and its Christian personality, as exemplified by the palace of Emperor Charles V. The division Lorca perceived in his native city echoes the contradictions that he himself experienced between instincts and reason, passion and spirit, language and reality, not only in these early writings but throughout his career.

This early book contains impressions about music as well. Lorca was well versed in classical music, especially in piano, which he had played since childhood, as well as in the popular and traditional songs of his country. However, he despised some of the popular rhythms (*pasodobles, habaneras, cuplés* [two-step], Cuban, and pop songs, *IL* 71), viewing them as musical forms pleasing to the vulgar taste of the middle class, the social group he frequently attacked for its conventionality. Hearing these tunes being butchered by the driver of the car taking the group on tours was more than he could tolerate.

Leaving aside the debt of this first book to Lorca's readings of authors from the modernist, Romantic, and symbolist traditions, and from the 1898 generation (Azorín, Machado, Unamuno),[6] several aspects stand out: themes and concerns about religion, art, and music that are announced here will recur throughout Lorca's career; a social consciousness is displayed that will only increase with time; and, above all, a strong position about his art is staked out. The Lorca of *Impressions and Landscapes* emphasizes the artist's need to transform reality by informing it with his feelings and emotions. His landscapes are directly and consciously affected by the artist's gaze, which converts the mere scene into a seen landscape from which their artistry originates.

Lectures

Lorca's lectures offer invaluable information for the understanding of his artistic production and the development of his aesthetics. He began to lecture early in his career, in 1922 in Granada, when he spoke about Deep Song, and continued throughout his life in Madrid, New York, Cuba, Buenos Aires, Montevideo, Barcelona, and other cities.[7] Lorca's aim in lecturing was to establish a chain of spiritual solidarity with others (*OC* 1:1106). Thus he repeatedly stated his wish to break away from the evils normally affecting lecturers and lecture-goers, that is, pretentiousness on the part of the lecturer who does not make any attempts to communicate with his listeners, and the resulting boredom and unresponsiveness on the part of the audience (*OC* 1:1083). Therefore, for him, lecturing was not a mere presentation of a topic for which the lecturer had studied and prepared, but a means of communicating through art. Lorca counted on generating enthusiasm in the audience by using poetry as a weapon against intellectual laziness and indifference. As Marie Laffranque indicates, Lorca's lectures are prose pieces carefully crafted with a clear didactic and aesthetic-social intent.[8] The same attempt to communicate and enlighten through art is evident in the prologues of many of Lorca's plays, in which he addresses the public directly, in his frequent poetry recitations and readings of his plays to friends, and in the way all barriers came down when he sat at the piano to play and sing popular Spanish songs. The links in the "chain of spiritual solidarity" with the audience were actively connected throughout the various manifestations of Lorca's artistic career.

The first version of his lecture "Deep Song: Primitive Andalusian Song," delivered in 1922 as part of the events surrounding the Festival of Deep Song (see chapter 1 of the present study), was repeated almost unchanged in Cuba, Spain, and Buenos Aires between 1930 and 1933 (*DS* 23–41) under the title "Architecture of the Deep Song." Deep Song attracted Lorca because of its "marvelous artistic truth" (*DS* 23). Like his friends also involved in the Deep Song Festival, Lorca was committed to salvage this art form from the false notions that confined it to seedy taverns. Lorca's lecture is based on Manuel de Falla's research on the subject. Part of the approach is to emphasize the ancient roots of Deep Song and the historical facts that contributed to its development. The scholarly tone is intended to restore to this art form the prestige and value it had been losing by its association with other, more popular, forms, like flamenco. The lecturer points to the origin of Deep Song in the primitive musical systems of India. These songs carry in their notes "the naked, spine-tingling emotion of the first oriental races" (*DS* 25). Deep Song is profound, *jondo,* or deep, coming "from the first sob and the first kiss" (*DS* 30).

Deep Song did not result simply from a transplantation from the East to the West, but from a merging of many sources. The similarities between Deep Song and some songs from India are found in enharmonic modulation, restricted melodic range, and the almost obsessive reiteration of one single note (*DS* 26). Always following Falla's research, Lorca points to three historical factors that contributed to the emergence and development of Deep Song: "The Spanish Church's adoption of Byzantine liturgical chant, the Saracen invasion" and occupation of the Iberian Peninsula from 711 until 1492, "and the arrival in Spain of numerous bands of Gypsies" in the middle of the fifteenth century (*DS* 26). These groups were able to fuse their own songs with the musical substratum they found in Andalusia, producing the Deep Song.

Historical research can establish the antiquity of Deep Song. However, the other aspect of Lorca's approach to this topic has to do with the connection between Deep Song and his own artistic views. The dominant mood in Deep Song is sorrow or pain, as in Lorca's writings. Its corollaries—love, death, and the terrible question of the mystery of human existence—are found at the root of all these songs and of Lorca's art. The popular poet composing these songs is able to condense in three or four lines the complexity of life's most intense emotional moments. These musical expressions depict only emotional extremes. In these songs, Lorca also found the fusion of form and pathos for which his art strived. The lecturer remembers the marvelous *cantaores,* or singers, of Deep Song. Their voice is a zigzag emerging from their soul, charged with a deep religious feeling as if they were celebrating a solemn rite. Thus they function like a medium through whom the people's pain is voiced. The *cantaor* is for Lorca the epitome of the artist as martyr on the altar of the passion he feels and expresses in his singing. This lecture condenses Lorca's aesthetic position during the period 1920–1925; as Laffranque indicates, Lorca was concerned with tradition and with the latest expressions in art.[9] But it also reveals the coincidences between Deep Song and what were already Lorca's views on art and the artist. Deep Song offered the most authentic artistic manifestation of the Andalusian spirit in a form that combined emotion with the stylization and restraint that the new generation of poets were attempting to create in their works.

That group of poets, commonly referred to as the generation of 1927, found in the aesthetics of seventeenth-century Spanish baroque poet Luis de Góngora the epitome of their search for an art form pure in form and execution (see the introduction to the present study). In 1926 Lorca delivered his lecture "The Poetic Image of Don Luis de Góngora," and he gave it again in 1927, the year commemorating the tercentenary of Góngora's death (*DS* 59–85). Lorca sees in Góngora the artist who conquers time by constructing a new type of beauty solidly founded on the quality and perfect fit of poetic images. The Gongorine model describes the artistic process as a hunting expedition: the artist hunts images in nature, and takes them to the dark chamber of the mind, in which, in a state of calm inspiration, away from external excitement, they are recreated and transformed into autonomous artistic entities. Góngora's art departs from nature to create, with all the arrogance and responsibility of the artist convinced of the capabilities of his craft, another world. This artistic assuredness attracted Lorca's generation of young poets, who were totally dedicated to the ideal of pure poetry and who shared Góngora's concern with poetic images as separated from nature; weaving them together would create the solid fabric of the work of art impervious to time. By what Lorca describes as "an equestrian leap of the imagination" (*DS* 66), the metaphor fuses two apparently opposed realities, resulting in a new one, that of the artistic image as a world apart, carefully and consciously crafted, antinatural and antirealistic. Góngora never allowed himself to be carried away by the dark forces of the subconscious, but always kept his imagination bridled. Lorca recognized, as did Góngora, the role that sensorial reality plays in the work of art, but he also acknowledged the need for the artist to avoid being controlled by it. He has to be the one directing the senses toward the achievement of an image whose formal beauty will construct the artistic edifice with which to defy the destruction of time.

In 1926 Lorca presented the lecture "Paraíso cerrado para muchos, jardines abiertos para pocos (Un poeta gongorino del siglo XVII)" (*OC* 1:1026–33; A Paradise Closed to Many, Gardens Open to a Few [A Gongorine Poet of the Seventeenth Century]), about the author Don Pedro Soto de Rojas. A native of Granada, Soto de Rojas represents the Granadine aesthetics of preciosity, of preference for small objects, for intimacy, for detailed descriptions in which, as in Góngora, reality is placed at a distance from the artistic creation. Soto is an interesting figure for Lorca because his work articulates the tempo and personality of Granada, a city whose identity plays a central role in Lorca's writings. Lorca finds in Soto the elements that characterize the Granadine temperament and that he had already explored in some of the essays in his *Impressions and Landscapes:* preference for seclusion and isolation, for small spaces, as represented in the typical Granadine architecture of the *carmen,* or secluded garden, of contemplation rather than action. Soto embraced the ideal of pure and abstract poetry defended by Góngora, but instead of dealing with immense spaces—ocean, forests—as found in the work of his contemporary, Soto remained in his garden, ordering nature according to a domestic sensibility. The Granadine temperament is the opposite to the Sevillian, for while Seville is the enclave of sensuality, of political intrigue, of external reality and triumph, Granada is a city of retreat and withdrawal, of sexual repression and frustration.

During this period Lorca underwent profound changes in the theory of his art. The increasing popularity of *The Gypsy Ballads* was becoming a source of embarrassment for Lorca (*SL* 94), because it gained for him a reputation as a popular Gypsy poet, while the artistry of the poems was ignored. He felt oppressed in the provincial and narrow-minded atmosphere of Granada and ill at ease with his work: "encuentro en todo una dolorosa ausencia de mi *propia y verdadera* persona" (I find in everything a painful absence of my *own and true* being), he wrote to a friend (*OC* 2:1099; emphasis in the original). His involvement with the surrealistic magazine *gallo* was aimed at awakening Granada from its romantic and sentimental sleep to the new currents in art. As mentioned earlier, his stay in Catalonia with Dalí during the spring and summer of 1927 had a crucial impact on the evolution of Lorca's aesthetics.

Lorca's letters to his friend, the Catalan critic Sebastiá Gasch, in the summer of 1927 after his return from Catalonia, attest to the poet's profound aesthetic meditation during this time. He says he is drawing intensely as a way of better understanding the world around him *(SL* 121). He also repeatedly affirms his resistance to losing control over his work by falling into the world of dreams and the unconscious as proposed by the surrealistic program. Lorca is defining his aesthetic position, one distant from the old Romantic and sentimental poetry as well as from a blind adherence to the new surrealistic modes. His work and aesthetics take a new course in 1928, as expressed in his correspondence from that year. Lorca says he is fully involved in the creation of a type of poetry that evades the limitations imposed by objective reality. The new writing demands opening up one's veins (*SL* 139); this writing is a painful activity stemming from the core of the poet's being, a new, spiritual manner of writing (*SL* 135) free from logical control but endowed with its own poetic logic.

The lecture "Imaginación, inspiración, evasión" (*OC* 1:1034–40; Imagination, Inspiration, Evasion), delivered in Granada in 1928, elaborates on the aesthetic principles expressed in Lorca's letters of that same year. Imagination, and its daughter the metaphor (the essential tool in Gongorine art), are placed here at the most basic level in the creative process, since they depend on reality, from which they normally need to originate. The true artist must move from imagination to inspiration, and its poetic logic, which gives rise to the poetic fact or event. This poetic fact is a kind of artistic miracle, since it is ruled by its own internal laws and stands as a manifestation of artistic truth. Through inspiration, poetry is liberated from analogical constraints with outside reality, thus allowing for the flight into the realm of poetic reality. There, the poetic fact, as the articulation of poetic truth, stands free of any mimetic links with banal reality.

These ideas, as they apply to the plastic arts, continue to be elaborated in "Sketch de la nueva pintura" ("Thoughts on Modern Painting"), delivered also in 1928. In this lecture, the end of modern Gongorine aesthetics is seen as coinciding with that of cubism. Lorca recognized the important role played by both artistic manifestations—Góngora's and the avant-garde's—in returning to art its autonomy. Thanks to them, art stopped being merely the realistic rendition of the object and was directed at capturing the object's artistic nature. However, cubist attention to "pure" and geometric forms in painting led, according to Lorca, to cerebralism. By way of reaction, surrealism allowed modern art to supersede the level of objective reality by delving into the instinctive and subconscious areas. But rather than rejecting the control of logic altogether, as surrealism proposed, Lorca's superseding of reality, as stated in "Imaginación, inspiración, evasión," calls for a new type of writing, in contact with instincts and with the center of the soul, but endowed with its own poetic logic.

Also from 1928 comes the lecture on Spanish lullabies, "Añada. Arrolo. Nana. Vou veri vou. Canciones de cuna españolas" ("On Lullabies," *DS* 7–22). These are songs Lorca compiled during his trips to different Spanish regions. Bored with cathedrals and dead stones, he looked for these songs, for they artistically captured life in all its trembling present. Lorca points to the sadness that characterizes the Spanish lullaby, and to the fact that Spanish children are put to sleep by melodies in which the expression of loneliness prevails over the expected manifestations of tenderness and love in children's songs. In Lorca's view, the explanation for this unusual kind of lullaby is found in its origin; these songs are the invention of wretched women for whom having children is more a burden than a source of happiness. In the lullabies the women cannot help but voice their resentment of the child and their weariness with life.

This aggressive element in the lullaby must have attracted Lorca, who always recognized the painful and wounding nature of true art. Lullabies are compared to an artistic expedition: through the lullaby, the mother takes the child away into a new reality, the realm of art, a space that recalls those of inspiration and evasion discussed in "Imaginación, inspiración, evasión." And no one is better equipped to go on this journey than the child, who for Lorca is endowed with a poetic sense of the first order. The child lives in an inaccessible poetic world, a plane of horror and acute beauty with "its nerve centers exposed" to the air, and where a "snow-white horse" (like the horse in *Blood Wedding*'s lullaby) falls injured with "a swarm of furious bees at its eyes" (*DS* 15). This astonishing image of the poetic realm of the child describes Pegasus, the white horse of imagination and poetry, being attacked by the fury of its own poetic potential—the bees and their honey of creation. Horror and extreme beauty, sweetness and cruelty, fuse in the poetic realm. There, conventional reason and logic have no place.

The period from 1929 until Lorca's death in 1936 includes his trip to New York, where the poet's aesthetic position consolidated and he became keenly aware of his responsibilities as an artist. His humanity—the pain, suffering, and love—is at the core of his creative activity and in solidarity with that of his public. From this period comes Lorca's lecture "Juego y teoría del duende" ("Play and Theory of the *Duende*," *DS* 42–53). In Andalusia, a bullfight, a dance, certain music, or a person is said to have *duende* when marked with a type of grace and passion mixed with mystery and danger. For Lorca *duende* is found in extreme situations, in the "black sounds" of dissonant music, on the borders where life and death mingle. *Duende* is a mysterious power, a struggle of never-resolved, opposing forces. Different from artistic virtuosity or technical competence, the *duende* ascends from within the artist, possessing him.

Lorca establishes the difference between three types of artistic inspiration: the *duende,* associated with Spain, the muse (connected with Germany), and the angel (with Italy). While the muse dictates to and awakens the artist's intellect—often an enemy of poetry—and while the angel flies over the poet's head, showering him with grace and light, the *duende* moves in subterranean provinces of death from which both muse and angel flee. The inspiration of the muse and the angel comes from without, while that of the *duende* comes from within, from the depths of human nature, from the spirit of the earth. By the time of this lecture Lorca has clearly moved from emphasizing the realm of imagination and metaphor to concentrating on the dark inspiration of the *duende,* which puts the artist not in a state of calm and repose as described in his Góngora lecture, but in a state of struggle and vigilance. Through the *duende,* the artist evades objective reality and moves into the center of being, a realm of unknown and inexpressible norms and emotions where no logical rules work.

Although any artistic manifestation may arise from *duende,* Lorca finds its most authentic expression in music, dance, and spoken poetry: artistic forms that require a moving body. In Lorca's view, Spain is particularly receptive to *duende,* because it is a country open to death. Death, which Lorca finds all around him—in the razor, in the lace-covered statues of saints, in the naked moon, in flies, on moist pantry shelves, and in torn-down buildings—wounds the sensitivity with the awareness of man's temporal nature, marking artistic expression with its void. While muse and angel flee when they see death approaching, the *duende* does not come unless death appears: "the *duende* enjoys fighting the creator on the very rim of the well" (*DS* 50). The *duende* wounds, and art emanates from the attempts to heal that wound, which never closes. *Duende*-inspired art is a succession of newly created forms in search of unknown landscapes. It is here that Lorca's art moves, the liminal areas where desire encounters frustration, where the healing is never complete and desire never fulfilled.

Lorca's lectures present a summary of some of his artistic interests, showing both the development as well as the continuity of his aesthetic views. Although the Gongorine model is superseded by the aesthetic model presented in "Imaginación, inspiración, evasión," Gongorine tenets concerning form continued to play an important role in Lorca's later writings. Thus, these lectures show more than a mere superseding of old ideas by newer and better ones; there is a tension, as in

Lorca's own writings, maintained among these various aesthetic approaches.

Prose Poems

Soon after the publication of *The Gypsy Ballads,* Lorca began to express his discomfort at being labeled a Gypsy poet (*SL* 94). He wanted to distance his person from his artistic endeavors, his biography from his production. *The Gypsy Ballads* did not interest him any longer, for his poetry had now taken another turn, becoming more personal and intense (*SL* 136). Around this time (September 1928), he mailed to a friend several prose poems, including *Nadadora sumergida* (*Submerged Swimmer, CP* 613–14) and *Suicidio en Alejandría* (*Suicide in Alexandria, CP* 615–16). As Lorca explained, these prose poems responded to his new way of writing, a spiritualist manner of pure and naked emotion freed from the control of reason but endowed with the greatest poetic logic (*SL* 135). He denied that they were surrealistic poems, because the clearest consciousness illuminated them. There are six known prose poems, or narrations—or seven if one considers *Degollación de los Inocentes* (*Beheading the Innocents*) and *Degollación del Bautista* (*Beheading the Baptist*) as two separate poems rather than as two parts of the same one.[10]

In *Submerged Swimmer,* the speaker, in a dialogue with a Contessa, tells her that he is in love with a woman who left half of her body in the northern snow—possibly the submerged swimmer. That woman could be the embodiment of an aesthetic ideal that the speaker identifies with the old literature he is now giving up. The new artistic program will have to inject old norms with new life. Perspectives will be challenged, as well as the conventional link between the work of art and reality: "The elephant must see through the eyes of a partridge, and the partridge walk with the hooves of a unicorn" (*CP* 614). The Viennese waltz, a representation of old European values, will become the American waltz, implying the overthrowing of the old for the sake of the new. At the end, the Contessa is found dead on the beach with a fork stuck in her nape. No one knows the identity of her "marvelous killer," so her death is attributed to her love of swimming. Like the woman half submerged in the snow, the Contessa embodies a type of decadent aesthetics that the speaker has abandoned.[11]

Suicide in Alexandria consists of short paragraphs with numerals inserted between them, starting in pairs, with 13 and 22, and reducing each by one until it reaches the pair 1 and 10, and ends in vertical form, a countdown from 9 until 0. If one adds both numbers in each pair, the outcome is the same for both parts: "13 and 22," 13: 1+3 is 4; 22: 2+2 is 4, and the same with the rest. The even and odd difference between the numbers of the pairs is eliminated through the operation of adding their elements. The addition of the elements of the last pair, 1 and 10, is 1, which could signify the merger of the two lovers who, through their embrace, become one. Likewise, the vertical countdown could be a numerical representation of the life leaving their bodies, until 0, signifying death. The use of numerals counteracts the emotionally charged short paragraphs about suicide and despairing love. It is also contrasted with the surrealistic images (a severed head, whips, eyes threaded on a string), with the world of Romantic and idealistic poetry (the "roses" and the typical love scene at the end), and with the cultural codes implicit in the references to the Eiffel Tower, London, and Alexandria. The numerals thus create the distancing effect that Lorca wants to achieve in all these prose poems. The narration refers to a *they* whose only wish is to commit suicide, to end it all. This desperate position, together with the mixing of those various cultural and literary codes, raises the question of personal knowledge in the midst of so many different and conflicting messages.

Amantes asesinados por una perdiz (*Two Lovers Murdered by a Partridge, CP* 617–19) is a homage to French novelist Guy de Maupassant, famous in the school of Realism for his bourgeois characters and settings. In Lorca's prose poem, the realistic technique is echoed in the melodramatic tone of the opening dialogue between a lady and a character named Luciano, and in the detailed description of different body parts of the couple making love. However, the realistic convention is overturned by the dismemberment of the two bodies in the description, by mixing romantic details of the couple with references to the world of science (the law of gravity, chemists, the element mercury), and by juxtapositions that break all links with objective reality (a man becomes a little piece of earth, then an elephant, a child, and a bulrush). Christological allusions (a sponge of honey and vinegar, a governor eating nonchalantly in spite of the tragedy) place the couple in the context of Christ's crucifixion, turning this pair into an image of love in the midst of an indifferent world of science and intellectualism. The partridge is associated with a very cruel dove from whose beak, or song, comes the pale moon, described as a transatlantic ship. The kiss of that dove, which in Lorca's early poetry promised grace and happiness in the form of the Holy Ghost, becomes the pale ship of the moon, an image of life's fatal cycle. The lovers die, assassinated by the kiss of that partridge/moon. This prose poem offers an unexpected rendition of a conventional love story. The mixture of disparate elements creates a poem whose coherence, as in the other narrations, is not established in relation to the outside world but within its own structure.

159

As Terrence McMillan and others have remarked, the title prose poem *Santa Lucía y San Lázaro* (*St. Lucy and St. Lazarus*, *CP* 619–24), establishes two aesthetic positions: that represented by Saint Lucy, patroness of sight and example of spiritual enlightenment, the virgin who cut her eyes out and gave them to a pagan suitor on a platter rather than consenting to his sexual advances; and that of Saint Lazarus, knowledgeable of the other world since he was resurrected from the dead.[12] The speaker is a traveler stopping at an inn to rest from his journey. This journey is soon recognized as an artistic pursuit, which in Lorca is identified with love. He arrives at the inn at midnight, at a crucial point in his journey. St. Lucy's eyes offer him the guidance of an objective light. To follow it would entail a rejection of subjective passion and love fulfillment for the sake of purity and emotional detachment.

The next day, at noon, the scene is the market, a public and visible place. The traveler goes for a walk and witnesses all the activity typical of a city—markets, bars, and traffic—while in the church, Saint Lucy, who is described somewhat androgynously, defends the luminous dove of the Holy Ghost. Streets are filled with optical shops and the whole scene is situated in a visual realm. Saint Lucy is the guardian of the "seen," of the established and officially accepted.

Saint Lazarus, by contrast, is at a train station, a place of transition where identities are not definitely fixed. He represents the polar opposite to Saint Lucy's objectivity and assurance about what is real. His world is that of the candle and casket, both elements of the dead. He is extremely pale and delicate, contrasting with Saint Lucy's physical vigor. While glasses are Saint Lucy's distinctive possession, the *guardapolvos,* or dust cover, is Saint Lazarus's protection from dust, from life's hustle and bustle; this garment is very similar to a shroud.[13]

The traveler is confronting two different aesthetic positions: one aimed at capturing reality in an objective way devoid of emotion, the other seeking after a more internal, subjective reality. At the end, he is at home gazing at the glasses, with "their rigid lines and flat steadiness," as well as at the dust cover, "with an almost inhuman remoteness" (*CP* 624). This narration reflects the intense aesthetic meditation that occupied Lorca starting in 1925, the year he was exposed to surrealism and to frequent conversations with his friends Dalí and Gasch.

Beheading the Innocents and *Beheading the Baptist* can be read as two parts of the same prose poem. The backdrop is provided by the biblical stories of the Sacrifice of the Innocents, ordered by King Herod, and the beheading of John the Baptist, indirectly brought about by the Jewish princess Salomé. The first part is presented as a surgical procedure; the second is narrated as though it were a soccer game in which the two teams exchanged expressions of pain, like *ay,* or words alluding to such objects as a razor, knife, or blade.

Beheading is a frequent term in Lorca's poetry; it commonly refers to the speaker's sacrifice on the altars of love and art to a repressive society. In the first part of *Beheading the Innocents,* blood is predominant; nothing seems to be able to stanch it. Since the speaker refers only to boys, there is the implication that homosexuals are the sacrificial victims. The force of the Innocents' blood can be heard in the *g* sound of the word *sangre* (blood). It is in that sound that the full meaning of the word *sangre,* as life, is contained. This fusion of life and language, or reality and writing, is implied in the biblical story that serves as a backdrop to this narration. Lorca's extended description of the blood flowing is juxtaposed with its petrification in the written word of the story narrating it. Hence, at the end, the blood triumphantly takes over things made of marble, pervading their solid structure.

John the Baptist announced Christ's coming but was silenced by a jealous woman. In Lorca's prose poem, the Baptist, possibly a representation of the poet himself, confronts the blacks and the reds, emblematic colors of death and of blood (or passion). The soccer game is played by the poet, a lonely figure attacked by Salomé's "seven sets of false teeth" (*CP* 627), a reference to her dance of the seven veils, a game of seduction that will lead to decadence and death. This dance recalls the peeling off of masks and costumes in some of Lorca's plays. It is also a representation of the reflective nature of the poetic image. The Baptist/poet is beheaded for rejecting the deceitful play of the poetic image in favor of a word whose truth society represses.

The Baptist/poet is this referred to as "the child who died in jail," whom the speaker calls "my son," a representation of his creativity and passion. This child, who is word and love, has to stay hidden inside because of his unorthodox nature. The reds, or blood, are the winners, indicating the strength of conventional heterosexual passion over any deviant manifestation: "the executioner has no friend of emeralds" (*CP* 627, the "green" Lorca associates with unconventional love, as in"Sleepwalking Ballad"). In the image of the knife Lorca concentrates the horror of official rules. At the end "little girls" dye their cheeks with the red, and "the boys" paint their ties (an image of their penises) with the blood from the Baptist's jugular vein (*CP* 628). His spilled blood is used to give the conventional couple (the boys and girls as a picture of heterosexual love) renewed vigor. Society's conventions are thus maintained by the sacrifice of those who dare go against them.

The last narration, *La Gallina (Cuento para niños tontos) (The Hen [Story of Foolish Children], CP* 628–29), as the title indicates, is presented as a tale for foolish children. *Gallina* is the term used in Spanish to describe a cowardly attitude or behavior (like *chicken* in English). This *gallina* is an idiot; it did not like eggs—it wanted them to be devoured by foxes—but it did like roosters. The Spanish word for *egg* is also a term used to refer to the testicles, and it could be that the *gallina* is a reference to a male too cowardly to express himself openly. He likes roosters, or other males, therefore he may be a homosexual, but he hates his own egg, which could be construed as a rejection of his true self. The end of the narration takes place during a night full of violent sexual encounters, with the rooster and the hen fighting for eternity. This is the ceaseless struggle between the hen, who does not want to accept its homosexual nature, and the rooster as the paradigm of macho virility.

These narrations reflect Lorca's search for new ways of artistic expression. While the avant-garde was rejecting the sentimentality and excessive emotionalism of old Romantic and symbolist literary forms, Gongorine aesthetics proposed the construction of an autonomous work of art solidly built upon an elaborate process of metaphorization. Lorca's Gypsy ballads provide superb examples of Gongorine metaphors, as well as their limitations. Imagination can perceive unexpected associations in the world and articulate them in startling metaphors, but it remains dependent on that world. As these narrations and Lorca's correspondence indicate, *The Gypsy Ballads* was followed by an intense exploration into the realm of inspiration, of the poetic fact, an artistic space whose coherence did not depend on its link with the outside world, but rather on its own internal system. Metaphorical artistry was insufficient to articulate the alogical instincts and passions that these narrations develop by mixing cruelty, violence, blood, and murder with tenderness and lyricism. Normal logic has no place in these stories, which like Lorca's later works of poetry and theater, explore these inner realms through a language that negates expected connections with the world in order to articulate their own nonrepresentational code.

Visual Arts

Drawings

Drawing occupied Lorca throughout his life. Poetic images often originated in drawings before they were articulated verbally. In 1927 twenty-four of his drawings were exhibited at the Josep Dalmau Gallery, a leading gallery for modern art in Barcelona. In 1974 some of Lorca's drawings were exhibited in Madrid as part of a show entitled "The Origins of the Spanish Avant-Garde:

1920–1936," including works by Dalí and others.[14] Lorca's drawings continue to be exhibited; some ninety-five were shown in 1991 at various universities in the United States. Helen Oppenheimer describes Lorca's creative process in the drawings as, first, "the idea or emotion, then the visual image or drawing, and lastly the verbal image or metaphor."[15] Mario Hernández perceives in the drawings a process of essential refinement in three stages: the early ones (dating before 1925) depicting *manolas* (women from the poorer, working-class districts of Madrid), clowns, and fruit bowls; those of a more cubist style (1926–1929), during Lorca's contact with the Catalan group associated with the avant-garde journal *L'Amic de les Arts* (Friends of the Arts), to which Dalí contributed; and more personal ones after his stay in New York (1929–), characterized by economy of lines and a tragic sense.[16]

In his lecture "Thoughts on Modern Painting" Lorca credits cubism with giving the final blow to art as the realistic representation of a theme or subject.[17] After cubism, surrealism directed artists toward instinct, chance, and pure inspiration. Modern art goes beyond the mere representation of reality, says Lorca, for it transcends the objective world to move "on the borders of death."[18] Thus Lorca envisions artists as struggling between the poles of content (or theme) and of form. He described his own drawings as "very human," because they depict the human struggle to go beyond masks, mirrors, and conventions to the very dangerous truth; in fact, the artist can be fatally wounded just in searching (*SL* 121).

In his correspondence of 1927, Lorca wrote that when a subject was too long or it had a poetically trite emotion, he resolved the problem by drawing with pencils (*SL* 115). He confessed finding great joy and amusement in this activity. Writing and drawing poems, words and lines on the page, became *one* activity. However, drawing seemed to be a succinct way of expressing an idea before giving it a verbal form. Drawings seemed free from the traditional connotations affecting words, hence they were more "innocent." Drawings allowed capturing reality in a stylized form. Lorca often expressed his rejection of so-called direct painting, because he perceived it as an anguished struggle with forms in which the artist and the work inevitably lost (*SL* 121). Attempting to copy reality results in a dead work of art, because no artistic transformation has taken place. But when the drawing creates its own reality, then the interplay between its artistic fact and objective reality becomes inexhaustible.

As Lorca repeatedly stated, his drawings demanded a full commitment of hand and heart, technique and emotion (*SL* 119–20). He characterized them as lineal metaphors intended to capture the essential features of emotion and form. His drawings were beautiful metaphors that sometimes came about unexpectedly, at other times found after "fishing" for them. The line in a drawing is like the fishing line on which the fish, or subject matter, is caught; then the artistic fact can emerge. Lorca remarked that his drawings of 1927 were executed with a poetic-plastic or plastic-poetic criterion; their technique, or form, was identified with the emotion, or theme, they represented.

The emotion of Lorca's drawings resides on the line (*OC* 2:1189). Against the white page the line becomes the inscription of the search for artistic truth, with all the curves, meanderings, entanglements, stumbling, and falls of a self-reflexive search. The lines in these drawings continue uninterrupted, forming in their course different and unexpected shapes. Early drawings depict somewhat pathetic male figures, hermaphroditic types wearing a kind of skirt with pantaloons underneath; clowns; women with Spanish mantillas and fans, looking with a straight glare, as if transfixed by some law of fate beyond themselves; or women secluded in convents. The overall effect is of oppression, fatalism, despair, and resignation to an unconquerable fate. Severed hands predominate, possibly symbols of the pain marking the support, love, and creative activity that hands connote. Roots also appear frequently, as a reminder to always keep close contact with the earth. Masks, as in his written work, signal the opposition between the social and the inner, or true, self. Similarly, women with fans that open and close (like the folding screen in some of his plays) connote the constant fluctuation from one self to the other. Sailor figures evoke freedom from social restrictions, although they often appear as suffering because those restrictions inhibit their desire. Some sailor figures are formed from lines coming out of vases while the sailors, in turn, have flowers or vines with leaves coming out of their eyes and falling down toward the earth. In an endless cycle, the lines metamorphose into flowers, into sailors, into flowers. According to David K. Loughran, the basic imagery of roots, hands, vines, sailors, and arrows seems to point to the "essential struggle and polar tension between desire and its limitations."[19] In the more experimental drawings, lines are somewhat less curvy, and human figures become schematic. These drawings are presented in their simplicity and nakedness as a reality in their own right. Later drawings go back to more personal and emotional depictions, such as red beasts or horses apparently attacking the poet, who in turn is seen surrounded by the ominous buildings of New York. If the sailors had flowers coming out of their eyes, now human figures have empty stares, the eyes being hollow cavities from which dry vines emerge.

The primary issue in all of these drawings is not what the line depicts, the subject matter, but the line itself as it unwinds in its own search. Lorca is concerned with the act of creation itself, with how the line evolves, moves, progresses across the white page—the emptiness, or void—where its form is always threatened with dissolution. In his drawings, the artist confronts his images with space. This confrontation is a central concern in his poetry as well, in which images often articulate spaces of anguish and suffering. The drawings are linear metaphors in which Lorca seems to have reached a great artistic independence from objective reality. Lines allowed him to evade the connotations normally attached to words and thus move in a free artistic realm. However, this same autonomy of the line is also the mark of its alienation from reality. Lorca's drawings show an interplay between line (or form) and emotion, abstraction and pathos. They depict in visual form the tension between art's autonomy and its link to the world that Lorca articulates in his poetry and theater.

Trip to the Moon

Lorca shared the interest of his generation in films. As Kevin Power indicates, in his film script *Viaje a la luna* (*Trip to the Moon, CP* 631–39), Lorca was not merely trying to shock the spectator with unexpected images but rather was attempting to find new ways to express his personal and artistic search.[20] The key to understanding this script lies in Lorca's aesthetic concerns during the years between 1928 and 1931, as evidenced in the narrations and in *The Public*.[21] Lorca wrote this script in one-and-half days in New York and left it with Emilio Amero, a Mexican painter and filmmaker he met there. It is very possible that Buñuel and Dalí's film *Un chien andalou* (An Andalusian Dog, filmed in 1929 and premiered in Paris in June that year) was in the back of Lorca's mind when he wrote his own script, although he had not actually seen it. It seems Lorca believed that the dog in the title, a name used in the Resi for the residents from Andalusia, referred to him, and he felt hurt by the designation.

This script is a series of takes in which images are not described but presented as visual poetic images.[22] Just as in the drawings the line moves on the white page, forming different and unexpected configurations and combinations, these visual images follow one another according to cinematic principles of movement, superimposition, and simultaneity. Most are recurring images in Lorca's poetry and drawings. According to Laffranque, the plot includes a trip away from this world, as the title indicates, identified with an anguished search for sexual love through three frustrated attempts, ending in disappointment and death.[23] The white bed in the first take is an allusion to the white page, or screen against which the trip is going to take place. The *paños* (cloths) are the sheets as well as the shrouds of pain and suffering on which the sexual dance of the numbers 13 and 22 takes place. As in *Suicide in Alexandria,* numbers indicate the equalizing of the difference between odd numbers and even: 1+3 in 13—an odd number—and 2+2 in 22—an even number—both adding to 4; perhaps they will be united in that white bed of the text/screen. Yet the presence of ants, frequent in surrealistic paintings and films, as well as in Lorca's narrations, indicate the failure of the encounter.

The seeker in the script is a Harlequin-like figure running through a long corridor with New York as background (takes 6–7). At the end, he encounters an eye-fish, the eye looking into and becoming the fish (take 13), a sign of sexual sterility and frustration or of unsuccessful union, as in *The Public*. Children's heads in take 20 are spotted with ink, indicating the spotting of all childhood dreams, like the blood-stained cat in *As Five Years Pass*. The women lamenting and crying in takes 31–32 are a clear picture of desperation. There are also signs carrying the name Elena (take 35). According to Ian Gibson, Elena could easily refer not only to the Greek Helena, the cause of so much destruction, but also to Dalí's wife, Gala, whose real name was Helena Dimitrievna Diakonava.[24] Women's arms going up and down, as the camera descending and ascending the stairs in a double and triple exposure form a spiral shape that suggests that feelings are pent up (takes 35–38).

A naked boy at the top of the stairs is the same Harlequin boy, the seeker (take 44). The fact that his circulating blood is visible may suggest his inner suffering and vulnerability. He loses himself in a night street, the dark night of his search. There the dominating symbol is the moon that three mysterious men look at (take 46)—a possible reference to the Fates, like the three woodcutters in *Blood Wedding* or the card players in *Once Five Years Pass*. A man with visible veins, who is shown crucified, is clearly a suffering Christ figure. An allusion to the chalice of Christ's blood appears in the bar scene of take 51. The waiter pours wine that the boys in the bar cannot drink, as if they could not partake of Christ's sacrifice and salvation. Similarly, even though the man with the visible veins is gesturing, no one pays attention; everyone falls asleep. When everyone vomits in the bar, it may be in reaction to the Harlequin's leaving with a girl. The departure itself is typical of Hollywood films, in which the search for love ends in the conventional romance with the girl in white. When both ascend in an elevator, modern technology counteracts the romantic overtones and points to the artificiality of their union; their kiss is a typical Hollywood kiss, devoid of authenticity (takes 57–59). The vomiting is also a recurring motif in Lorca's drawings of this period and in the New York poems. It is a sign of the artist's reaction to the corruption and artificiality of his surroundings.

Nevertheless, conventionality does not last long: the young boy bites the girl in the neck and pulls her hair violently while guitar strings are cut, marking the end of the romance (takes 60–62). When the man takes off his jacket and wig, the man whose veins can be seen appears as he is, free of masks. Consequently, the girl becomes a white plaster bust, the petrification of woman, frozen into an unattainable ideal (take 64). The name *Elena* appears again, while the man with the visible veins is now lying dead on a pile of abandoned newspapers. This may indicate that he, like the daily news, will also soon be forgotten (takes 66–68). A couple kissing and laughing over the dead body suggest the oblivion into which the corpse will necessarily fall (take 70). The end is the moon, the death scenery where all quests fail.

Music

Music was Lorca's vocation until 1916, when he decided to concentrate on literature. As a child, Lorca learned from servants and peasants in his native village the songs that he would later incorporate into his writings. Music is an intrinsic part of Lorca's literary work, especially in his theater, where songs are often interwoven into the fabric of the play. He said he had written *Blood Wedding* with one of Bach's cantatas in the background [25], and *Don Perlimplín* and *The Shoemaker's Prodigious Wife* are plays supported by music. Lorca was well acquainted with the *cancioneros* (collections of popular songs) that had been published in Spain since the beginning of the century, and he himself compiled and harmonized songs from different regions where he had traveled. Lorca played piano for six records of popular old Spanish songs sung by Encarnación López Júlvez, "La Argentinita."

In his early article, "Divagación. Las reglas de la música" (Divagation: The Rules in Music; *OC* 1:1115–18), Lorca defined music as passion and vagueness, as an art above and beyond rules and technique. Although the young artist recognized the need for rules at the beginning, human drama and passions soon surpass them (*OC* 1:1116). The artist is clearly superior to any type of rule; no norm can hinder the flow of his creative spirit.

Lorca's research on various types of songs responds to an interest that goes beyond historical preservation. In these musical expressions, Lorca finds the inner voice—what Unamuno would call the *intra-history*—of a people or country. He spoke of songs as creatures that require extreme protection because of the marvelous but fragile example of equilibrium they provided (*OC* 2:942). In the fabric of the song, Lorca found the trembling present meeting with the emotion of history. Thus the song became a type of circulatory system through which the blood, life, and passion of a people run. In his lecture "Cómo canta una ciudad de noviembre a noviembre" ("How a City Sings from November to November," first delivered in 1933), Lorca sought to draw a true portrait of his city, Granada, through songs.[26] The different seasons of the year are marked by songs whose melodies express the ever-turning wheel of time in its cycle of the seasons. A similar effort to find cultural roots directs Lorca's study of lullabies, "the reverend mothers of all songs," as he called them, quoting Spanish poet and archaeologist Rodrigo Caro (1574–1647) (*DS* 7). With these songs, Lorca attempted to weave the musical tapestry of Spain and its regions, for lullabies, more than monuments or cathedrals, capture the immemorial history of the country. Similarly, Deep Song represented for Lorca the umbilical cord that kept the connection with the nurturing fundamentals of human nature. In that primitive music, which he described as "a stammer, a wavering emission of the voice" (*DS* 25), Lorca searched for the key to deciphering the existential manuscript.

Lorca's collaboration with musician Manuel de Falla resulted in the Deep Song Festival in 1922, the puppet play at the poet's house in 1923, and the uncompleted project for a comic operetta in one act entitled *Lola, la comedianta* (Lola, the Comedienne). According to Piero Menarini, Lorca worked on the libretto in 1923; Falla only made notes on the margins. Lorca left the libretto unfinished, and it has now been reconstructed from different scripts.[27] He conceived it as a parody of Italian opera and romantic sentimentality.[28] Lola, a comedienne, and her new husband, a poet, are on their honeymoon. To entertain themselves, they weave a web of tricks to make a Marquis fall in love with Lola and then drop him in humiliation at the end. Lola's eyes are described as "two little ropes" with which she is going to trap the poor Marquis in her web.

Lola is different from other Lorcan heroines in that she acts more freely and is satisfied with her husband. Her proclivity for laying traps, and her use of different masks, make her similar to the moon as Lorcan symbol, beautiful but destructive. Menarini indicates how Lorca's libretto differs from others in that it does not depend on music; this comedy can stand on its own as a play.29

Notes

1. Between 1917 and 1920, Lorca authored various works of prose besides *Impressions and Landscapes,* some of which are still unpublished. In an article about Lorca's early prose writings ("Sobre la prosa temprana de García Lorca [1916–1918]" [On García Lorca's Early Prose], *Cuadernos Hispanoamericanos* 433–34 [1986], esp.

15, 19), Christopher Maurer calls attention to the lack of genre definition of these writings. They are meditative, a type of spiritual diary for the young author, and as Ian Gibson notes (*Federico García Lorca: A Life* [New York: Pantheon, 1989] 65), they center on two main topics: Lorca's rejection of the Catholic orthodoxy and his sexual anguish. Starting in 1917, Lorca wrote *Fray Antonio (Poema raro),* (Friar Anthony [Strange Poem]), in reality a novel with autobiographical references; *El patriotismo,* (Patriotism), possibly Lorca's first text in prose, in which he fiercely attacks the militarism and war that often accompanies patriotism and accuses the church of supporting the war plans of the government; and *Mi pueblo,* (My Village), which shows Lorca's early awareness of social injustice, inequality, and human suffering (see Eutimio Martín, *Federico García Lorca, heterodoxo y mártir* [Madrid: Siglo XXI, 1986] 161–75, 150–54, 175–76). *Místicas (de la carne y el espíritu)* (Mystical Writings [of the Flesh and the Spirit]) is a series of meditations written between 1917 and 1918. Contrary to its title, it does not describe any ecstatic state but one of deep conflict between faith and the demands of the flesh, Christ and Satan, good and evil (see Maurer, "Sobre la prosa temprana" 19).

    2. See pp. xi–xii of *Impressions and Landscapes,* trans. Lawrence H. Klibbe (Lanham, New York, London: UP of America, 1987). Page references to this translation, abbreviated *IL,* will be cited parenthetically. For a critical reading of this work, see Klibbe's *Lorca's "Impresiones y Paisajes": The Young Artist* (Madrid: José Porrúa Turanzas, 1983). References to "Granada (Paraíso cerrado para muchos)" (Granada [A Paradise Closed to Many]) and "Semana Santa en Granada" (Holy Week in Granada) come from volume 1 of *OC,* where they appear under the heading "Other Impressions and Landscapes" (see Klibbe, *Lorca's "Impresiones y paisajes"* 6).

    3. Cited in Klibbe, *Lorca's "Impresiones y paisajes"* 43.

    4. Klibbe, *Lorca's "Impresiones y paisajes"* 101.

    5. Klibbe, *Lorca's "Impresiones y paisajes"* 104–6.

    6. For an elaboration on Lorca's influences, see Klibbe, *Lorca's "Impressions and Landscapes"* 13–24.

    7. See Marie Laffranque, "Una cadena de solidaridad. Federico, conferenciante" (A Chain of Solidarity. Federico, Lecturer), *Trece de nieve,* 2d series, 1–2 (1976) 132–40. Whenever the lecture or letter under discussion is not translated in *Deep Song* or *Selected Letters,* I shall refer to the Spanish original included in *OC.* The most thoroughly critical editions of the lectures and letters are those edited by Christopher Maurer in Spanish: *Epistolario* (Correspondence) (Madrid: Alianza, 1983), 2 vols.; *Conferencias* (Lectures) (Madrid: Alianza, 1984), 2 vols. "Sketch de la pintura moderna" appears translated as "Thoughts on Modern Art" in Helen Oppenheimer, *Lorca: The Drawings. Their Relation to the Poet's Life and Work* (New York and Toronto: Franklin Watts, 1987) 127–35.

    8. Laffranque, "Una cadena de solidaridad" 133–40.

    9. Laffranque, "Una cadena de solidaridad" 135.

10. As Maurer indicates (*CP* 837), these narrations were written in 1927–1928 but never published as a book. All page references to these works, and to the film script *Trip to the Moon,* are to *CP.* They will be cited parenthetically.

11. See Gibson, *A Life* 218–20.

12. Terence McMullan, "Federico García Lorca's 'Santa Lucía y San Lázaro' and the Aesthetics of Transition," *Bulletin of Hispanic Studies* 67.1 (1990): 13–14.

13. For an in-depth analysis of *Saint Lucy and Saint Lazarus,* to which my reading is indebted, see *Federico García Lorca: Santa Lucía y San Lázaro,* ed. Julio Huélamo (Málaga: Centro Cultural de la Generación del 27, 1989), especially pp. 53–54 for the images of glasses and dust cover and 26–27 for the aesthetic meaning of the traveler's trip.

14. See Patrick Fourneret, "Los 'dibujos humanísimos' de Federico García Lorca" (The Very Human Drawings of Federico García Lorca), *Trece de nieve,* 2d series, 1–2 (1976): 158. For a catalog and critical analysis of Lorca's drawings, see Mario Hernández, *Line of Light and Shadow: The Drawings of Federico García Lorca,* trans. Christopher Maurer (Durham and London: Duke UP, 1991). Also see Cecelia J. Cavanaugh, *Lorca's Drawings and Poems: Forming the Eye of the Reader.* Forthcoming (Lewisburg, Pa.: Bucknell UP, 1995).

15. Oppenheimer 87.

16. Mario Hernández, "El arte del dibujo en la creación de García Lorca" (The Art of Drawing in the Works of García Lorca), *Federico García Lorca: Saggi critici nel cinquantenario della morte,* ed. Gabriele Morelli (Fasano, Italy: Schena Editore, 1988) 125, 120.

17. Oppenheimer 127–35.

18. Oppenheimer 134.

19. David K. Loughran, *Federico García Lorca: The Poetry of Limits* (London: Tamesis, 1978) 204.

20. Kevin Power, "Una luna encontrada en Nueva York" (A Moon Found in New York), *Trece de nieve,* 2d series, 1–2 (Dec. 1976): 147, 142.

21. See also C. B. Morris, *The Dream-House (Silent Films and Spanish Poets)* (Scotland [Hull]: U of Hull, 1977), and Marie Laffranque's edition and interpretation of this film script (*Viaje a la luna [Guión cinematográfico]* [Loubressac: Braad Editions, 1980]).

22. Laffranque, *Viaje a la luna* n.p.

23. Laffranque, *Viaje a la luna* n.p.

24. Gibson, *A Life* 276.

25. Gibson, *A Life* 334.

26. Federico García Lorca, *How a City Sings from November to November,* trans. and ed. Christopher Maurer (San Francisco: Cadmus Editions, 1984).

27. *Lola, la comedianta,* ed. Piero Menarini (Madrid: Alianza, 1981) 61, 70–71.

28. Cit. in *Lola, la comedianta* 85.

29. See Menarini's preliminary study to *Lola, la comedianta* esp. 78–80, 83–85, 89.

Conclusion

Within the limitations of a general introduction, this study has attempted to elucidate Lorca's rationale of art and what he set out to accomplish in his varied production. The material has been organized according to genres, and each particular work has been read with attention to the development of Lorca's writing through its major poetic signs. Lorca's poetry, plays, drawings, and lectures—all his fields of artistic expression—show his craft, and by that craft, his understanding of art and reality. Many accounts of Lorca given by friends and acquaintances attest to the magic of his personality. His charm and capacity for communication are often remarked on, as well as the aura of mystery that counterbalanced his apparent openness and accentuated his ultimate inaccessibility. That conflictive meeting of expression and its boundaries, of the inner and outer realities, of what is seen or present and what is suggested although absent, as embodied by Lorca, is what his writings articulate. To read his various works is to accept the invitation to probe beyond that threshold where objective reality meets with mystery, the door to an entirely untrodden ground.

From the beginning of his career, Lorca was very aware of the impact art has on the audience. His various works articulate the need to communicate without sacrificing artistic demands. This duality in the work of art, that is, its autonomy versus its link to the world, is expressed in different ways at various times during his productive life. It is articulated as the conflict between the private and social realms of the self; as between imagination, instinct, and fantasy, on the one hand, and on the other, the constraints imposed by reason and common sense (the great enemy of poetry, as Lorca said); as between desire and reality; as between the theater in the open-air and the theater beneath the sand that the author explored in *The Public;* as between the concepts of inspiration either by the muse (or the angel), which the author places at the level of objective reality, or by the *duende,* always bordering on death. When we read Lorca, we sense and hear the voice of human desire aspiring to fulfillment but remaining unable to transcend itself. If, with certain poetic signs (the star, the Host, nature), Lorca attempted to create a language in which word and object coincide, more frequently his texts are articulated through signs of fragmentation, so that the depicted reality is dispersed in a myriad of reflections, just as the word displays its refractory nature. In analyzing Lorca's famous line "Green, oh how I want you green," ("Sleepwalking Ballad," from *The Gypsy Ballads*), his brother Francisco indicated how the desire expressed there is one whose fulfillment meets its inception, whose completion is but the point where the process begins anew. Francisco García Lorca states how that verse articulates the longing not for green as such, but for the idea of green yet to be created, hence unreachable and unidentifiable.[1] In its obsessive reiteration throughout the poem, that line encapsulates the unending desire pervading Lorca's multi-faceted oeuvre and that moves all his characters on their quests.

The year 1928 was crucial in Lorca's aesthetic and personal development. His letters confirm a new artistic awareness that he termed "poetry of opening up one's veins." Poetry writing is linked to the body in its innermost element, blood. For Lorca, the poet writes with the ink/blood of his passion and suffering; the Christian implications are obvious. The pathos that Lorca considers fundamental to his art runs parallel to the highest artistic demands as expressed in his concept of the *hecho poético* (poetic event or fact), also articulated in that year. The *hecho poético* is an artistic creation endowed with its own poetic logic. It can arise from the inspiration of the *duende,* a theme that Lorca developed a few years later. The *duende* strives to express what is in itself inexpressible, and in the meantime, it wounds the poet with the desire to express forever newly created forms. The *duende* is power—as well as the struggle that the artist fights in every step of his/her work. It is the realm of true poetry, where the creator is confronted with the desire for expression and the limitations of the medium, with wanting to live and wanting to die. Form and pathos, structure and emotion, the poem as a formal construct that will pierce the heart like an arrow: these are the tenets of Lorca's aesthetics. In the figure of Saint Sebastian, as evidenced in drawings and in his correspondence with Salvador Dalí, Lorca offers a visual expression of that fusion of form and pathos he was seeking for his art. As form, Saint Sebastian's beautiful body pierced by arrows unites a precision of execution with suffering and eroticism. The figure of the saint appears to emerge from a trance-like balance between the pain of his wounds and the ecstasy that those same wounds suggest. That tension is what the Director in the play *The Public* termed "un dificilísimo juego poético" (an extremely difficult poetic trick). Art is inescapably linked with form, which the artist seeks to maintain alive, away from the static nature of artistic inscription, by bringing forth the "fuerza oculta" (hidden force) of love and pathos behind the exterior, or manifest, form. This tension is reenacted by the reader/spectator who is engaged intellectually and emotionally by the work. The work of art offers itself not as a mimesis of reality but as an articulation of the duality

172

and ambivalence intrinsic to life.

That duality is also evident in the constant dialogue that Lorca's text establishes with a wide range of artistic traditions and forms. Lorca's plays are articulated in the form of farce as well as drama, tragedy, tragic poem, and romantic, popular, or historical plays. His characters are animals, puppets, and human beings placed in contexts that range from artistically adapted history and tradition to the world of the movies, from rural Andalusian and middle class bourgeois urban settings to dreams. His poetry is voiced through various meters, is expressed as drawings or musical variations (*cante jondo,* suites, songs), or adopts surrealistic tones. In his dialogue with literature as a tradition and institution, Lorca calls on the reader to approach his works according to the particular formal designation he chose to give them. Through that designation, Lorca established a set of expectations as well as a semiotic orientation for the reader. Lorca's careful attention to the form, to the work as an artistic construct, is also an attempt to surpass it, to push it forward in search of ever-new fields of meaning. His conception of poetic language is marked by tension, by a trance-like quality that results from using the word both communicatively and self-reflectively, for pathos and form. Desire and reality, the word and its referent, play an endless game that keeps the planes shifting, much as his dramatic characters do. This poet, who so often has been called popular, is highly aware of the problems and possibilities implicit in his craft. As he himself responded to a question about his poetry: "if it is true that I am a poet by the grace of God—or of the devil—it is also true that I am a poet by the grace of technique and effort, and by being totally aware of what a poem is" (*OC* 1:1141; translation my own).

Note

1. Francisco García Lorca, *In the Green Morning: Memories of Federico,* trans. Christopher Maurer (New York: New Directions, 1986) 137–38.

Works Cited

Spanish editions of Lorca's works are listed here mainly because of the unavailability of these works in English. Secondary sources include a selection of books, articles, book chapters, and special issues of journals devoted mainly but not exclusively to Lorca, in various languages, but primarily in English and Spanish.

Works by Federico García Lorca

Spanish-language Editions

La casa de Bernarda Alba. Ed. Herbert Ramsden. Manchester and New York: Manchester UP, 1983.

Conferencias. Ed. Christopher Maurer. 2 vols. Madrid: Alianza, 1984.

Diván del Tamarit. Llanto por Ignacio Sánchez Mejías. Sonetos. Ed. Mario Hernández. Madrid: Alianza, 1981.

Epistolario. Ed. Christopher Maurer. 2 vols. Madrid: Alianza, 1983.

Libro de poemas. Ed. Ian Gibson. Barcelona: Ariel, 1982.

Lola, la comedianta. Ed. Piero Menarini. Madrid: Alianza, 1981.

Obras completas. Ed. Arturo del Hoyo. 18th ed. 2 vols. Madrid: Aguilar, 1973. Abbreviated *OC* in parenthetical citations.

Oda y Burla de Sesostris y Sardanápalo. Ed. Miguel García-Posada. Ferrol: Esquío, 1985. Includes a textual analysis and interpretation, and transcriptions of three manuscripts of this ode. The appendix includes "Oda al toro de lidia" (Ode to the Fighting Bull) and transcriptions of two manuscripts for this ode.

Oda a Salvador Dalí. Obras completas. Ed. Arturo del Hoyo. Vol. 1. Madrid: Aguilar, 1973. 752–55.

Oda al Santísimo Sacramento del Altar: "Exposición" y "Mundo." *Revista de Occidente* 22.66 (1928) 294–98.

Poeta en Nueva York. Con cuatro dibujos originales. Poema de Antonio Machado. Ed. José Bergamín. México: Séneca, 1940.

El público. Ed. María Clementa Millán. Madrid: Cátedra, 1987. Critical edition after the only existing manuscript of *The Public,* published in 1976 in a facsimile edition by

Rafael Martínez Nadal, with well-documented and explanatory prologue.

Santa Lucía y San Lázaro. Ed. Julio Huélamo. Málaga: Centro Cultural de la generación del 27, 1989.

Sonetos. ABC Edición internacional (Madrid), 21–27 March 1984: 35–45. First authorized publication of Lorca's *Sonnets,* with illustrations and various critical articles by different authors.

Suites. Ed. André Belamich. Barcelona: Ariel, 1983.

Teatro inconcluso: Fragmentos y proyectos inacabados. Ed. Marie Laffranque. Granada: Universidad de Granada, 1987.

Viaje a la luna (Guión cinematográfico). Ed. Marie Laffranque. Loubressac: Braad Editions, 1980.

English-language and Bilingual Spanish-English Editions

Collected Poems (bilingual Spanish-English edition). New York: Farrar, Straus & Giroux, 1991. Vol. 2 of *The Poetical Works of Federico García Lorca.* Ed. Christopher Maurer. Trans. Francisco Aragón et al. 2 vols. Essential edition of all of Lorca's poetical works—with the exception of *Poet in New York*—plus the film script *Trip to the Moon* and "Prose Poems and Narrations." Solid and useful editor's introduction, notes to the poems, and bibliography.

Deep Song and Other Prose. Ed. and trans. Christopher Maurer. New York: New Directions, 1980. Besides "Deep Song," this volumes includes "Elegy for Marie Blanchard," "On Lullabies," "Play and Theory of the *Duende,*" "Holy Week in Granada," "Sun and Shade," "The Poetic Image of Don Luis de Góngora," "A Poet in New York," "On the *Gypsy Ballads,*" "A Talk About Theater," "Greeting to the Crew of the Juan Sebastián Elcano," "Conversation with Bagaría," "From The Life of García Lorca, Poet." Abbreviated *DS* in parenthetical citations.

Five Plays: Comedies and Tragicomedies. Trans. James Graham-Luján and Richard L. O'Connell. New York: New Directions, 1963. Includes *The Butterfly's Evil Spell, The Billy-Club Puppets, The Shoemaker's Prodigious Wife, The Love of Don Perlimplín and Belisa in the Garden,* and *Doña Rosita, the Spinster.*

Four Puppet Plays, Play Withoug a Title, The Divan Poems and Other Poems, Prose Poems and Dramatic Pieces. Trans. Edwin Honig. Riverdale-on-Hudson, N.Y.: Sheep Meadow Press, 1990.

How a City Sings from November to November. Trans. and ed. Christopher Maurer. San Francisco: Cadmus, 1984.

Impressions and Landscapes. Trans. Lawrence H. Klibbe. Lanham, New York, London: UP of America, 1987.

"Lecture: A Poet in New York." Trans. Christopher Maurer. *The Poetical Works of Federico García Lorca.* Ed. Christopher Maurer. Vol. 1. New York: Farrar, Straus & Giroux, 1988. 181–98. 2 vols.

Mariana Pineda. Trans. Robert G. Havard. Warminster, Wiltshire: Aris and Phillips, 1987.

Ode to Salvador Dalí. Trans. William Bryant Logan.*Collected Poems* (bilingual Spanish-English edition), ed. Christopher Maurer. New York: Farrar, Straus & Giroux, 1991). Vol. 2 of *The Poetical Works of Federico García Lorca.* 588–95.

Once Five Years Pass and Other Dramatic Works. Trans. William Bryan Logan and Angel Gil Orrios. New York: Station Hill Press, 1989. Includes three dialogues, "Buster Keaton's Outing," "The Maiden, the Sailor and the Student," and "Chimera," the film script *Trip to the Moon,* a translation of "Leyenda a medio abrir" ("Half-Open Legend"), a poem dated 6 June 1918, and a translation of "En el bosque de las toronjas de luna" ("In the Forest of the Grapefruits of the Moon"), from *Suites.*

The Poet in New York and Other Poems of Federico García Lorca (bilingual Spanish-English edition). Trans. Rolfe Humphries. New York: W. W. Norton, 1940.

Poet in New York. Trans. Greg Simon and Steven F. White. New York: Farrar, Straus & Giroux, 1988. Vol. 1 of *The Poetical Works of Federico García Lorca.* Ed. Christopher Maurer. 2 vols. Very useful introduction and notes to the poems. Includes the lecture "A Poet in New York" and "The Poet Writes to His Family from New York and Havana," trans. Christopher Maurer.

The Public and Play Without a Title: Two Posthumous Plays. Trans. Carlos Bauer. New York: New Directions, 1983.

Romancero Gitano: A Ballad Translation and Critical Study. Trans. Carl W. Cobb. Jackson: UP of Mississippi, 1983.

The Rural Trilogy: Blood Wedding, Yerma, and The House of Bernarda Alba. Trans. Michael Dewell and Carmen Zapata. New York: Bantam, 1987.

Selected Letters. Ed. and trans. David Gershator. New York: New Directions, 1983. Abbrev *SL* in parenthetical citations.

Songs. Trans. Philip Cummings, with the assistance of Federico García Lorca. Ed. Daniel Eisenberg. Pittsburgh: Duquesne UP, 1976.

"Thoughts on Modern Art." *Lorca: The Drawings. Their Relation to the Poet's Life and Work.* Text by Helen Oppenheimer. New York and Toronto: Franklin Watts, 1987. 127–135.

Three Tragedies: Blood Wedding, Yerma, Bernarda Alba. Trans. James Graham-Luján and Richard L. O'Connell. Intro. Francisco G. Lorca. New York: New Directions, 1955. Standard translation of the trilogy.

Critical Works

Books

Allen, Rupert C. *Psyche and Symbol in the Theater of Federico García Lorca.* Austin and London: U of Texas P, 1974. A study of Lorca's dramatic characters in *Perlimplín, Yerma,* and *Blood Wedding* as psychic entities whose conscious and unconscious elements unfold through a complex symbolical network.

―――. *The Symbolic World of Federico García Lorca*. Albuquerque: U of New Mexico P, 1972. A study of symbols and their transformation into poetry in several poems selected from various collections and from the play *Once Five Years Pass*.

Anderson, Andrew A. *Lorca's Late Poetry: A Critical Study*. Leeds, Eng.: Francis Cairns, 1990. Close readings of each of the poems in Lorca's collections published from 1931 to 1936, with a thorough introduction preceding each collection and useful notes.

―――. *La Zapatera Prodigiosa*. Critical Guides to Spanish Texts. London: Grant and Cutler, 1991. A well-documented study guide to *The Shoemaker's Prodigious Wife*, addressing its different versions, productions, sources, language, characters, dramatic qualities, themes, and motifs.

Barthes, Roland. *S/Z*. Paris: Seuil, 1970.

Brenan, Gerald. *The Spanish Labyrinth: An Account of the Social and Political Background of the Civil War*. Cambridge, Eng.: Cambridge UP, 1974. A rigorous analysis of Spanish history between 1874 and 1936.

Carpentier, Alejo. *La música en Cuba* (Music in Cuba). México: Fondo de Cultura Económica, 1946.

Cecelia J. Cavanaugh. *Lorca's Drawings and Poems: Forming the Eye of the Reader*. Forthcoming. Lewisburg, Pa.: Bucknell University Press, 1995.

Cirlot, Juan Eduardo. *A Dictionary of Symbols*. Trans. Jack Sage. New York: Philosophical Library, 1962.

Cobb, Carl W. *Lorca's 'Romancero Gitano': A Ballad Translation and Critical Study*. Jackson: UP of Mississippi, 1983. Part one includes an introduction to the Spanish and English ballad traditions, as well as English translations of Lorca's eighteen ballads along with the original Spanish. Part two deals with the formative influences, and part three features an analysis of each ballad, with special attention paid to their psychological overtones.

Correa, Gustavo. *La poesía mítica de Federico García Lorca* (The Mythic Poetry of Federico García Lorca). Eugene, Ore.: U of Oregon Publications, 1972. A structural approach to *Yerma* and *Blood Wedding* and to Lorca's major poetry collections as different artistic expressions unified by a central mythical view.

Craige, Betty J. *Lorca's Poet in New York: The Fall Into Consciousness*. Lexington: UP of Kentucky, 1977. A study of the New York poems as an expression of both the poetic speaker's alienation of consciousness from nature's wholeness and his journey toward regaining identification with the universe.

Derrida, Jacques. *Of Grammatology*. Trans. Gayatri Chakravorty Spivak. Baltimore and London: Johns Hopkins UP, 21976.

Domenech, Ricardo, ed. *La casa de Bernarda Alba y el teatro de García Lorca* (*The House of Bernarda Alba* and the Theater of García Lorca). Madrid: Cátedra, 1985. Ten essays by various critics on Lorca's theater, mostly *The House of Bernarda Alba*.

Dolfi, Laura, ed. *L'"imposible/posible" di Federico García Lorca* Atti del convegno di studi, Salerno, 9–10 maggio, 1988. Napoli: Edizioni Scientifiche Italiane, 1989. Seventeen essays by different critics on various aspects of Lorca's life, works, and correspondence.

Edwards, Gwynne. *The Theatre Beneath the Sand*. London, Boston: Marion Boyars, 1980. An overview of Lorca's theater.

Eich, Christoph. *Federico García Lorca, poeta de la intensidad* (Federico García Lorca, Poet of Intensity). Madrid: Gredos, 1976. A study of Lorca's writings as a cohesive totality whose interpretative key is the experience of time as a unique moment of plenitude.

Enciclopedia Universal Ilustrada Europeo Americana. Apendice VII. Madrid: Espasa Calpe, 1932.

Fernández Cifuentes, Luis. *García Lorca en el teatro: La norma y la diferencia* (García Lorca in the Theater: The Norm and the Difference). Zaragoza: Prensas Universitarias, 1986. An acute evaluation of the originality and novelty of Lorca's theater in relation to the norms of the conventional theater of his time.

García Lorca, Francisco. *In the Green Morning: Memories of Federico*. Trans. Christopher Maurer. New York: New Directions, 1986. Translation of *Federico García Lorca y su mundo*, written by the poet's brother, without the sections on poetry, essays, and other texts included in the Spanish-language version. Part one includes fourteen essays based on memories of the poet's early years in Fuente Vaqueros, Valderrubio, and later in Granada, from his school and university years, up until his departure for Madrid. Part two includes ten essays, each devoted to an analysis of one of Lorca's plays.

García-Posada, Miguel. *Lorca: interpretación de Poeta en Nueva York* (Lorca: An Interpretation of *Poet in New York*). Madrid: Akal, 1981. An exhaustive textual and stylistic analysis of *Poet in New York* and *Earth and Moon* as two separate collections.

Gibson, Ian. *Federico García Lorca: A Life*. New York: Pantheon, 1989. The standard biography of Lorca.

———. *Granada en 1936 y el asesinato de Federico García Lorca* (Granada in 1936 and the Assassination of Federico García Lorca). Barcelona: Editorial Crítica, 1979. In-depth study of the situation in Granada at the outbreak of the Spanish Civil War and of the circumstances surrounding the poet's assassination.

Góngora y Argote, Luis de. *The Solitudes of Luis de Góngora* (bilingual Spanish-English edition). Trnas. Gilbert F. Cunningham. Baltimore: Johns Hopkins UP, 1968.

Hernández, Mario. *Line of Light and Shadow: The Drawings of Federico García Lorca*. Trans. Christopher Maurer. Durham and London: Duke UP, 1991. English-language translation of the 1990 original Spanish-language book produced for the "The Drawings of Federico García Lorca" exhibition at the Duke University Museum of Art in association with the Federico García Lorca Foundation in Madrid. Includes an introduction and eight interpretive essays on the prevailing themes in Lorca's drawings. Features high-quality illustrations and good documentation.

Howatson, M. C., ed. *The Oxford Companion to Classical Literature*. Oxford and New York: Oxford UP, 1989.

Huélamo, Julio, ed. *Federico García Lorca: Santa Lucía y San Lázaro* (Federico García Lorca: St. Lucy and St. Lazarus). (Málaga: Centro Cultural de la Generación del 27, 1989).

Jackson, Gabriel. *The Spanish Republic and the Civil War, 1931–1939.* Princeton, N.J.: Princeton UP, 1972. The standard study of this critical period in modern Spanish history.

Jakobson, Roman. "What Is Poetry?" *Semiotics of Art.* Ed. Ladislav Matejka and Irwin R. Titunik. Cambridge, Mass., and London: MIT Press, 1976. 164–175.

Klibbe, Lawrence H. *Lorca's "Impresiones y Paisajes": The Young Artist.* Madrid: José Porrúa Turanzas, 1983. An interpretive study of Lorca's often overlooked first book.

Lima, Robert. *The Theater of García Lorca.* New York: Las Américas, 1963. A critical study of all of Lorca's plays available in print at the time of its writing.

Loughran, David K. *Federico García Lorca: The Poetry of Limits.* London: Tamesis, 1978. An overview and analysis of Lorca's main poetry collections as stemming from the speaker's alienation of reason and self-consciousness from the unconscious and natural rhythm; also includes one of the earliest study-chapters, with illustrations, devoted to Lorca's drawings.

Marcilly, Charles. *La burla de Don Pedro a caballo de Federico García Lorca* (The "Joke About Don Pedro on Horseback" by Federico García Lorca). Paris: Librairie des Editions Espagnoles, 1957. Close reading in French of Lorca's enigmatic ballad "Joke about Don Pedro on Horseback."

Martín, Eutimio. *Federico García Lorca, heterodoxo y mártir* (Federico García Lorca: Heterodox and Martyr). Madrid: Siglo XXI, 1986. An interesting approach to Lorca's writings—especially his unpublished juvenilia production—as the expression of an unorthodox messianic-chivalric concept of literature.

Martínez Nadal, Rafael. *Lorca's "The Public": A Study of His Unfinished Play and of Love and Death in the Work of Federico García Lorca.* London: Calder and Boyars, 1974. The first part of this two-part study analyzes Lorca's unfinished play, *The Public.* Part two concentrates on general themes in Lorca's plays, such as horse symbolism and theater-within-the-theater.

———.*Federico García Lorca. Autógrafos II: El público* (Federico García Lorca. Autographs II: The Public). Facsimile edition. Oxford: Dolphin Book Co., 1976.

Miller, Norman C. *García Lorca's Poema del Cante Jondo.* London: Tamesis, 1978. Important study of the origin and history of *Deep Song* and of the content, structure, and vocabulary of the book by way of a detailed analysis of a representative poem from each of the work's major sections.

Morelli, Gabriele, ed. *Federico García Lorca: Saggi critici nel cinquantenario della morte.* Fasano, Italy: Schena Editore, 1988. Twelve essays by different critics on various aspects of Lorca's works, marking the fiftieth anniversary of his death.

Morris, C. Brian, ed. *"Cuando yo me muera...": Essays in Memory of Federico García Lorca.* Lanham, New York and London: UP of America, 1988. Seventeen essays by different critics on various aspects of Lorca's works.

———. *The Dream-House (Silent Films and Spanish Poets).* Scotland [Hull]: U of Hull,

1977. A study of the influence of silent films and of cinematic techniques on Spanish artists of the 1920s and 1930s.

Newton, Candelas. *Lorca: "Libro de poemas" o las aventuras de una búsqueda* (Lorca: *Book of Poems* or The Adventures of a Quest). Salamanca: Universidad de Salamanca, 1986. Close textual reading of Lorca's first published book of poems and a consideration of its often overlooked importance in Lorca's corpus.

―――. *Lorca, una escritura en trance: Libro de poemas y Diván del Tamarit* (Lorca, Writing in a Trance: *Book of Poems* and *The Divan at the Tamarit*). Amsterdam and Philadelphia: John Benjamins, 1992. Analysis of a series of poetic signs through contextual readings of *Book of Poems* and *The Diván at Tamarit* seen as the initial and final stages of Lorca's career.

Oppenheimer, Helen. *Lorca. The Drawings: Their Relation to the Poet's Life and Work.* New York and Toronto: Franklin Watts, 1987. An introduction to Lorca's drawings.

Predmore, Richard L. *Lorca's New York Poetry: Social Injustice, Dark Love, Lost Faith.* Durham: Duke UP, 1980. An exploration of the poetic symbolism and thematic structure of *Poet in New York* in light of the symbolism developed in earlier books and of Lorca's own aesthetic ideas.

Ramsden, Herbert. *Lorca's "Romancero gitano": Eighteen Commentaries.* Manchester and New York: Manchester UP, 1988. A poem-by-poem guide to Lorca's *The Gypsy Ballads,* with a brief introduction, a reference to different critical views, and a select critical bibliography for each commentary.

Santos Torroella, Rafael. *La miel es más dulce que la sangre. Las épocas lorquiana y freudiana de Salvador Dalí* (Honey Is Sweeter Than Blood: The Lorcan and Freudian Periods of Salvador Dalí). Barcelona: Seix Barral, 1984. A study of the "Lorcan" and "Freudian" periods in Salvador Dalí's paintings.

Schonberg, Louis. *Federico García Lorca: L'homme, L'oeuvre* (Federico García Lorca: The Man, His Work). Paris: Plon, 1956. Study of Lorca's life and works.

Soria Olmedo, Andrés, ed. *Lecciones sobre Federico García Lorca* (Lessons on Federico García Lorca). Granada: Comisión Nacional del Cincuentenario, 1986. A collection of essays marking the fiftieth anniversary of Lorca's tragic death.

Stanton, Edward F. *The Tragic Myth: Lorca and Cante Jondo.* Lexington: UP of Kentucky, 1978. An in-depth study of *Deep Song,* the traditional music of Lorca's native Andalusia, and of the close relation of literature and music in the author's production. Good analysis of the mythic quality of Lorca's art in connection with *Deep Song.*

Trece de nieve. 2d series, 1–2 (Dec. 1976). Important journal issue devoted to Lorca. Includes unpublished texts and letters, homages to Lorca, replies by various authors to questions about the poet, and critical essays.

Articles and Other Short Studies

Aguirre, J. M. "El sonambulismo de Federico García Lorca" (Sonambulism in Federico García Lorca). *Bulletin of Hispanic Studies* 44.4 (1967): 267–85. An important early analysis of the main symbols of Lorca's "Sleepwalking Ballad."

Aleixandre, Vicente. Prologue. *Obras completas.* By Federico García Lorca. Ed. Arturo del Hoyo. 18th ed. Vol. 2. Madrid: Aguilar, 1974. ix–xi. 2 vols. Personal reminiscences about Lorca by a contemporary poet and friend.

Allen, Rupert. "An Analysis of Narrative and Symbol in Lorca's 'Romance sonámbulo'." *Hispanic Review* 36.4 (1968): 338–52. An explanation of the dramatic action and an interpretation of the narrative and symbolic elements in "Sleepwalking Ballad."

Alonso, Dámaso. "Federico García Lorca y la expresión de lo español" (Federico García Lorca and the Expression of Spanishness). *Poetas españoles contemporáneos.* Madrid: Gredos, 1958. 271–80. Personal memories of Lorca by a contemporary poet and friend.

Anderson, Andrew A. "*El Público, Así que pasen cinco años* y *El sueño de la vida*: Tres dramas expresionistas de García Lorca"(*The Public, Once Five Years Pass* and *The Dream of Life*: Three Expressionst Dramas of García Lorca). *El teatro en España. Entre la tradición y la vanguardia, 1918–1939.* Ed. Dru Dougherty and Francisca Vilches de Frutos. Madrid: CCIC, Fundación García Lorca, Tabapress, 1992. 215–26. Important discussion of Lorca's *The Public, Once Five Years Pass,* and the unfinished drama *The Dream of Life* (also known as *Play Without a Title*) as plays within the tradition of expressionism, rather than surrealism, as is frequently believed.

———. "Los primeros pasos de 'La Barraca': Una entrevista recuperada, con cronología y comentario" (The First Steps of 'La Barraca': an Interview with Chronology and Commentary). *L'"imposible / posible" di Federico García Lorca.* Ed. Laura Dolfi. Napoli: Edizioni Scientifiche Italiane, 1989. 177–99. Well-documented chronology of the development of the university theater company "La Barraca." Includes a previously unpublished 1931 interview with Lorca on "La Barraca."

———. *Poeta en Nueva York una y otra vez"* (*Poet in New York* Once Again). *El Crotalón. Anuario de Filología Española* 2 (1985): 37–51.

———. "The Strategy of García Lorca's Dramatic Composition 1930–1936." *Romance Quarterly* 33.2 (1986): 211–29. A revisionary approach to the "centrality" of Lorca's trilogy and a reconsideration of his compositional motives during the crucial period 1930–1939.

———. "Who Wrote *Seis Poemas Galegos* and in What Language?" *"Cuando yo me muera . . .": Essays in Memory of Federico García Lorca.* Ed. C. Brian Morris. Lanham, New York and London: UP of America, 1988. 129–46. A well-documented assessment of the textual problems of Lorca's *Six Galician Poems.*

Barnes, Robert. "The Fusion of Poetry and Drama in *Blood Wedding.*" *Modern Drama* 2.4 (1960): 395–402. Perceptive analysis of the poetic element as enhancing the dramatic structure of Lorca's play.

Barthes, Roland. "Style and Its Image." *The Rustle of Language.* Trans. Richard Howard. New York: Hill and Wang, 1986. 90–99.

Belamich, André. "Claves para *El público*" (Keys to *The Public*). *Federico García Lorca: Saggi critici nel cinquantenario della morte.* Ed. Gabriele Morelli. Fasano, Italy:

Schena Editore, 1988. 107–15. Interpretive reading of some "clues" to Lorca's enigmatic play *The Public.*

Cabrera, Vicente. "Poetic Structure in Lorca's *La casa de Bernarda Alba.*" *Hispania* 61.3 (1978): 466–70. A study of *The House of Bernarda Alba* as a poetic drama in spite of its subtitle, "A photographic documentary."

Cano Ballesta, Juan. "Historia y poesía: Interpretaciones y sentido de 'Grito hacia Roma'" (History and Poetry: Interpretations and Meaning of "Cry to Rome"). *Revista Hispánica Moderna* 39.4 (1976–1977): 210–14. An elucidation of the historical events related to Lorca's ode "Cry to Rome," from *Poet in New York.*

Cernuda, Luis. "Federico García Lorca (Recuerdo)" (Federico García Lorca [Reminiscence]). *Hora de España* 18 (1938): 13–20. Personal reminiscences about Lorca from a contemporary poet and friend.

DeLong-Tonelli, Beverly J. "The Lyric Dimension in Lorca's 'Romance sonámbulo'." *Romance Notes* 12.2 (1971): 289–95. An attempt to resolve the interpretive challenges of "Sleepwalking Ballad" by identifying the basic speaker and the lyrical dimension of his language.

Domenech, Ricardo. "Símbolo, mito y rito en *La casa de Bernarda Alba*" (Symbol, Myth, Ritual in *The House of Bernarda Alba*). *"La casa de Bernarda Alba" y el teatro de García Lorca.* Ed. Ricardo Domenech. Madrid: Cátedra, 1985. 187–209. A study of the symbolical code of *The House of Bernarda Alba.*

Feal, Carlos. "El Lorca póstumo: *El público* y *Comedia sin título*" (The Posthumous Lorca: *The Public* and *Play Without a Title*). *ALEC* 6 (1981): 43–62. A study of these later plays as exponents of Lorca's major artistic and existential concerns.

———. "El sacrificio de la hombría en *Bodas de sangre*" (The Sacrifice of Manhood in *Blood Wedding*). *Modern Languages Notes* 99.2 (1984): 270–87. A study of Lorca's play as the destruction of the male characters (Leonardo and the Groom) by the women (the Mother and the Bride).

Fourneret, Patrick. "Los 'dibujos humanísimos' de Federico García Lorca." *Trece de nieve.* 2d series, 1–2 (1976): 158–64. An analysis of Lorca's drawings and their link to his written work that considers their importance as interpretive clues to the authors's artistry.

García Lorca, Francisco. "Primeros escritos de Federico" (First Writings by Federico). In *Federico García Lorca y su mundo.* Translated as *In the Green Morning.* Trans. Christopher Maurer. New York: New Directions, 1986.

———. Prologue. *Three Tragedies: Blood Wedding, Yerma, Bernarda Alba.* By Federico García Lorca. Trans. James Graham-Luján and Richard L. O'Connell. New York: New Directions, 1955. An overview of Lorca's career by his brother Francisco, with personal reminiscences of Lorca's theatrical beginnings in childhood games and rural surroundings. Emphasis on the fusion of poetry and drama and on the importance of tradition in Lorca's theater.

———. "Verde" (Green). *Homenaje a Casalduero.* Ed. Rizel Pincus and Gonzalo Sobejano. Madrid: Gredos, 1972. 135–39. Perceptive reading of the opening line of "Sleepwalking Ballad," "Verde que te quiero verde" (Green oh how I love you green).

García-Posada, Miguel. "Sonetos de Lorca. Un monumento al amor" (Lorca's Sonnets:

A Monument to Love). *ABC Edición internacional*. Madrid. 21–27 March 1984: 33–34.

Glasser, Doris M. "Lorca's 'Burla de Don Pedro a caballo'" (Lorca's "Joke About Don Pedro on Horseback"). *Hispania* 47.2 (1964): 295–301. A reading of Lorca's ballad "Joke about Don Pedro on Horseback" within the tradition of the historical legend.

Guillén, Jorge. "Federico en persona" (Federico in Person). *Obras completas*. By Federico García Lorca. Ed. Arturo del Hoyo. 18th ed. Vol. 1. Madrid: Aguilar, 1973. 2 vols. xv–lxxxi. Personal memories of Lorca by a contemporary poet and friend.

Heilbrun, Carolyn, and Catharine Stimpson. "Theories of Feminist Criticism: A Dialogue." *Feminist Literary Criticism: Explorations in Theory*. Ed. Josephine Donovan. Lexington: UP of Kentucky, 1975. 61–73.

Hernández, Mario. "El arte del dibujo en la creación de García Lorca" (The Art of Drawing in the Works of García Lorca). *Federico García Lorca: Saggi critici nel cinquantenario della morte*. Ed. Gabriele Morelli. Fasano, Italy: Schena Editore, 1988. 117–34. An approach to Lorca's drawings as a stylization of his tormented inner world.

———. "La muchacha dorada por la luna" (The Girl Turned Golden by the Moon). *Trece de nieve*. 2d series, 1–2 (1976): 211–20. Relevant analysis of the traditional theme of the "love bath" in relation to "VIII. Qasida of the Golden Girl," from *The Divan at the Tamarit*.

Herrero, Javier. "The Father Against the Son: Lorca's Christian Vision." *Essays on Hispanic Themes in Honour of Edward Riley*. Ed. Jennifer Lowe and Phillip Swanson. Edinburgh, Scotland: Department of Hispanic Studies, U of Edinburgh, 1989. 170–99. A study of Lorca's conflicts between flesh and spirit and between personal desire and authority as reflected in the image of the sacrificed Son against a cruel Father.

———. "'La luna vino a la fragua': Lorca's Mythic Forge." *De los romances villancicos a la poesía de Claudio Rodríguez: 22 ensayos sobre las literaturas española e hispanoamericana en homenaje a Gustav Siebenmann*. Ed. José Manuel López de Abiada and Augusta López Bernasocchi. Madrid: José Esteban, 1984. 175–97. A study of the image of the forge in the "Ballad of the Moon, Moon."

———. "The Spider-Moon: The Origin of Lorca's Lunar Myth." *Studies in Honor of Bruce W. Wardropper*. Ed. Dian Fox, Harry Sieber, Robert TerHorst. Newark, Del.: Juan de la Cuesta, 1989. 147–62. A study of the central Lorcan image of the moon as originating from the author's early writings.

Ilie, Paul. "Three Shadows on the Early Aesthetic of Lorca." *"Cuando yo me muera . . ." Essays in Memory of Federico García Lorca*. Lanham, New York and London: UP of America, 1988. 25–40. An analysis of "Three Portraits with Shading" (*Songs*) as a foreshadowing of Lorca's later irrationalism.

Jerez-Farrán, Carlos. "La estética expresionista en *El público* de García Lorca" (The Aesthetics of Expression in *The Public* by García Lorca). *Anales de la literatura española contemporánea* 11.1–2 (1986): 111–27. Enlightening discussion of the avant-garde movement of expressionism as a more appropriate tool than surrealism for explaining the themes and techniques in *The Public*.

Klein, Dennis A. "'Así que pasen cinco años': A Search for Sexual Identity." *Journal of*

Spanish Studies XXth C. 3.2 (1975): 115–23. Emphasis on the main character of *Once Five Years Pass,* the Joven (Young Man), and his struggle with his own sexuality.

Knapp, Bettina L. "Federico García Lorca's *The House of Bernarda Alba*: A Hermaphroditic Matriarchate." *Modern Drama* 27.3 (1984): 383–94. A reading of the "house" in *The House of Bernarda Alba* as the concretization of Bernarda's consciousness and desire to force others into a static position.

———. "Federico García Lorca's *Yerma*: A Woman's Mystery." *Women in Twentieth-Century Literature: A Jungian View.* University Park and London: Pennsylvania State UP, 1987. 11–24. Archetypal reading of *Yerma* within the framework of the play as a dramatization of secret doctrines and initiation rituals.

Laffranque, Marie. "Una cadena de solidaridad. Federico, conferenciante" (A Chain of Solidarity. Federico, Lecturer). *Trece de nieve.* 2d series, 1–2 (1976). 132–40. An evaluation of Lorca's prose as the expression of his persistent need to communicate with his audience, to establish a "solidarity link," by sharing his reflections about his work and about art in general.

———. "Federico García Lorca, de *Rosa mudable* a la 'Casida de la rosa' " (Federico Garcia Lorca, from Changeable Rose to "Qaside of the Rose"). *Lecciones sobre Federico García Lorca.* Ed. Andres Sona Olmedo. Granada: Comisión National del Cincuentenario, 1986. 279–300. An analysis of the connection between the dramatic fragment "Changeable Rose" with *Dona Rosita, the Spinster* and " Qasida of the Rose."

Lyon, John. "Love, Imagination and Society in *Amor de don Perlimplín* and *La zapatera prodigiosa.*" *Bulletin of Hispanic Studies* 63.3 (1986): 235–47. An important essay that compares in *Perlimplín* and *The Shoemaker's* the role of imagination and its connection with love and reality.

Martín, Eutimio. "Federico García Lorca, ¿un precursor de la 'teología de la liberación'? (Su primera obra dramática inédita)" (Federico García Lorca, A Forerunner of the "Theology of Liberation"? His First Play, Still Unpublished). *Lecciones sobre Federico García Lorca.* Ed. Andrés Soria Olmedo. Granada: Ediciones del cincuentenario, 1986. 27–33. An analysis of Lorca's social concerns in his early writings as an expression of an evangelical, messianic view of literature.

———. "Hacia una lectura de 'Burla de Don Pedro a caballo'" (Towards a Reading of "Joke About Don Pedro on Horseback"). *Hommage/Homenaje a Federico García Lorca.* Toulouse: Université de Toulouse-Le-Mirail, 1982. 173–88. An interpretive reading of "Joke about Don Pedro on Horseback," with special attention to the identification of the character.

Maurer, Christopher. "The Black Pain." Rev. of *Federico García Lorca: A Life,* by Ian Gibson. *New Republic* 1 Jan. 1990: 29–34. Interesting brief account of Lorca's life and works within a review of Gibson's biography; includes a perceptive analysis of the elegiac character of Lorca's writings.

———. "Sobre la prosa temprana de García Lorca (1916–1918)" (About Lorca's Early

Prose Writings [1916–1918]). *Cuadernos Hispanoamericanos* 433–34 (1986): 13–22. An important article about Lorca's early prose writings and their generic indetermination; includes an appendix of never before published texts.

McMullan, Terence. "Federico García Lorca's 'Santa Lucía y San Lázaro' and the Aesthetics of Transition." *Bulletin of Hispanic Studies* 67.1 (1990): 1–20. A study of "Santa Lucía y San Lázaro" as the expression of two different aesthetic positions. Also views the piece as permeated by a religious satire stemming from Lorca's first prose work, *Impressions and Landscapes.*

Miller, Norman C. "Lorca's 'Nana del caballo grande': A Psychological Perspective." *Hispanófila* 3.93 (1980): 37–46. A study of the prophetic-symbolic content of the lullaby of act I, scene 2 of *Blood Wedding,* and of the lullaby's function within the play.

———. "'Romance sonámbulo,' An Archetypal Drama." *Hispanic Journal* 7.2 (1986): 17–24. Perceptive study of "Sleepwalking Ballad" as a miniature psychological drama.

Morris, C. Brian. "Lorca's *Yerma* and the 'beso sabroso'." *Mester* 10.1–2 (1981): 68–81. An analysis of the semiotic implications of Juan's kiss to Yerma.

Newton, Candelas. "Los paisajes del amor: Iconos centrales en los *Sonetos* de Lorca" (Love's Landscapes: Important Icons in Lorca's *Sonnets*). *Anales de la literatura española contemporánea.* Special Issue in Honor of Federico García Lorca. 11.1–2 (1986): 143–59. A study of poetic signs in Lorca's sonnets.

Palley, Julian. "Archetypal Symbols in *Bodas de sangre.*" *Hispania* 50.1 (1967): 74–79. A reading of *Blood Wedding*'s mythic projections through the archetypes of the knife, horse, moon, blood, wheat, and orange blossom.

Power, Kevin. "Una luna encontrada en Nueva York" (A Moon Found in New York). *Trece de nieve.* 2d series, 1–2 (Dec. 1976): 141–52. A study of Lorca's film script, *Trip to the Moon.*

Ramsden, Herbert. "Round Perspective and Lyric Tension in *Romancero gitano.*" *"Cuando yo me muera . . . ": Essays in Memory of Federico García Lorca.* Ed. C. Brian Morris. Lanham, New York and London: UP of America, 1988. 89–104. A reading of various gypsy ballads as examples of the interplay between lyric tension, narrative, and images.

Rubia Barcia, J. "El realismo 'mágico' de *La casa de Bernarda Alba*" (Magic Realism in *The House of Bernarda Alba*). *Federico García Lorca.* Ed. Ildefonso Manuel Gil. Madrid: Taurus, 1973. 301–21. A study of *The House* as a play where realism fuses with poetic and unlikely elements from the unconscious.

Ucelay, Margarita. "De las aleluyas de Don Perlimplín a la obra de Federico García Lorca." *Federico García Lorca: Saggi critici nel cinquantenario della morte.* Ed. Gabriele Morelli. Fasano, Italy: Schena Editore, 1988. 89–106. A discussion of the influence of popular and children's literature in Lorca's *Perlimplín.*

Valente, José Angel. "Pez luna" (Moon Fish). *Trece de nieve.* 2d series 1–2 (1976): 191–201. A study of the image of the unborn or dead child in Lorca's production.

Walsh, John K. "The Social and Sexual Geography of *Poeta en Nueva York*." *"Cuando yo me muera..."*: *Essays in Memory of Federico García Lorca*. Ed. C. Brian Morris. Lanham, New York and London: UP of America, 1988. 105–27. A consideration of the social and personal context surrounding the writing of *Poet in New York*.

Wells, C. Michael. "The Natural Norm in the Plays of F. García Lorca." *Hispanic Review* 38.3 (1970): 299–313. An analysis of the norm of nature (the instinctual or primal existence) in Lorca's plays versus divergent forms of life such as illusion or social convention.

Index